SEX, KIDS, AND POLITICS

Health Services in Schools

SEX, KIDS, AND POLITICS

Health Services in Schools

CATHERINE EMIHOVICH

and

CAROLYN D. HERRINGTON

Foreword by Irving Lazar

Teachers College
Columbia University
New York and London

Published by Teachers College Press, 1234 Amsterdam Avenue, New York, NY 10027

Library of Congress Cataloging-in-Publication Data

Emihovich, Catherine.
    Sex, kids, and politics : health services in schools / Catherine Emihovich and Carolyn D. Herrington.
        p.   cm.
    Includes bibliographical references and index.
    ISBN 0-8077-3635-X (paper : alk. paper). — ISBN 0-8077-3636-8 (cloth : alk. paper)
    1. School health services—United States—Case studies. 2. Politics and education—United States—Case studies. 3. Education and state—United States—Case studies.
    I. Herrington, Carolyn D. II. Title.
    LB3409.U5E55   1997
    371.7′1′0973—dc21   97-16422

ISBN 0-8077-3635-X (paper)
ISBN 0-8077-3636-8 (cloth)

Printed on acid-free paper
Manufactured in the United States of America

04   03   02   01   00   99   98   97   8   7   6   5   4   3   2   1

Contents

Foreword

The school nurse was, historically, the first professional outside of education to play a regular and resident role in American public schools. She largely disappeared as budgets got tighter and other kinds of expenses were given higher priorities by local school boards. Along with many of the services of local health departments, school health services were seen as unnecessary because, it was argued, students had access to private health care and health care was a responsibility of the home. The passage of the Medicaid program further justified dropping health care from the school since the poorest students could be served by these federal funds. Of course, this access eroded as fewer and fewer physicians would accept Medicaid reimbursement and as more working-class families found themselves unable to afford health insurance. We faced a simultaneous increase in demand for health services, the spread of AIDS, the increase in teenage pregnancies, and the increasing restrictions of managed care as health care decisions were transferred from physicians to insurance companies. It was clear that health status affected learning, that the media culture was increasingly violent and sexual, and yet it was the school that was under increasing attack for the poor performance of many students.

Increasing the pressure on the schools were the effects of the legislative and judicial decisions that schools were required to provide educational services for disabled children. They could no longer be expelled or segregated into special facilities but were to be accommodated in regular classrooms. Teachers found themselves needing to administer medication and needing to cope with children with a wide variety of special needs, many of them health-related.

At the same time, the nation was going through what appears to be a 30-year cycle of rediscovering that human services are fragmented, duplicative, inefficient, and increasingly inaccessible. The banners of coordination of services, or better, service integration, were dusted off, and a new round of quests to reach that holy grail of the human services got underway. As has been the case in the past, the public schools were seen as a likely base for such efforts, and new tries at school-based social and health services blossomed across the country.

This volume is a thoughtful and careful examination of such an effort. Spurred by legislative concerns about teenage pregnancy rates and concerns by educators and health professionals about the decreasing access to and increased demands for health care, the state of Florida undertook a pilot program of funding school-based health services, staffed largely by nurses and designed to reduce health-related barriers to school performance and to reduce teenage pregnancy rates.

This straightforward and humane purpose unleashed a myriad of value conflicts, turf battles, religious and cultural conflicts, and professional role dilemmas. Even the name of the service became a cause of conflict, and the term *school clinic* had to be replaced with the phrase *health room*. The legislature ducked the battles by writing very general language and passing the buck—and the determination of details—to school boards. Many school boards tried to pass the buck to the principals. The study reported here examined the ways in which different counties implemented the program, and three case histories represent a range of solutions, from one county that would not permit the use of the word *condom* to another in which nurses showed classes how they were to be used.

The study investigates the variety of differences among the players, the intergovernmental issues, interprofessional and turf issues, political and ideological conflicts, and the particular problems of asking principals of schools to relinquish some of their authority over what goes on in "their" school. The preventive and educational responsibilities of the nurses meant that they didn't stay in the clinic all day and that the principal had no control over their activities. The nurses, on the other hand, were often reluctant to do what they saw as necessary for fear of arousing resentment in the school.

Two very thoughtful chapters then explore the sources and implications of the efforts, the conflicts, and the achievements of the program. They suggest approaches to resolving the conflicts it found and point out, from within the study, successful practice. Opposition to service was more imagined than real, and the children's needs were greater than was imagined. With the mass media serving as the most important socializing influence in children's lives today, and our national inability and unwillingness to limit the media's instructional barrage of mayhem and rampant sex, the schools are truly limited as transmitters of a civil culture. Just as this example of an effort to increase access to critically important health and safety information spawned conflicts across the whole range of our cultural differences—even nutrition education was opposed as an attack on family and ethnic eating traditions—so too must we begin to reexamine the future of our schools, the heavy costs of their isolation from political accountability, and the increasing choices and more complex needs that parents and their children face.

Drs. Emihovich and Herrington have provided the raw materials for a sensible discussion of these problems and the scholarly materials for understanding their origins and implications. Used well, this book can be an effective tool in helping students, parent groups, and concerned citizens move the process of change forward and in reducing the duplication of old tries that don't work.

Irving Lazar, Ph.D.
The Santa Fe Institute

Acknowledgments

Writing is often conceived of as a solitary action, but in reality the assistance of many people is needed to bring a book to fruition. We owe a debt of gratitude to our colleagues, graduate students, and family members, whose research on our behalf and/or thoughtful comments throughout the process encouraged us to believe that this topic was worth pursuing. First and foremost, we'd like to thank Jan Basile, who has been involved in this study with us for over four years, and who tirelessly tracked down sources of information, fielded endless phone calls from school districts and state agency personnel, coordinated the paperwork, and wrote insightful comments on multiple drafts of both the state report and this book. Above all, her humor kept us sane, and we honestly couldn't have managed this study without her.

We also would like to thank our graduate students who worked on different stages of the project: Lenora Jean Dona, Scott Gilbert, Eliana Montero, Gwendolyn Quinn, Lisa Sullivan, and Kay Um. Their assistance was greatly appreciated.

In the field, we would like to thank all the state agency personnel from both the Florida Department of Health and Rehabilitative Services and the Department of Education who expanded our thinking on this issue from a statewide policy perspective. Especially helpful were conversations we had with Mary Apple, Donna Barber, Jean Battaglia, Sylvia Bryd, Risa Fogel, Paula Schneider, John Tolliver, and Mae Waters. Because we don't want to compromise people's identities in the places we visited, we cannot name all the school and public health personnel who generously gave us time in interviews and who, more than anyone, made us realize the importance of school health services in children's and families' lives. We hope that this book adequately reflects the depth of their commitment that was so clearly evident on all our visits.

The comments of our editor, Brian Ellerbeck, on our first draft were so encouraging we were more motivated than ever to complete the final draft. We also appreciate the fact that he was so supportive of this topic and our approach to writing about it in ways that belied the concept of the dispassionate social scientist.

Finally, we would like to thank our spouses and children who tolerated our long absences during field visits, and whose pointed questions about the end ("Aren't you ever going to finish that book?") kept us on track despite the distractions of professional and familial obligations. For Catherine, it was her husband, Ron, and sons, David and Benjamin, who kept her attention focused; for Carolyn her husband, Robert Bradley, and children, Elizabeth, Michael, Carolyn, and Robert.

Chapter 1

Losing Ground

Children's Welfare in Decline

America's enormous strengths and distressing weaknesses are nowhere more evident than in the lives of its children and families.
—National Commission on Children, 1991

The United States can be no stronger than measured in the well-being of
its children. Yet it is now well documented that many children living in
the world's remaining superpower are growing up deprived of the basic
resources necessary for leading healthy, productive, and fulfilling adult
lives. For over a decade, the Children's Defense Fund, with an insistent
combination of grim statistics and graphic metaphors, has been chronicling the declining condition of American children's lives, lives that rival
many Third World countries in their destitution and despair. Just to give
a few examples, approximately 1 in 5 children live in poverty, in 1992
there were 850,000 substantiated cases of child abuse or neglect, and the
homicide rate for teens more than doubled between 1970 and 1992
(Gleick, 1996b). The fact that these conditions exist in the world's wealthiest nation is a national disgrace.

These concerns received official imprimatur from the federal government with the 1991 release of the National Commission on Children
report:

> Although many children grow up healthy and happy in strong, stable
> families, far too many do not. They are children whose parents are too
> stressed and busy to provide caring attention and guidance. They are
> children who grow up without the material support and personal
> involvement of their mothers and fathers. They are children who are
> poor, whose families cannot adequately feed and clothe them and pro-
> vide safe, secure homes. They are children who are victims of abuse
> and neglect at the hands of adults they love and trust, as well as those
> they do not even know. They are children who are born too early and
> too small, who face a lifetime of chronic illness and disability. They are
> children who enter school ill prepared for the rigors of learning, who
> fail to develop the skills and attitudes needed to get good jobs and be-
> come responsible members of adult society. They are children who lack

1

hope for what their lives can become, who believe they have little to lose by dropping out of school, having a baby as an unmarried teenager, committing violent crimes, or taking their own lives. (National Commission on Children, 1991, pp. vii–viii)

The consequences to American society of failing to provide adequately for its children's welfare are severe. Doug Nelson, the executive director of the Annie E. Casey Foundation, described it well:

It may well be that this nation cannot survive—as a decent place to live, as a world-class power or even as a democracy—with such high rates of children growing up into adulthood unprepared to parent, unprepared to be productively employed and unprepared to share in mainstream aspirations. (quoted in Gleick, 1996b, p. 33)

With less stirring rhetoric but equally heartfelt anguish, groups of citizens, community leaders, and public officials in cities and towns throughout the country have been banding together to better understand what is happening to their children. Teachers, police officers, social workers, religious leaders, and parents are alarmed over the growing numbers of children who come to school unprepared and unkempt, over kindergartners who lack immunization against ordinary childhood diseases, over young children living with only their mother and teenagers living alone, and over disturbingly high levels of sexual precocity, substance abuse, and violence. In both official and unofficial reports at all levels of government, there is a steadily growing conviction that a generation of children are growing up in environments lacking the essential material, social, and spiritual resources that nourish bright, happy, and productive young people. Without question, the quality of life of children today has declined and the structures that sustain the quality of life have been weakened. The forces to hold responsible are difficult to amend: large-scale economic changes that have brought considerable stress to young families because of lost jobs and the disruption of entire communities, along with the emergence of a predominantly service-oriented economy whose employment for the less educated offers low wages, part-time work, and often no benefits. This economic shift has led to a growth in the number of the working poor who are caught in the middle, ineligible for Medicaid but having no health insurance, and has disproportionately affected inner-city dwellers, racial minorities, and these with a less than high school education.

Before discussing the specific program that this book investigates, the Florida Supplemental School Health Program, it is important to identify the issues facing the country to which this program was an attempt to respond and offer some understanding as to why this particular programmatic strategy emerged at this time.

CHILDREN'S HEALTH CARE

Of all the problems that children today face, none is more essential than maintaining and improving their health through routine health care. Regular physical exams identify and can lead to the correction of conditions that otherwise might result in serious or permanent impairment. A common earache, for example, left untreated, can lead to significant hearing loss; an uncorrected vision problem can impair a child's academic and social development. However, it is estimated that 20% of children in the United States have no yearly contact with a physician. For low-income and minority children, the percentages are significantly higher (National Commission on Children, 1991).

Increasing costs have placed health care out of reach of lower- and middle-class families except through public and private health insurance. The majority of families with a working parent obtain health insurance coverage through their employer. Medicaid covers some of the cost for the poor. However, many children have no coverage at all. These are typically children from families with a single parent or two parents who work in low-wage jobs. The National Commission on Children characterized children's relationship to the private insurance system as "fragile." Over the past 10 years, the percent of employees who paid for dependent coverage in full declined from two-fifths to one-third. Furthermore, fewer than 60% of children who are eligible for Medicaid on the basis of family income receive services (Center for the Future of Children, 1992). It is estimated that approximately 8.3 million children, or 13% of all children under the age of 18, lack health insurance protection.

Efforts to improve children's health often overlook the central role that the educational sector plays in children's lives and how their overall health status is conditioned by their attitudes and behaviors toward health as much as their actual physical condition. A now-established body of research has shown that the greatest health threats facing children today come from risky behaviors. The National Commission on Children (1991) emphasizes the critical role of behavior in the health of children and their later health as adults:

> Malnourishment, obesity, and the incidence of many illnesses are related to nutritional intake. Sexually transmitted diseases, accidents and injuries, and physical and mental impairments are directly attributable to early, unprotected sexual activity, drug and alcohol use, and delin-

quent behavior. Many of the health problems that afflict Americans in adulthood, including cancer, stroke, heart disease, and AIDS, are profoundly influenced or caused by how they conduct their lives. In fact, better control of a limited number of risk factors—among them diet, exercise, and the use of tobacco, alcohol, and other drugs—could prevent at least 40 percent of all premature deaths, one-third of all short-term disability cases, and two-thirds of all chronic disability cases. Changes in health behaviors can also reduce medical costs and limit losses in productivity. (pp. 126–127)

It is increasingly clear that the goals of educational and health institutions are inextricably linked. We know that a child with a health problem—malnourishment, vision impairment, child abuse—does not learn as readily or as well as a healthy child. And a sound education about healthy behaviors and lifestyles may be one of the most powerful deterrents to unhealthy lifestyle choices. Children and adolescents can be taught how to maintain their own health through diet, exercise, and avoidance of risky behaviors.

Linking Schools and Health Services

The realization of the strong link between health and education has led to an emergent interest in using the school as a community site for providing linkages and/or delivering health services for children and youth. Arguments in favor of this approach have been well articulated (Kirst, 1994). The most compelling is that schools offer the most sustained contact with children of any social institution and can thus provide continuity of care not possible anyplace else. Because of their proximity, school staff may be the first to identify emerging health problems, and school-linked health services may be reinforced with education about and promotion of healthy lifestyles. Since many of the health problems facing children today are behavior-based, education is often the key to prevention. Also, locating services in the schools effects a change in strategy from problem-based need to geographical area, which may be more appropriate for problems that have root causes in poverty or impoverished community support systems.

Furthermore, since the 1978 Education for All Handicapped Children Act, schools have expanded their responsibilities in the areas of physical treatment for children. The fragility of some of these children who now attend schools was graphically illustrated by school nurses' testimony at a recent conference. One session addressed issues surrounding the case of children who are terminally ill and attend school with DNR (do not resuscitate) orders (Annual Conference of School Nurses, 1996).

At the same time, the fields of both health care and education are experiencing significant crises in public support because of public perceptions of ineffectiveness and inefficiencies. The increasing concern about inadequate academic achievement in the public education system is matched by concerns about inequitable access in the health care system. Both systems are concerned about rising costs and inadequate outcomes. Working together, both systems might be able to address these criticisms. The health system faces a new set of challenges brought on by societal changes. Major improvements in health are more likely to occur because of better access to services and reduction of risk behavior, rather than through further advancement in knowledge and technology. The growing realization of the interrelationships between behavior and health is putting new pressures on the health services delivery system. Reducing risky behaviors to improve health calls for a different set of skills and different service settings than treating individual patients who need acute-care services. Promotion and education become more critical to improving health outcomes and community-based delivery sites more critical to reaching underserved populations (Center for the Future of Children, 1992).

The education system is receiving increased criticism for its inability to graduate a larger segment of the population and for insufficient achievement among those who do graduate. As the number of jobs that require only limited reading, number, and problem-solving skills shrinks, a higher success rate in elementary and secondary education becomes critical for economic self-sufficiency. Furthermore, research clearly indicates that the physical and mental condition of children and their out-of-school experiences and behaviors are powerful influences on their in-school performance (Center for the Future of Children, 1992). In-school health programs offer the promise of helping to widen access to primary health care for needy children and at the same time strengthen children's ability to learn.

Health services in schools are politically appealing because of the long and relatively uncontested role of schools and school nurses. Throughout most of the century, schools have served as sites for visual screening, hearing screening, TB screening, immunizations, and other public health efforts, and their role has not generated much controversy. In fact, today's adults probably went to schools that routinely had school nurses and health clinics. Schools are currently involved in a good deal of education about healthy lifestyles and behaviors. A survey conducted by Holtzman and colleagues (1992) found that 80% of all school districts in the United States required a comprehensive health education program as part of the curriculum, and that 67% of all school districts in 1990 required that HIV education policies be put in place. A broader role for schools in promoting student health and reducing teenage pregnancies is supported by a majority of the population. A 1993 Gallup poll indicates that 60% of the American public favor the free distribution of condoms in public schools (Elam, Rose, & Gallup, 1993). As is well documented in political science research, new programmatic directions are always better received by the electorate if they appear to be additions to existing programs or modest expansion of services that are already established and well received politically (Peterson, Rabe, & Wong, 1986). School health services qualify under these conditions.

Many mainstream national commissions and associations have called for closer linkages between schools and health service providers, including the National Governors' Association, the National School Board Association, the National Commission on Children, the Carnegie Council on Adolescent Development, the National Alliance of Business, the National Commission to Prevent Infant Mortality, the Education Commission of the States, the Council on Economic Development, and the Council of Chief State School Officers.

New Morbidities and New Controversies

The health problems facing children and young people today differ in source and in treatment from the ones prevalent just a few generations ago. The advances of science and technology have eradicated or considerably reduced the ills that have traditionally plagued children. Tuberculosis, smallpox, diphtheria, whooping cough, and polio have retreated before the advance of new and powerful detection, prevention, and treatment technologies. However, in their wake have appeared a set of new threats that also endanger, impair, weaken, and sometimes kill today's children. Now often referred to as the "new morbidities" or "social morbidities," these threats are induced by behavior more than biology. These threats include accidents, homicide, suicide, child abuse, street violence, obesity, substance abuse, too-early childbearing, and unprotected sex. These new health issues, unlike the old ones, are less amenable to purely technical interventions. Their treatments often require the voluntary support of the child, may involve the parents, and may require highly subjective assessments on the part of the health practitioner (e.g., when does an overweight child go from chubby to obese?). The new morbidities raise questions about individual rights and personal responsibility, test the boundaries between school and parent jurisdiction over the behavior of young people, and blur distinctions between unhealthy behavior and immoral behavior. For example, should a student's request for confidentiality be respected when discussing sexual activity or substance abuse with the school nurse? In this sense, the new morbidities inhabit more treacherous and socially contested terrain than their predecessors and link the delivery of school-based health service with thornier issues of values, control, authority, and legitimacy.

Expanded Role of School Health Personnel. The Florida Supplemental School Health Program was an attempt to address these new morbidities through supplementing basic school health practices with a more activist and preventive approach. The goal of school-based health services has always been to balance reaching adulthood in good physical and psychological health while maximizing educational achievement. However, the methods and processes to achieve this have evolved over time (Strehlow, 1987). As described by Kolbe (1986) and Newton (1989), the model of school-based health services, which developed as school health services originated in the 1900s, aimed for providing minimal protection of the public's health through prevention of the spread of contagious disease and for providing schools some protection from legal liabilities associated with injuries in the playground or to school athletes.

In this model, the role of the school and of the school nurse is strictly defined. The major responsibilities of the school nurse or an aide are to ensure that students have the required immunizations and are screened as needed. The nurse is also responsible for maintaining records and for follow-up. However, with the increasing success of efforts to control communicable childhood diseases and the appearance of the new social threats to children's health, the mission of school health services was broadened and required a reconceptualization of the role of school-based health personnel.

A more expanded role for the school nurse began to appear in the 1970s. In addition to the activities of the traditional model, the school nurse is involved in providing primary health care, including the diagnosis and treatment of common health problems of students. This new role changed the nature and frequency of school nurses' interactions with educators, the health community, and parents. It requires active linkages with the medical community for consultation and referral and with community health facilities, including hospitals, for backup and inpatient care. It also often involves the nurse as a part of child support teams that also include teachers, school administrators, health aides, psychologists, social workers, nutritionists, mental health care providers, health educators, and case managers.

Services provided by school nurses in this expanded model include athletic physicals; emergency care; immunizations; general health assessments; weight-reduction and other nutrition programs; health education programs in relation to smoking, alcohol, and drug use; and family-planning services (George, 1992). Moreover, the new role includes an expanded involvement of the school nurse in other aspects of the school's activities. As health educator, the nurse spends more time in classrooms lecturing on and discussing the risk of certain behaviors. Finally, because many of the new morbidities arise from problems with or challenges facing families, such as child abuse or malnutrition, the new role requires more consultation with students' families.

This new role has proven much more controversial. For one thing, it involves more subjective professional judgments. Particularly at the secondary level, the school nurse assumes a role that is at times closer to that of a counselor than a health technician. While the possibility for effective intervention in the lives of young people under this model is greater, the risk of conflict with classroom teachers and with the students' parents is also much greater.

New Roles for Schools. Schools have always been turned to as a location for delivering services other than education for children. As documented by the educational historian David Tyack (1992), there was considerable use of schools around the turn of the century in the country's large urban areas to deliver health and social services to the city's immigrants and the children of the rapidly growing urban poor. In the early part of the century these services continued as needed. Tyack notes in particular that school-linked health services expanded even during the Great Depression. In the 1960s schools were seen as critical sites in the War on Poverty. Greater efficiency and effectiveness through the integration of children's services was one of the major goals of the program designers of the Great Society. One of the most politically enduring of all the Great Society programs has been Head Start. Public opinion polls repeatedly have provided evidence that society is willing to underwrite the costs of this program. In one of the most dramatic examples of social science research driving public policy, a consortium of researchers under the direction of Irving Lazar in the late 1970s compiled a sample of Head Start–type program graduates to determine if they displayed any long-term effects of the programming they had received as preschoolers. Their report documenting significant outcomes compared to a control group resurrected the program from a near-death (Lazar, Darlington, Murray, Royce, & Snipper, 1982). Head Start and other programs that combined education and health services for preschoolers were remarkably successful both in improving children's condition and in maintaining political viability (Zigler & Muenchow, 1992).

The situation today is less clear. On the one hand, pressures on the school to expand health personnel are increasing. The declining number of children who have insurance coverage through their family and the logic that schools are where the children can be found are compelling arguments. And the federal mandates regarding handicapped children have resulted in more children with more complicated medical needs in attendance.

But the strongest pressure, from an educator's perspective, is the increasingly strident clamor from public leaders, the business community, and parents for greater educational achievement. Increased use of standardized testing and increasing public scrutiny of the scores are putting unprecedented stress on educators. Healthier students may result in better achievement scores. However, there are risks for educators as well. These may be summed up as follows: (1) School personnel have not traditionally had to coordinate their educational programs with other community service providers and may be wary of a different set of professionals and services on their sites; (2) it is not clear how parents and other community members will react to the expansion in availability of health services to children; and (3) schools will need to sort out how these new responsibilities may be assumed without its appearing that schools are overburdening themselves at a time when they appear to be having trouble handling their primary mission (Center for the Future of Children, 1992).

Moreover, educators are expected to be successful with all students for the entire span of schooling. Toleration that once may have existed for lower performance by certain groups—such as minority, poor, or handicapped students—or for some students dropping out before completing high school is disappearing. And because the research is unambiguous that poor health impairs learning—and that this is true for the traditional health problems such as poor vision or hearing as well as the new morbidities such as unprotected sexual activity, substance abuse, or other risk-taking behaviors—educators are more inclined to support the early identification of health problems that may impair learning and more aggressive efforts to address them.

Family Role. Another unsurprising consequence of the new morbidities and the type of school health services they require is a need for the greater involvement of parents and the attendant potential for greater conflict between parents and schools. The new morbidities involve the family in unprecedented ways. For example, some of the new health risks facing children may result directly from the family, such as child abuse, neglect, or malnutrition. Others necessitate the involvement of the family as an active partner in treatment. These include most mental health–related areas, such as suicide, substance abuse, and eating disorders. The role of school nurses in middle and high schools, in fact, is often a direct result of issues that arise as teenagers become less dependent on their parents. These issues include having more control over one's nutrition, maturation (socially and biologically), sexual behavior, and substance abuse. Once the family becomes involved either as the recipient of services or as a partner with the school in addressing a student's problems, the potential for conflict rises sharply.

The family is seen as central by virtually all people concerned with children. However, the role that families should play and the relative authority that should be given to schools or families in dealing with children are perceived very differently by different groups. Advocates of system reform (primarily liberals) call for children's services to be family-centered, which means involving other family members in both defining the problems and determining the services needed. In addition, they support expansion of existing public services, criticizing only the relative inefficiencies in a system that is often uncoordinated. They also show considerable tolerance, if not support, for diversity in what defines a family. Conservatives equally stress the importance of the family; but for them, it means that the family should be providing services rather than being a partner in determining what services should be provided by the government. In general, they are leery of expanding public services in areas where the family has traditionally provided the service (such as preschool education, child care, character development, and sexuality education). They also support parents' rights to determine what is best for their children (such as a parent's right to choose spanking as a family discipline policy). At the same time, they show little toleration for departure from traditional family structures and oppose curricula that condone divorce and single-parent or homosexual families.

Clashes of Policy, Politics, and Culture

Although school-based health services appear to be a promising response to the growing numbers of children who do not receive routine health care, and although schools have the institutional infrastructure and at least some professional incentives to provide them, there are a number of thorny ideological as well as pragmatic obstacles that make realization of such a program exceedingly problematic. First, despite the undisputed relationship between good health and learning, the institutional capacity of schools at this time to take on new roles is under question. The same economic problems that have resulted in declining percentages of American children with health insurance coverage (e.g., the decline of manufacturing, intense global competition, and the emergence of low-wage, service-based economies) have also weakened fiscal support for schools. Although evidence clearly indicates that per-pupil appropriations for schools have increased over the last three decades, there is no evidence of any slack in the system. Class sizes are intolerably large, facility construction lags behind need, demands for huge infusions of computer and related technologies are backing up, and restructuring efforts are placing enormous stresses on the institutional stability, cohesiveness, and overall strength.

Second, schools are already enmeshed in a cultural battle as they struggle to respond to the higher academic demands placed on them by political leaders and businesspeople. As pointed out by public opinion pollsters:

> The drive to improve students' academic performance has also hit unexpected detours in a number of districts where discussion about how to improve skills has taken a back seat to debates about what should be taught. Bitter controversies over the content of history and science courses, selection of textbooks and library books, and most prominently, sex education and AIDS prevention policies have surfaced in communities in all parts of the country. . . . At the core are values— what values Americans want to transmit to their children and what role they want the school to play in teaching these values. (Johnson & Immerwahr, 1994, p. 8)

Third, schools are being asked to become a partner in one of today's most controversial public responsibilities—health care for the indigent. The reason so many children have unaddressed health problems is because the American public is intensely divided over the role of government in subsidizing health services. We are the only industrialized country without a comprehensive public health system, and that is because there is neither a societal consensus nor the political will to adequately fund primary care from public coffers. In the absence of any resolution of this issue, can a shift in location—from public health offices to school buildings—be sufficient to result in real improvements for children?

Fourth, school-based health services are emerging at a time when public cynicism about the effectiveness of governmental programs, particularly programs for the poor, is at record high levels. Few welfare programs today can marshal the administrative and public support necessary for long-term effectiveness or even survival. Moreover, for some segments of the population, governmental programs are not just ineffective—they are themselves the source of many of the problems they are designed to address (Murray, 1984). For these critics, problems such as teenage pregnancy, sexually transmitted diseases, and substance abuse are the result of wrong-headed governmental programs such as Aid to Families with Dependent Children, subsidized child care, and family-planning services that reward irresponsible behavior, weaken family ties, and blunt the force of community sanctions. Furthermore, to many of these same critics, school-based health services such as sexuality education and AIDS education are part of a larger social trend in public education to promote social views not shared by the critics (Hunter, 1991). To these people, the legitimate role of schools is to teach skills of literacy and numeracy and the factual body of knowledge in the various disciplines. They view attempts to develop attitudes (such as toleration of diversity or support for environmental conservation) or to develop character traits (such as self-esteem, values clarifications, or critical stances on received knowledge) as an illegitimate intrusion of the public sector into areas rightfully reserved for the family.

School-based health services programs touch upon virtually all these controversies. The most politically charged areas are sexual activity and sexually related health problems, such as sexually transmitted diseases and unwanted pregnancies. The confusion and uncertainty about how schools should respond reflect society's uncertainty. Public opinion polls, on the one hand, indicate that support for sex education is strong and getting stronger. According to a poll conducted by the Planned Parenthood Federation of America, 85% of Americans approve of sex education in the schools (Carter et al., 1994). In 1988, 73% favored making birth-control information and contraceptives available through school-based clinics (Kirby, 1991). And, according to Kirby (1992), when controversy has arisen, it has been around what should be taught, not whether it should be taught.

On the other hand, these issues have resulted in highly contentious and divisive political battles in some school settings. One of the foremost educators in the country, Joseph Fernandez, the chancellor of the New York City schools, was forced to step down in the wake of a controversy over making condoms available to high school students. He was not alone in this struggle. School personnel from Boston and New York as well as in the South have shared accounts with us of how the attempt to place even the most modest level of health services in schools has been met with vocal and sustained opposition from groups that see the availability of these services as an attack on parents' rights and family values. The most recent example concerned a family in rural Georgia who filed suit against a school district because the counselor had taken their two daughters to a local pharmacy to have birth-control prescriptions filled ("Telling tales," 1996).

In several cases the curriculum struggle was overly prolonged because of the timidity of school officials in confronting a small but highly vocal group who believed that their views should dominate the programs developed to meet a broad range of children's needs even though safeguards were put in place to protect their interests. As one northeast school superintendent stated in an interview, "these parents always had the right to opt their children out of any services they didn't want. The parents could attend any meeting to obtain more information about a given service, and that the school's policy was to treat all children with dignity" (Helfrich, 1996, personal communication). He always believed that the board made a mistake by not passing the health curriculum immediately, instead of giving the opposition time to organize by dragging the issue out for four months. In the end, only two parents opted out of the service, and the sexuality curriculum has been in place for over 10 years.

ARRESTING DECLINE: ONE PROGRAMMATIC APPROACH

Over the last few years the authors of this study have been involved, in different ways, in research on children's issues in the community and in schools. As researchers, we were becoming increasingly interested in the interactions between schools and communities in trying to address the problems facing children. We had both previously written on issues such as poverty, teenage pregnancies, dropping out, school discipline, day care, and strategies that involved the use of schools, such as full-service schools, integrated children's services, and increased parent involvement. Herrington (1991a) completed a comprehensive look at children in one state, Florida, that documented the alarming increases in childhood poverty, lack of access to health care, and decline in two-parent families. Her research had also examined intergovernmental issues involved in integrated children's services and the linkages among local public health offices, city police departments, welfare programs, and schools (Herrington, 1991b, 1994; Kochan & Herrington, 1992). Emihovich completed several evaluation studies of community-based programs designed to reduce teenage pregnancy in a low-income area (Emihovich, 1993; Emihovich & Davis, 1994) and from this work raised troubling questions about the politics of morality in social service evaluations (Emihovich, 1994).

In 1991, we were contacted about conducting an evaluation of a program in Florida whose objective was to expand the health personnel and services in schools serving at-risk communities. The program was statewide and involved the use of school nurses and other health personnel placed in schools to attempt to curb the number of teenage pregnancies, to promote better student health, and to improve school performance and attendance. Undertaking the evaluation provided us with an opportunity to analyze how statewide policies might be structured to attack some of the problems children are facing. At the same time, it gave us a unique opportunity to visit with people at the local level and observe how the state policies actually took shape in different settings and how different professionals were asked to translate them into tangible supports. Interestingly, the dynamics of the evaluation process itself—the hammering out of a methodology acceptable to state-level agency personnel, local program implementers, and academic researchers—further served to illuminate the problems and potential of governmental efforts to improve children's lives through school-based interventions. The idea for this book evolved from our growing conviction that this particular program was representative of efforts in other states and localities that addressed concerns regarding children's health and upbringing. Drawing upon the analyses and data from our earlier evaluation, to which was added a fresh set of site visits in three local communities three years later, we present a heretofore unavailable description and analysis of the politics, pitfalls, and promises of using a school-based service strategy to improve the condition of children.

What Works for Children

We were drawn to the program because it seemed to incorporate many of the elements that previous research had suggested were critical to intervention programs likely to make an enduring mark on children's lives. In particular, it met the set of criteria elaborated by Lizabeth Schorr in her important research on what works in social interventions for children (Schorr & Schorr, 1989). Schorr, after identifying and analyzing successful programs for at-risk children and youth, had determined that a few features—comprehensiveness, intensity, and flexibility—are critical to success. Within certain limits, the state program could be said to adequately meet these criteria. The program attempted to be comprehensive in that its policy objectives were very broad: reduce teenage pregnancy and improve student health. Health was interpreted to mean both physical and mental health and included explicitly broad sub-objectives such as increasing student self-esteem. Virtually all health, social, and educational services services were included, either directly or through referral. The intensity of the program was questionable. It could be intense within the school setting but was limited in community and family relations. Finally, it was designed to be very flexible, allowing the funds to be used for an extensive range of services (health, social, educational) and modes of service (individual consultation, referral, classroom instruction, peer-group activities, and others). This program shared these features.

The program we were working with was titled the Florida Supplemental School Health Program. The term *supplemental* referred to the fact that it was structured as an addition to the already existing basic school health program. That is, it was designed to expand the function of school health personnel beyond the basic, or more traditional, areas of immunization, personal hygiene, and emergency care for cuts and bruises. The program was unique in a number of ways. It included a feeder pattern of schools (elementary, middle high, and high schools), required community and parental involvement, and required collaboration between the county public health unit and the local school district. It maintained a special focus on reducing teenage pregnancy, which was viewed by many in the state legislature and in local communities as a problem that lay at the core of today's economic and social troubles. The program reached about 9% of Florida schools and an equal percent of Florida's schoolchildren. As such, it operated at a scale sufficient to make a sizable impact on the lives of the children and on the schools, families, and communities in which they live throughout the state.

Other states investigated either had many fewer schools involved or broader goals, such as family and community health improvement. The only two significant state-financed intervention programs that are school-based both had much broader policy objectives. A New Jersey program, which includes grants of $250,000 per school, is limited to high schools and must include services such as job training and employment in addition to physical and mental health services. The Kentucky Family Resource and Youth Services Centers, a critical component of that state's 1991 education reform act that made available $75,000 per school, also had much broader goals, including significant family and community outreach, and had different service emphases in the elementary and high schools. There were other local programs that affected only one city or county and other state programs that financed only a few model or pilot sites. The Florida program was unique in its emphasis on a feeder pattern of schools; its focus on prevention of teenage pregnancy within a broad social, educational, and health context; and its coverage of almost 10% of the state's schoolchildren.

Even more interestingly, this program anticipated the new alignments among federal, state, and local governments that undoubtedly will define America's human services policy structure in the next century (Agranoff, 1986). As Washington, for reasons of ideology as well as in pursuit of efficiency, shrinks from policy and program responsibilities for helping the indigent, increasingly it will fall to the states to structure and fund such programs and to the local communities to assume the responsibility for making the programs work. It is unlikely that states will simply adopt the same structures as the federal government. On the contrary, they are already rethinking their new roles and a consensus is emerging that the role should be more targeted and more constrained. Many argue that states should concentrate on providing resources, establishing goals and program objectives, and assuring accountability. As states define their roles more narrowly, local governments and community organizations benefit from greater discretion in how they choose to implement programs. In turn, they will be called upon to forge local and site-based leadership structures to assure program effectiveness and survival.

Research and Policy Issues

These issues, in particular, we believed had been inadequately documented to date. As we became more familiar with the program and followed its political and programmatic deployment, we saw the program as potentially providing insight into one of the major public policy questions of the day—will decentralization work?—and one of the major social policy questions of the day—how to structure governmental supports to help poor children?

The questions to which we addressed ourselves as researchers were: Given the new politics of decentralization and increasing numbers of children needing help, how do the local actors—in this case, educators and personnel in the schools, health providers at the local public health units and the community at large—transform state-level program requirements and resources into meaningful supports for young people? More particularly, how do they assure that the programs developed respect local community values and remain supportive of local institutions such as schools, public health clinics, and neighborhood organizations? Furthermore, how do teachers and school administrators, nurses and physicians, and local community members find common ground in their search for bettering children's lives when their own understandings and values differ and their ability to understand others' points of view remain imperfect at best?

Our aim for this book was to integrate an analysis of the political, intergovernmental, and bureaucratic systems that structure governmental programs with a highly personalized investigation of how such programs are actually implemented in different contexts. We believed it important to complement our structural and institutional analyses with understandings gleaned from personal interactions with school, agency, and community people. It was important to us to preserve the individual voices of the actors—the teachers, the school board members, the school nurses. These men and women are breaking paths through new governmental, professional, and ideological landscapes, creating as they go, designing new mixes of services, institutional arrangements, and political accommodations to meet the ever-evolving needs of today's children. Our hope was that the juxtaposition of the analyses of institutional structures and political realities with the struggles of the individual actors would point the way to new understandings and new accommodations that might hold promise for helping children and strengthening the families, communities, and institutions on which they depend.

OVERVIEW OF CHAPTERS

In the next four chapters, we describe the policy design of the Florida Supplemental School Health Program and then report on the activities and observations of the personnel involved in implementing this program in three communities. In Chapter 2, we explore the structure of the program as created by the state lawmakers, describing the responsibilities given to the state agencies for policy direction, program selection and oversight, and the relation established between the state and the local providers. We also provide a detailed look behind the scenes of the evaluation process and describe how decisions were reached with the key stakeholders as to the scope of the evaluation design. Chapters 3, 4, and 5 focus on implementation issues as viewed through the perspective of the program providers. Through field interviews we explore how this policy structure is fleshed out at the local level and how the intent of the designers is supported or thwarted by the quotidian realities of the local institutions. We pose questions about the degree to which the potential of this program is realized and what issues arise in implementation.

In Chapter 6, we focus on what we call the discourses of dissent, as we examine the intersection between school health services and community values. The interplay between the narratives collected on-site and the analytic perspectives based on current research illustrate the vexing decisions faced by public officials in making policy decisions that attempt to address a wide spectrum of community concerns without alienating key constituent groups. Finally, in the last chapter, we sketch out a framework to assess the overarching issue: Is this type of program a feasible, effective, and viable model for meeting the need for routine primary care for children from impoverished communities who lack other health resources? If not, what solutions can be developed to deal with the overwhelming needs of poor families?

Chapter 2

Pursuing Social Justice Through Contested Territory

THE POLITICS OF DESIGN

In 1990 the Florida legislature established a program through House Bill 1739 to provide funds to "school districts and schools where there was a high incidence of medically under served high-risk children, low birth weight babies, infant mortality or teenage pregnancy." The purpose of the funding was to "phase in those programs which offer the greatest potential for promoting the health of students and reducing teenage pregnancy." Services were not to include the promotion of elective termination of a pregnancy, and parents could exempt their child from any services provided by the programs.

While on the surface the bill appeared to establish a relatively simple program with clear-cut objectives—health services for needy children— it became evident from the ensuing debate that the proposed program made visible complex, fundamental, and value-laden questions regarding the purpose of government, the mission of schools, the funding of health services, and the public sector's role in sex education, all questions over which our country is deeply divided. As the Florida legislature sought to address the issue, it joined elected officials throughout the country who, by the end of the 1980s, found themselves pressured to respond to a virtual flood of grim statistics chronicling the worsening condition of children throughout the country. While these reports clearly demanded a policy response, another set of voices were also arguing that many of the problems the children were facing were in fact the result of wrong-headed government programs to begin with, programs that had left a legacy of declining personal responsibility, increased dependency, and weakened family ties.

CONTESTED TERRITORY

As the Florida legislators quickly learned, the issue of teenage pregnancy and health services in school drew together in one policy locus

19

some of the most contentious and problematic issues facing the country. Despite virtual unanimity across the political and ideological spectrum that too early childbearing is destructive to the individual and to society at large, the formulation of policy to prevent teenage pregnancy is fraught with emotional and ideological controversy. Adolescent girls (and their partners) who bear children too early not only cut short their own future prospects but also risk the health and well-being of the babies involved, thus endangering two generations. While foremost a social problem, it is a serious problem for educators as well. Pregnancy is one of the major causes of young women dropping out of school, and children raised by too-young parents are at greater risk of not being ready to benefit fully from schooling when they come of age (National Commission on Children, 1991). School-based pregnancy-prevention policy formulation also thrusts one of the most sensitive and private areas of human behavior—sexuality—into the largest public bureaucracy in the country—the public schools. These broad issues of the role of government, the role of schools, and the role of personal responsibility collide in unpredictable ways when elected officials attempt to formulate policy responses. This became evident in 1990 when the Florida legislature addressed a proposal to promote health services in schools as a means of reducing teenage pregnancy.

Policy Making for Children and Youth: Barriers and Strategies

To understand the difficulties that confront legislative bodies when they undertake policy proposals seeking more effective programs to serve children, it is necessary to review briefly the increasingly persuasive body of literature documenting the difficulties experienced over the years by federal, state, and local policy makers. Reviewing scores of governmental policy reports and scholarly research programs on policy making for children, dating back to the 1909 White House Conference on Children, it becomes clear that children's policy development has been chronically hampered by deep-seated ideological differences among Americans on the appropriate role of government in helping those who are most vulnerable (Tyack, 1974; Zigler, Kagan, & Klugman, 1987). Policy making for children forces confrontations among differing philosophical beliefs about human nature and individual responsibility, differing political beliefs about the role of government in the economic and social well-being of the citizenry, and pragmatic concerns about what public institutions can achieve and how high taxes can be raised. For the purpose of this study and drawing upon previous research, we have characterized these barriers to effective policy making for children and youth as being ideo-logical, intergovernmental, and professional in nature.

Ideological Barriers. Ideology, the prevailing belief system in a cul-ture, has split the American polity over how to respond to the worsening condition of children and youth in the country (Zigler et al., 1987). Con-servative and liberal ideologies have increasingly polarized policy devel-opment. At the risk of oversimplification, it can be said that during the last 30 years policy development among liberals has focused on the eco-nomic plight of children and their families but neglected the issue of family values, while conservatives have stressed values but downplayed the need for economic support. As Kamarck and Gaston (1990) have pointed out:

> Liberals tend to reach for bureaucratic solutions even when they are counterproductive; conservatives tend to reject government responses even when they would work. (p. 3)

Social conservatives stress the importance of changing individual be-havior and articulating clearer societal norms about what is best for chil-dren. They argue that governmental services, including services for chil-dren, create negative consequences for the recipients, often leading to increased dependency on governmental support. For example, in the in-fluential book *Losing Ground,* Murray (1984) posits the "law of unintended rewards: Any social transfer increases the net value of being in the condi-tion that prompted the transfer." The "law of net harm" asserts that "the less likely it is that the unwanted behavior will change voluntarily, the more likely it is that a program to induce change will cause net harm" (p. 175). For example, the higher the welfare payments, the more people go on welfare, and the greater the availability of school-based health ser-vices, the more pregnancies among unmarried teens. Conservatives also argue that certain areas, such as sexuality education and distribution of contraceptives to adolescents, are not legitimate areas of public debate but are and should remain the sole purview of the family.

Liberals, affirming that governmental services are both legitimate and viable mechanisms for serving children, emphasize the need to im-prove the system by increasing its scope as well as its effectiveness through better coordination. To adherents of this point of view, the current deliv-ery system is inadequate as well as fragmented. It slights front-end pre-ventive measures and favors intervention only when need becomes acute, creating unnecessary costs. Reform under this perspective emphasizes sector coordination and provision of services at the most appropriate time through better assessments and follow-through. School-based health services would thus appear to be an effective mechanism for reaching needy children because providers can target the right mix of health, social, and educational services to the child; they would also appear to be an efficient mechanism because much of the infrastructure (clients, professionals, and facilities) is already in place (Kirst, 1991). The difference in these two perspectives result from ideological cleavages that run deep and too often result in an impasse in which no governmental action is taken or in governmental programs that are internally self-contradictory.

Intergovernmental Barriers. The ideological divisions are compounded by the complex intergovernmental context in which the policies and programs for children and youth are formulated, funded, and operated (Herrington, 1991a). Federal, state, and local governments all have significant and overlapping responsibilities in developing policies, determining eligibility, regulating and delivering services, and raising revenues (Gold, 1989). The sheer magnitude and complexity of the intergovernmental array of services impacting children are a barrier to sound policy. Shifts in funding levels, regulatory requirements, and the political constituencies behind them ripple through the federal, state, and local systems, confusing programmatic intent and bewildering policy makers and program personnel. Furthermore, at the local level, federal and state programs are increasingly structured as partnerships with other local governmental programs and private or nonprofit community agencies, thus creating complexity in program delivery as well as policy design. Traditionally, health services for the indigent have been the responsibility of federal and state governments in partnerships, education has been the responsibility of state and local partnerships, and teenage pregnancy-prevention programs have been the responsibility of local government or community-based nonprofit agencies.

In addition to being complex, the intergovernmental context at the local level has become very dense over the past 20 years. Human services programs grew in numbers and size dramatically during the 1960s, and complexity accompanied growth. Categorical grant programs from state and federal governments brought into being or increased the size of a host of local governmental and nongovernmental providers, including city and county program offices, local offices of state departments, and nonprofit and private community agencies. Stress on the intergovernmental landscape was further increased by the worsening condition of children in the 1980s, governmental cutbacks in program to serve these children, and the devolution of human service responsibility to the local level. Decreasing resources, increasing need, and increased responsibility have forced local governmental actors to seek more effective and efficient service delivery through increasing partnerships and cooperation. However, as closer working relationships are sought, the clashes among differing regulatory structures, financing mechanisms, and accountability requirements have grown (Agranoff, 1982). Some researchers have suggested that the inability to manage the intergovernmental context is the most serious impediment to improving conditions for children and youth (Pizzo, 1983).

The intergovernmental challenges posed by a program that consists of placing a health program run by the local public health unit within the school walls are considerable. The organizational and bureaucratic research literature has substantiated the tensions involved when established governmental offices or organizations are called upon to extend their mission, to take on additional responsibility, or to collaborate with other entities (Owens, 1991). Schools are notoriously hidebound institutions. Since the turn of this century, public schools have been separated from other local governmental and community social service agencies. Stimulated by both urban educational reform movements and attempts to professionalize school administration, school systems became increasingly separate and then isolated from the municipal and county governments that served the same children (Cremin, 1988). Furthermore, the public school system since the latter part of the nineteenth century has developed into a centralized, rationalized, and bureaucratized service delivery system. It has attained a relatively privileged and protected status (Tyack, 1974).

Proponents of placing social and health services in the school system argue that its sheer size and monolithic structure make it one of the most stable and dependable resources acting on behalf of children. Schools can be home to a broad array of services because they are large, relatively well-funded, and stable, with an extensive network of personnel and facilities throughout virtually all communities with children. On the other hand, critics charge that precisely because of their large size and bureaucratic structure, public schools lack accountability for their actions and flexibility to respond to changing conditions. Their independent and dedicated funding sources and political autonomy from other governmental and community agencies mean that they have neither the professional culture nor political incentives to collaborate. In order to attain the enhancements and efficiencies promised by a collaborative approach to program delivery, program administrators would have to overcome formidable intergovernmental and organizational barriers to coordination of services.

Professional Barriers. The ideological and intergovernmental divisions often reflect and are shaped by differences in the professional orientations of the service providers. Professionals from the health and educational sectors have been defined in terms of an association of individuals possessing valid and useful knowledge in certain areas and incorporating an ethic of service (Kimball, 1992). Exponential growth in scientific knowledge over the last century has spurred the growth and advanced organization of professions, including specialized vocational preparation, governmental licensure and certification, and varying degrees of professional autonomy in practice and in peer evaluation. This growth has led to the increasingly frequent charge of professionalism being used to translate one set of scarce resources—special knowledge and skills—into another—social and economic rewards. This charge has frequently been leveled at the health field. Professionalism has also been accused of legitimating the deliberate manipulation of expertise to make specialized knowledge artificially abstruse in order to intimidate and exclude others, a charge often leveled at educators. Both education and health care have experienced significant development in the professionalization of their fields in this century, including increasingly lengthy periods of preparation, restrictions on who may enter the profession, increasing bureaucratization of the practice site, and unprecedented growth in the knowledge base and the technology of practice.

Strategies for Overcoming Barriers. As concern for children's well-being has heightened over the last few years; and as the barriers mentioned above have become better understood, strategies to improve the quality, effectiveness, and efficiency of children's services have emerged. These strategies are not new to either public policy or to children's concerns in particular; what is new is the growing conviction of the inadequacy of the current delivery system and the urgency of creating new intergovernmental, organizational, and professional structures. Policy analysts specializing in children and youth issues have attempted to identify strategies to overcome these barriers. The strategies all share a common thread of forcing some sort of shared activity. Three were particularly influential in the design of the Florida program. These included coordinated planning and policy development, case management, and co-location of services approaches.

Coordinated planning and policy development requires agencies serving children to develop policies and programs in conjunction with other agencies that have similar responsibilities. Mandating cooperation at the point of service delivery—case management—is another approach to achieving increased coordination among agencies and improved responsiveness to individual needs. Case management allows each individual's needs to be assessed by a third party, who then outlines a service plan, drawing upon all the resources and funding streams available in the community as dictated by the assessment of the child. Finally, co-location deals with situating existing services at the same locale to ease access on the part of children and their families. This approach does not require as much integration among existing service providers as program consolidation.

The program that emerged from the Florida legislature in 1990 bore the scars of attempts to design a program that would transcend the three barriers to effective policy making noted above. However, it was also surprisingly successful in drawing upon these three strategies in order to produce a viable program blueprint. The final product was a dynamic if flawed document that provided some funds and guidance to local communities in program planning and administration, even if it failed to resolve many of the ideological tensions.

The Calculus of Action: Teenagers and Politicians at Risk

Given the forbidding nature of policy development for children and youth, it can be argued that it takes a particularly strong set of pressures to force policy makers even to attempt to craft policy responses that can survive the often caustic tests of ideology and effectiveness erected by opponents. Precisely such a set of events existed in Florida in 1990. The issue of teenage pregnancy was thrust into the spotlight by an unexpected demographic phenomenon in Florida. While teenage pregnancy rates in Florida (as in most, particularly southern, states) had been unacceptably high for most of the century, they had been declining for at least two decades. This trend continued for the country as a whole but reversed itself in the mid-1980s in Florida (the reversal then occurred in the country as a whole as well, only later). This parting between Florida and the rest of the country became a key point repeated continuously in all the official documents related to this bill. In fact, House Bill 1739 began by stating:

> The Legislature recognizes that the birth rate for teenage girls aged 15–17 years in Florida is higher than the national birth rate and that it is increasing at the same time the national rate for the same age group is decreasing. Many teenage mothers drop out of school, remain undereducated and unskilled, and lack the ability to adequately educate and care for their own children.

Another key trend was the state's dropout rate. Again, it wasn't just the existence of a disturbing indicator—it was also Florida's position vis-à-vis other states. Indicators comparing states along a number of key statistics for educational performance were released in a press conference by the U.S. secretary of education in 1986. This was the first set of comparative state data officially released by the federal government. The indicator often perceived to be the most telling—the high school dropout rate—had Florida listed dead last. The media coverage of Florida's ranking was immediate and intense. The commissioner of education and other state policy makers proclaimed their intent to address the problem head-on and take whatever action necessary to reduce the rate. Their attention was immediately drawn to the issue of teenage pregnancy because research has repeatedly indicated the importance of pregnancy as a causative factor in girls dropping out of high school.

While these societal trends were powerful enough to propel further policy making, they were not the only factors setting the policy agenda. The awareness of these troubling trends emerged at a moment in time in which the state was already engaged in two other frays that were testing the body politic. These conflicts had already etched on the political landscape a set of programmatic preferences and political commitments.

In 1986, a school health clinic was opened at Shanks High School in Quincy, Florida. Quincy, in Gadsden County, is located only 25 miles from Tallahassee, the Florida capital. The county had one of the highest infant mortality rates (13.6 per 1,000 births in 1992) in the country. The population of Quincy was 58% black (28% African-American for the rest of the county), and 38.2% of the children lived below the federally defined poverty line. This largely agricultural community had sustained itself up through the 1960s primarily through tobacco growing, which offered living wages to unskilled workers. When tobacco prices fell, the tobacco economy collapsed and the community was plunged into a state of severe destitution from which it has yet to recover. Because of the desperately needy population and its close proximity to the state capital, the county has been the recipient of numerous governmental demonstration grants.

The school health clinic was an attempt to address in one program the county's disturbingly high infant mortality, teenage pregnancy, and high school dropout rates (Florida Center for Children and Youth, 1992). Controversy erupted, however, when it was learned that the school clinic would be offering family-planning services and distributing contraceptives, in addition to offering counseling and other health services. The year the clinic opened, 1986, there had been 44 pregnancies among the school's approximately 1,300 students. Under considerable pressure from groups who argued that the school clinic appeared to sanction premarital sex and immediate gratification and to distract the school from its primary function—teaching—then-Governor Robert Martinez ordered the clinic moved off the campus in 1987. The controversy was further fueled with the award of a federal grant from the Department of Health and Human Services for the opening of a school health clinic in Miami. The governor also opposed the state's receiving these funds. Eventually the funds were awarded to a nonprofit group that was then able to offer the services in the school. These controversies were heavily covered in the media and served to mobilize groups on both ends of the political continuum.

In 1988, after several unsuccessful attempts, abortion opponents successfully convinced the Florida legislature to enact provisions restricting teenagers' access to abortion without parental consent. They were further emboldened in 1989 when the Supreme Court, while reaffirming women's constitutional right to an abortion in *Webster v. Reproductive Health Services,* nonetheless upheld a Pennsylvania court ruling that state legislatures may impose restrictions on access to abortions without violating the Constitution. Limitations might include policies pertaining to waiting periods, spousal consent, or other provisions. In 1986 Florida had elected a Republican governor who, though considered relatively moderate, became the focal point for conservative groups whose hopes had been raised by the election of the second of only two Republican governors in Florida since Reconstruction. Governor Martinez, with the intention of making Florida the first state to act only three weeks after the Supreme Court's ruling, called a special session of the Florida legislature in October 1989 to adopt legislation restricting abortion rights in Florida. He was the only governor to do so. However, less than a week before the special session convened, the Florida Supreme Court overturned the 1988 law requiring parental consent for teenagers seeking abortion, based on a strong right-to-privacy clause in the Florida constitution. As a result, the session was, by any measure, a failure. The legislature was unable to come to any consensus on whether restrictions should be imposed; if so, what form such restrictions should take; and whether they could pass constitutional muster.

The session was politically and personally bruising for all involved. It was a considerable political failure for the governor because of the large amount of publicity generated by the attempt. All state media and large portions of the national media offered detailed coverage. The *New York Times* lead article termed it a "stunning political defeat" (Schmalz, 1989). The legislative coordinator for Florida Voice for Choice, Sam Bell, said, "There was no way to hammer out a compromise. It was important to make the governor lose on all counts" (quoted in Morgan & Nickens, 1989, p. 1). Legislators who may have worked together on other bills in the past found their tempers shortened and emotions frayed over the ideological battles and political skirmishes that ensued.

The session had a number of enduring effects on the political environment in Florida. Somewhat predictably, it emphasized the differences

between conservative and liberal ideological positions and served to mobilize both ends of the political spectrum to ward off future attempts to
push policy in one direction or the other. However, it also highlighted
the growing awareness on the part of policy makers and the public of the
problems of teenage pregnancy and the material and social costs to society of children whose parents are old enough to engender them but too
young to provide for them. The special session brought into focus the
common ground shared by conservatives and liberals in their commitment to reducing teenage pregnancy and the need to get past their differences on the issue of abortion. Teenage pregnancy emerged as a common
ground for policy activity that could reunite previously warring factions
and help smooth over the harsh feelings that had surfaced during the
special session.

Major Political Players. When the Florida legislature began its pre-
session committee meetings in January 1991, prior to the opening of the
session in April, the political environment consisted of a governor who
had been very outspoken in his opposition to public funds being used for
abortion and for school health services, a commissioner of education who
was a liberal feminist committed to broadening the role of schools in
meeting a range of community needs, and a legislature that while relatively conservative (as is the case in most southern states) had failed to
back up the governor in his earlier quest to limit access to abortions.

Governor Martinez, while on record as opposed to the provision of
contraceptives on school campuses and to unlimited access to abortion,
did not have a history of social conservatism. In fact, as a younger man
he had been a prominent official in a local teachers' union and had only
recently switched his political affiliation from Democrat to Republican.
He was, however, a Catholic who had strong ties to the Catholic church
and was personally opposed to abortion. The commissioner of education,
a Democrat and the first female to be elected to the post in Florida, was
a vocal proponent of women's rights and had a strong commitment to
addressing children's needs writ large. As a woman and as the beneficiary
of many well-organized women's political groups, she was philosophically
and politically attuned to progressive approaches to dealing with adolescent sexuality and the prevention of teenage pregnancy.

The legislature itself was split. The upper chamber was under the
leadership of a conservative Democrat, who had been put in office by a
coalition of Republicans and conservative Democrats and was becoming
increasingly conservative as Republican strength increased throughout
the decade. The House, on the other hand, was solidly in control of the
Democrats and had elected a progressive Speaker who had made chil-

dren—particularly young children—the number-one priority for the legislative session.

In January Representative Lois Frankel introduced in the House a bill to provide funds to schools for health clinics whose purpose would be the reduction of teenage pregnancy by offering health services and counseling to adolescents at the schools. Frankel was a veteran state representative from Palm Beach County, known as one of the legislature's few liberals and respected for her competence and persistence. Frankel had been asked by the Speaker to head a House-wide effort to look comprehensively at the needs of the children in the state and to design a wide-ranging and comprehensive set of legislation to address the identified needs. We asked her how she had become interested in these issues and why she felt it was important to sponsor legislation to respond to the pressing problems faced in Florida. After a pause, she responded:

> There were a couple of reasons. I myself had a personal interest in teenage pregnancy. It was also right after the time Governor Martinez had called a special session on abortion. He had established a task force to examine the issue of teenage pregnancy. Several Republican legislators, including George Albright, were on it. George wanted to get at this issue in terms of preventing unwanted pregnancies rather than limiting access to abortion. We heard a lot of testimony concerning the teenage pregnancy issue and basically realized there were no easy answers. And that we could look for one answer at the state level. So we wanted to design some experimental projects to try to get at this issue. The reason I was interested in teenage pregnancy was because of the concern of babies having babies and having two human beings starting off with really a lot of obstacles in front of them.

Under the aegis of the Speaker, House Bill 1739 was one of a number of bills introduced that session to follow through with the Speaker's designated priority of policies to serve children at risk. Although the primary intent of the legislation was to focus on ways of reducing teenage pregnancies, according to Representative Frankel, the issue of general student health was added to the bill so it would appear that something positive was being done. As she candidly told us:

> I don't remember if that was a combination of public policy politics. We didn't know if we had an answer to teenage pregnancy, but we felt that if nothing else if students could be healthier at least we'd be accomplishing something.

According to legislative staff interviewed, the bill was initiated by and remained the personal commitment of Representative Frankel, and the fact that it emerged at all, regardless of the compromises forced on it, was due to her remarkable political skills and sheer determination. However, she had a critical ally in a freshman Republican, George Albright, representing a relatively conservative and rural central Florida district. While Frankel was the official sponsor of the bill and shepherded it through the session, it fell to Albright to solicit support from other Republicans and conservative Democrats, particularly those in the Senate. Even more critically, after the bill had passed both chambers it fell to him to intercede with the governor to prevent a veto.

The Final Product. The bill reflected the confluence of interests typical in most legislation. It represented some of the best thinking available from policy and professional experts regarding the proximate and long-term causes of too-early child rearing as well as the politicized opinions and beliefs of the electorate as understood by their elected officials. The core content of the bill had three parts: (1) It was to add curricular information on human sexuality and reproduction, health, interpersonal skills, and parenting to the state-required curriculum for grades K–12; (2) it expanded the roles and responsibilities of the human services and education departments to include teenage pregnancy as an issue in their prevention programs; (3) it created and provided funds for the supplemental school health services program, which was to be a competitive grant program through which local public health units in conjunction with school districts would apply for state funds to provide supplemental health services at the school site. It came to be known as the Florida Supplemental School Health Program.

The legislation listed three types of program models from which school districts or schools could choose: school health improvement pilot project (SHIP), student support services team program, and full-service schools.

In addition, the legislation stipulated that "funding may also be available for any other program that is comparable to a program described in this subsection but is designed to meet the particular needs of the community." This language was critical in allowing communities to construct a program that reflected the values and beliefs of major players within the community, and it made the overall program much more context-sensitive to local differences. As evident in the case studies presented in later chapters, communities took full advantage of this provision to create programs that differed not only across regions but even across schools within the same district.

Funding was provided from the state's general revenue fund through the removal of a sales tax exemption on nonprofit physical fitness facilities (such as those run by hospitals). In 1990–91, $2.6 million was appropriated for a five-month period and, in 1991–92, $9,261,000 was appropriated. Twenty-eight projects were funded the first year and an additional 21 the second year.

The enacting legislation stipulated that the Supplemental School Health Program would be a collaborative program involving the state Department of Health and Rehabilitative Services and the Department of Education. The law stated that the heads of both agencies were to publicize the availability of funds and to form a joint committee to evaluate and select the school districts or schools to receive the funds. The enabling legislation also provided for an evaluation of the programs that would include analyses of effectiveness in meeting selected outcome objectives.

Conflicts and Accommodations

Disagreement centered on two major issues: (1) What was to be taught to students about human sexuality and reproduction? (2) what health services were to be provided in the schools?

K–12 Curriculum. The bill initially included abortion counseling as a component of the K–12 health education curriculum. This language was struck very early in committee deliberations by conservative opponents. A second point of contention was the degree of control and review given to parents. Opponents of the bill tried to insert language requiring parents to give explicit permission for their children to receive instruction on reducing teenage pregnancy. Although they were not successful, the final language did include a parent op-out clause. Parents could stipulate that their children were not to receive such instruction, but parents had to take the action. Permission did not have to be sought *a priori* by the school district. Amendments were introduced that provided considerable prescription of what school districts were to teach. They would be required to teach (1) that abstinence is the only 100% effective means of avoiding out-of-wedlock pregnancy, sexually transmitted diseases, and sexually transmitted AIDS, and (2) that all methods of contraception other than abstinence carry a risk of failure in the prevention of unwanted pregnancy. They would also be required to include discussion of the possible adverse emotional and psychological consequences of preadolescent and adolescent sexual intercourse outside of marriage and to instill respect for monogamous heterosexual marriage. These amendments failed.

Opponents were successful in including language to the effect that the instruction would deal not only with reduction of pregnancy but also with reduction of sexual activity. They were also successful in having language inserted that stated that "instruction in human sexuality must take into account the whole person, must present ethical and moral direction, must not be an expression of any one sectarian or secular philosophy, and must respect the conscience and rights of students and of parents."

Health Services on School Grounds. A second major objection was to having health clinics located on school grounds. Language deleting this key provision was introduced but did not pass at the committee level. However, the term *health clinic* was changed to *health room*. As noted by a supportive legislator: "The term *clinic* should never have been introduced to begin with. It was a red flag. Once we got rid of it, a lot of opposition died down." Attempts to insert similar amendments were introduced on the floor of the House as well. In fact, the opposition by then had became better organized and more aggressive. Amendments were introduced to head off abortion counseling and referral by having explicit language stating that such services could not be included. However, these amendments failed.

Personal and Political Commitment. Passage of the bill came down to the last few days of the legislature. As has been noted by other research, the fault line in society regarding the role of government in human sexuality cuts across other associations. This was certainly the case here. Support for the bill cut across divisions of gender, political affiliation, geography, and ideology.

The two most visible players in shaping the content of the bill and pressing for its adoption were an unlikely pair of House members. Lois Frankel, as mentioned earlier, was a veteran legislator, known as well for her liberal views as for her competence. Her success in advancing her positions over the years was remarkable given the conservative nature of the Florida legislature and its composition as a primarily male preserve. Intelligence, knowledge of the system, and persistence, along with a willingness to address disagreements head-on and to craft positions competing factions could support, had resulted in her being a formidable presence on the political scene. In this case she drew clout from being the Speaker's designee on children's issues and from expertise she had been developed over the years in the areas of health and women's issues. She also benefited from an informal caucus of female legislators whose cohesion had strengthened during the special abortion session and who were able to draw upon one another for support and arm-twisting when needed. She successfully shepherded the bill through the session, guiding it through the labyrinth of subcommittees, full committees, and appropriation committees—a structure whose primary purpose is to kill all but the heartiest of bills.

The other major supporter of the bill was equally effective, although the opposite in ideology and in experience. George Albright was a freshman legislator elected from a conservative rural district in central Florida, a Republican who was committed to socially and fiscally conservative approaches to government. His support of the bill was both pragmatic and personal. Like the governor, he was personally opposed to abortion. However, he came to believe that educating students about the risks and consequences of too-early sexual behavior was the best way of reducing the demand for abortions. He differed from other social conservatives in that he thought that *not* teaching young people about sexuality is what leads to irresponsible behavior. In an interview, he revealed that his support for the bill came from his own experiences as an adolescent. Although his parents divorced when he was 16, they were what he termed "educated, responsible parents." His mother, in fact, was a nurse. However, neither one ever mentioned sex to him. What he learned, he learned on the streets. He told us, "I thought the kids of Florida deserved better than this. If I didn't learn about sex at home, and my parents were good parents, what are the chances of other kids learning about it, too?"

Lois Frankel was the official "handler" of the bill; drawing upon her knowledge based on years of experience in the legislature and her clout based on being the Speaker's designee for children's issues, she led the bill through the process. Duties of garnering the votes necessary for the bill's passage were split between Frankel and Albright. Frankel mobilized the other liberal-leaning legislators and the women's political activists. However, because of Frankel's reputation as a liberal, Albright took responsibility for gathering support of not only his fellow Republicans but also the conservative Democrats. As a freshman, he was not well known but, by dint of working the bill through the House and the Senate, he not only came to know his fellow House members better but ended up meeting all 40 state senators as he lobbied them each—one by one—to support the legislation. The bill finally passed out of both houses in the waning days of the session. It passed 39 to 0 in the Senate and 76 to 40 in the House.

The fight was not over yet, however, because the governor's staff had placed the bill on the governor's veto list. Albright was again called into action. He appealed to the governor's chief of staff to reconsider, and he solicited the support of a number of wealthy constituents who had contributed to the governor's campaign. They placed a number of urgent calls to the governor asking that he at least reread the bill carefully and consider his position closely before vetoing it. In the end, the governor did not veto the bill, but neither would he sign it. It thus became law, but without his signature.

THE POLITICS OF DESIGN

The bill that resulted from the political conflict and personal ideologies of the various actors was a carefully crafted, delicate instrument of social policy. Its design features and policy components wove a careful path through the political and ideological minefields that studded the bill. What emerged was an innovative and experimental document whose potential effectiveness lay in the details of its design.

Intergovernmental and Professional Structure

The program erected an intergovernmental structure that was rather unique in its flexibility. The state role was narrow but clear. The state provided funds, designated eligibility criteria and program objectives, mandated intersector cooperation, and required an evaluation two years later. Eligibility criteria consisted of four indicators of need: high rates of medically underserved, high-risk children; low-birth-weight babies, infant mortality, and teenage pregnancy. The relative weights of these four indicators was not specified.

The local role was much broader and less narrowly defined. The legislation gave considerable flexibility to the local school districts and county public health units to determine the types of services to be offered and the personnel to be hired. The legislative language describing the first two models provided a long list of possible services, ranging from direct health service to counseling, educating, and providing referrals. The third model—the full-service school model—authorized virtually any service currently offered by the state's huge integrated health and human services department to be offered at the school site. Furthermore, a fourth option was allowed—the locally designed model—whose only prescription by the state was that it be "comparable" to the other ones and meet local community needs. The bill was very general in terms of defining community needs.

The legislative language regarding the program's goals and objectives was equally broad. It established in statute two overall goals—reducing teenage pregnancy and promoting student health—and five additional supporting objectives: decreasing self-destructive behavior, improving student health education, improving student counseling, improving extracurricular activities, and improving student self-esteem. These goals and objectives were broad enough that they excluded virtually nothing. By having such broad and numerous programs objectives mixed with considerable flexibility in project design, the state allowed the local school district and county public health unit to craft projects tailored to the health and social service needs of their communities, measured to the capacities of the local providers and responsive to the values and beliefs of community members.

Similarly, the agency structure was outlined only in broad strokes. Most details were left unspecified. The legislation required that the two executive agencies at the state level cooperate in evaluating proposals for the grant and in conducting a two-year evaluation. The state Department of Health and Rehabilitative Services was designated as the fiscal agent, and the funds were placed in that agency. Likewise, the legislation required a joint application from the local school district and the local county public health unit, but the county public health unit would serve as fiscal agent and would be the only agency authorized to expend the funds even though the services would be delivered on school campuses. It was silent on technical issues, such as who would be the employer of the personnel, who would own the equipment in the health room, and who would supervise and evaluate the personnel, as well as on more complicated issues, such as what restrictions might be placed on the health curriculum or the range of services and who was authorized to determine such restrictions.

The legislation was very inclusive in regard to professionals who would be eligible to work in the project. Clearly, one of the guiding principles behind the legislation was that today's children needed the services of both a nurse and more varied professionals. The aim of the legislation was to encourage educators, health personnel, and other related professionals (e.g., social workers) to work in more coordinated and presumably more effective ways for children's benefit.

The enabling legislation specified particular professionals in two of the models. The SHIP model detailed a staffing model consisting of school health aides and nurses and specified services such as providing student health appraisals, identifying health problems, conducting screenings and assessments, and working to coordinate health services for students with parent and other agencies (see Figure 2.1). However, services were not limited to these, all of which are broad to begin with.

The second model (see Figure 2.2) was also flexibly described. It encouraged a particular set of professionals and a particular set of services without being very restrictive. Called the student support services team

Figure 2.1
School Health Improvement Project (SHIP)

The model shall include basic health care to an elementary school, middle
school, and high school in a feeder system.

Program services shall include, but not be limited to:

- Planning, implementing, and evaluating school health services. Staffing
  shall include a full-time, trained school health aide in each elementary,
  middle, and high school; one full-time nurse to supervise the aides in the
  elementary and middle schools; and one full-time nurse in each high school.

- Providing student health appraisals and identification of actual or potential
  health problems by screenings, nursing assessments, and record reviews.

- Expanding screening activities.

- Improving the student utilization of school health services.

- Coordinating health services for students with parents or guardians and
  other agencies in the community.

program, it consists of a psychologist, social worker, and nurse; it focuses
on children who have mild to complex health, behavioral, or learning
problems affecting their school performance.

The third model (see Figure 2.3), the full-service school, located the
services available through the state's Department of Health and Rehabilitative Services on the school site. The legislation lists the services and
includes nutritional and health services, AFDC eligibility determination,
parenting skills, and education and abused children counseling.

The fourth model was a local option and made no mention of specific professions. All the models attempted to encourage integrated teams
of professionals who could serve a broad array of children's needs within
a local context as determined by need for services and local acceptability.

The bill contained features that reflected the best knowledge of the
experts in the substantive fields of education and health policy. The program was clearly designed to be responsive to locally defined needs and
to be locally administered. It defined services broadly, capturing the best
thinking about what causes early sexual activity and pregnancy. It recognized the psychological factors involved as well as the curricular activities.

Figure 2.2
Student Support Services Team Model

The model shall include a multidisciplinary team composed of a psychologist, social worker, and nurse whose responsibilities are to provide basic support services and to assist, in the school setting, children who exhibit mild to severely complex health, behavioral, or learning problems affecting their school performance.

Support services shall include, but not be limited to:

- Evaluation and treatment for minor illness and injuries

- Referral and follow-up care for pregnancy or chronic diseases and disorders as well as emotional or mental problems

- Referral care for drug and alcohol abuse and sexually transmitted diseases

- Sports and employment physicals

- Immunizations

- Preventive services intended to delay early sexual involvement and aimed at pregnancy, Acquired Immune Deficiency Syndrome, sexually transmitted diseases, and destructive lifestyle conditions, such as alcohol and drug abuse

The funds for this program are to be used to fund three teams, each consisting of one half-time psychologist, one full-time nurse, and one full-time social worker. Each team shall provide student support services to an elementary school, middle school, and high school that are a part of one feeder school system and shall coordinate all activities with the school administrator and guidance counselor at each school. A program which places all three teams in middle schools or high schools may also be proposed.

It recognized the limitations of didactic instruction in changing the behavior of young adolescents. It also recognized the importance of the institutional setting by stipulating that feeder patterns of schools should be involved, thus providing for continuity of services and care. Other positive points included required staff development for instructional components and a statewide policy advocacy group to review and make further

Figure 2.3
Full-Service Schools Model

The full-service schools model integrates the services of the Department of Health and Rehabilitative Services that are critical to the continuity-of-care process. The Department of Health and Rehabilitative Services shall provide services to students on the school grounds.

Services to be provided may include, but are not limited to the following:

- Nutritional services

- Medical services

- Aid to dependent children

- Parenting skills

- Counseling for abused children and education for the students' parents or guardians.

The full-service school model usually serves one specific school and is staffed by a variety of professionals and paraprofessionals including an ARNP, nurse, social worker, and/or physician.

---

recommendations to the legislature on further policy development in this area.

Ideological Accommodation Through Decentralization

The bill that emerged from the session was a delicately crafted instrument designed to accommodate a wide assortment of locally developed programmatic initiatives while striving to maintain cohesion and accountability to specified state policy objectives. It used the strongest incentive the state possesses—money—to encourage local initiative and local responsibility. It created a flexible policy mechanism to encourage and authorize local communities to seek their own accommodation through the contested grounds. It attempted to avoid ideological conflict at the state level through a strategy of decentralization. It allowed wide latitude in the mix and type of services, thus allowing for considerable local accommodation. It did not upset the prevailing administrative structures at the local level. The monies were to be spent using existing inter-governmental structures, existing bureaucratic units, and existing professional service providers.

But it also failed to resolve the substantives issues that divided the legislature (which was no doubt a prerequisite for passage). The ideological fault lines ran deep and were not amenable to rational or technical solutions. One group believed that instruction about sexuality should not be in the purview of a governmental institution and that doing so implicitly condoned sexual activity outside of marriage, misled young people into false security regarding unwanted pregnancy, and weakened parental authority. The other group believed that a failure to educate was an abdication of government's responsibility to step in where the health and safety of young people were at risk. The strong consensus over ends—the reduction of teenage pregnancy—masked a deeply divisive lack of consensus on means. Basically two philosophies were competing with each other. One group's solution was the other group's problem.

The means to break through the ideological and technical impasse was through a strategy of decentralization. The state would authorize the program but not prescribe its content. It would provide funds without mandating how the funds would be spent. It would force cooperation among service deliverers and integration of service delivery without prescribing the nature of the integration or of the services. The state both rose to the challenge of addressing the issue and at the same time recognized the limitation of its authority and legitimacy to prescribe programmatic features at the local level. However, the program's virtues were also its liabilities. The most controversial issues were simply ignored in the legislation and were left to the local communities to fight out.

Interrogating the Politics of Evaluation

Although the state refused to mandate specific program components at the individual level, it did amend Florida Statute 404.321 to direct the Department of Health and Rehabilitative Services (HRS) in conjunction with the Department of Education (DOE) to conduct an evaluation of the effectiveness of the Supplemental School Health Program. The emphasis was on determining whether selected program objectives centered on student health promotion and the reduction of teenage pregnancy were being met. Both departments were required to have a third party conduct the evaluation; they could not use their own staff, who were already engaged in internal program monitoring efforts. The contract was issued to the Learning Systems Institute at the Florida State University. In our initial conversations with our primary stakeholders—program personnel in HRS and DOE—we chose to make explicit our values in terms of how they would frame the evaluation of a program designed to provide comprehensive, school-linked health, medical, and social services to children. We subscribe to Guba and Lincoln's (1989) assertion that science is not value-free, nor are evaluations in a fourth-generation model. But such a position carries particular consequences for the evaluator in terms of how the worth of the evaluation will be judged, as well as consequences for those being evaluated.

Stakeholder Involvement. From the first meeting we had with personnel from both departments, it was clear to us that maintaining an "outsider" perspective would be extremely difficult, in terms of both our beliefs as to how evaluations should be conducted and the intense concern of both departments that the evaluation should yield information that would not only shape future program directions but also produce results so that the program would receive continued (and perhaps increased) funding. For the program personnel, these results translated into being able to demonstrate to legislators that the program made a discernible difference in the funded schools in reducing teenage pregnancy rates and promoting healthy behaviors among students. Although we were sympathetic to these concerns, we felt that our role included keeping everyone's attention focused on the fact that in the first 18 months of implementation, these results, if any, would be negligible. Our concern was reflected in the excerpt from the memo we sent concerning the rationale for the evaluation:

> This evaluation will be both process- and impact-oriented. However, during the first year of full-scale program operations, we believe the major emphasis should be placed on examining issues and problems related to implementation, and not on determining outcomes. In saying this, we are not suggesting that data on impact outcomes will not be collected. But the fact remains that the real outcomes desired from this program are long-term in nature and cannot be conclusively established except to demonstrate the beginning of a trend. The long-term outcomes we are referring to are positive changes in health care practices and behaviors, and a decrease in the teenage pregnancy rate. Even if impact outcomes are not the primary focus of the evaluation, a more likely scenario is that the process evaluation will reveal the ways in which students are beginning to change their behavior, and the factors which motivate them to do so. . . . The interrelationship among educational,

medical, and social services for children and their families who are under stress in modern society is so complex that any solutions to their problems must be multifaceted and extend over a period of several years. The era of the quick fix through one year of program operations is over. The best result that can be hoped for is to demonstrate that the program is making a difference in children's lives and to describe the ways in which components of the program can be strengthened or, if necessary, eliminated, and new ones put in place. (project memo, June 28, 1991)

Given the concerns expressed by both agencies, we felt that the evaluation should be structured around the utilization focused approach (Patton, 1986). This approach is based on five premises: (1) Concern for utilization should be the driving force in an evaluation; (2) concern for utilization is ongoing and continuous from the very beginning of the evaluation; (3) evaluations should be user-oriented; (4) once identified, the intended evaluation users should be personally and actively involved in making decisions about the evaluation; and (5) recognition is made of the multiple and varied interests surrounding any evaluation (Patton, 1986). While this approach incorporated some aspects of "formative" and "summative" evaluation, it also involved a much greater recognition of the negotiable aspects of the decision-making processes that occur during the course of the evaluation.

We also took into consideration these issues: (1) that program outcomes are contextualized with respect to factors present in local school districts and are not necessarily generalizable across all districts; (2) that program implementation may vary from one site to another; (3) that key stakeholders have different political investments in the success of programs; and (4) that agency officials have the delicate job of developing policies that allow for some uniformity across the districts in meeting the legislative requirements, while still maintaining the autonomy of local school districts to make adjustments based on local conditions that still comply with the mandates of the program.

While program staff from both agencies accepted the premises underlying the approach we had selected, they were especially concerned that we collect sufficient "hard" data that would demonstrate that the projects in the various schools were effective in meeting the two objectives of the program: reducing teenage pregnancy and improving student health. Working this issue through was the single greatest source of tension between us and the program personnel, and even between the two authors, since the first author was extensively trained in both quantitative and qualitative research methods, and was aware of the limitations in gathering "objective" data in field based studies, while the second author was an educational policy analyst who was acutely aware of the legislators' need to have defensible data on which to base future funding decisions.

We concurred with the opinion expressed by Lisbeth and Daniel Schorr (1989) in their book, *Within Our Reach*, that there was a premature rush to make quantitative judgments in social services, to want to convert program inputs and outputs to that which can be easily measured and, therefore, easily proved to be ineffective in statistical analyses. As the Schorrs note, "Many of the most effective interventions with high risk families are inherently unstandardized and idiosyncratic," and that "for many services, *how* they are delivered is as important as *that* they are delivered" (1989, p. 269). We also agreed with their conclusion:

> No single study, no single set of statistics, no single piece of evidence should be the basis of decisions to fund or not to fund, to abandon or replicate a project. Judgments about what works should be based on a thoughtful appraisal of the many kinds of evidence available. That means relying not only on quantitative but also on qualitative information, not only on evaluations by "objective" outsiders but on the experiences of committed practitioners, not on isolated discoveries but on understanding how consistent the findings are with other knowledge. Relying on common sense, prudence, and understanding in interpreting evidence does not mean sacrificing rigor in assessing information. But applying human intelligence may bring us closer to policy-relevant conclusions than reliance on numbers that have been manipulated in ways that ultimately conceal a basic ignorance of what is really going on. (1989, p. 270)

Evaluation Design. Just as the bill bringing the Supplemental School Health Program to life represented a compromise of ideological beliefs and accommodation to differences across regions, our final design was a compromise between process- and outcome-oriented approaches based on extensive negotiations over several months with agency program personnel. In a subsequent memo, we clarified the final design as follows:

> One critical issue discussed was the legislature's expectations concerning the results of the evaluation. It was decided that the evaluation should focus on meeting two goals: (1) to determine how well the services were being provided in the funded schools, which relates to quality of care issues; and (2) to determine whether this program was effective in promoting better student health and reducing the incidence of teen pregnancy. These two goals call for different evaluation strategies to be em-

ployed simultaneously, which are discussed below. The first goal emphasizes a process approach to the evaluation, one which will be handled primarily through the use of case studies of 12 funded projects. In this process, an important component will be the information acquired through the bimonthly reports submitted by each school. It was agreed that the evaluation team would work closely with the agency staff in the design of the report format to ensure that all schools are providing comparable information. At the same time, the evaluation team will be available for technical assistance to districts as needed to help them begin the process of internal evaluation. This latter step is necessary since each school has developed slightly different goals and objectives for their project, and they need to know how to monitor their own process after the evaluation team has completed its assessment. The second goal represents an outcomes orientation, and in our memo dated 6/28/91, it was noted that outcomes information will not be fully available for several years in order to determine that the program has been effective when compared to alternative models for achieving these same goals. However, a crucial element of the evaluation should be to lay the groundwork for collecting a database that will facilitate a more complex statistical analysis in the future. (project memo, August 5, 1991)

Other issues discussed at this meeting included replacing the term *school-based health clinics* with *school health room* because it was politically contested in several areas, and also examining the nurses' role in the school in terms of being educators versus health care providers. We also raised the issue of having all projects use common forms for collecting the outcome indicators, but that proved to be too politically difficult to enforce.

The final evaluation design drew primarily upon information collected from the following sources: (1) a survey of 2,572 students in 49 project schools; (2) site visits to 12 counties, where interviews with over 120 people were conducted, including focus group interviews with elementary and secondary students; and (3) a review of health activity logs maintained by all health rooms. In addition, documents including the authorizing legislation, project application forms, and individual project documentation (news clippings, internal reports and assessments, student attitudinal data, etc.) were reviewed. (For a more comprehensive description of the technical aspects of the process and the outcome data, see Emihovich & Herrington, 1993.)

Negotiating the Final Report. While we were able to reach consensus fairly quickly on how the data were to be represented in terms of formatting issues (e.g., which section appeared first, how much of the professional literature was cited, etc.), three issues proved particularly difficult to negotiate. These issues were the discussion of project cost-effectiveness data; interpretations of outcome indicators such as pregnancy, absenteeism, and dropout rates; and program recommendations.

When we identified the preliminary structure of the final report, the issue of establishing cost-effectiveness of one project model type over another quickly surfaced. The legislators had made it clear that they wanted to have data available on project costs, especially in reference to outcomes. We felt that providing this data from this perspective was not feasible, and we outlined our position by giving them two possible options that could be pursued. The first option was to provide a chart that detailed the type of project model, staffing configurations, number of students served, project funds requested, cost per student, and benefits or services provided. We were careful to tell them that this chart could be used for *descriptive purposes only* to provide a quick glance at differences among projects, and could not be used to support the conclusion, for example, that the team concept in one site was more cost-effective in providing services than the local design used by another site.[1]

We also mentioned that they should consider conducting a cost-benefit analysis to answer the question they had wanted us to answer: Which type of project model is most cost-effective in providing a given service? However, we cautioned them that a cost-benefit analysis was very complex, time-consuming, and expensive, and that insufficient funds had been committed to the evaluation to undertake this analysis. We suggested that since cost-benefit analyses are typically done several years after a project is up and running, because costs have stabilized after the initial implementation costs, and the outcomes are more clearly visible then, that the agency consider conducting such an analysis in the future. Ultimately, we were successful in having them accept the first option, and we mention this to illustrate some of the pressures evaluators face to provide information that is beyond the scope of the original design.

A second issue that needed to be resolved through extensive negotiations was the kinds of outcome indicators that would be discussed in the final report. The program personnel were anxious to include as much data as possible that could demonstrate program effectiveness, and one of our tasks was to remind them that inferences regarding effectiveness are dependent on the quality of the limited outcome data we are able to collect and the scope of the evaluation design. One issue that had to be resolved early in the process was our choice not to use the standard, experimental-group control design that Kirby, Waszak, and Ziegler (1989) used in their evaluation of six school-based health clinics. In a project memo we clarified our position:

1. After one year of full-scale program operations, there are unlikely to be major differences between clinic and nonclinic schools. Generally speaking, because of the type of behaviors that are being impacted, it takes several years of operations to demonstrate a trend. A comparison analysis done too soon is likely to have the unfortunate effect of being used politically to prove that no change *between* schools has occurred and that funding should be eliminated. We feel that it is possible to demonstrate that small-scale changes are occurring *within* schools and that a regression analysis between clinic and nonclinic schools can always be done at a later date when more information is available.

2. Finding an appropriate comparison school is extremely difficult in field-based studies for several reasons. One, since the evaluator does not control which school initially receives the program and which school does not, as would be the case in a true research design, the selection process is already biased. Second, the factors impacting on students' behavior in clinic and nonclinic schools are also not easily controlled, and statistical controls are a poor substitute. For example, in a small community with only two high schools, the school not receiving funds may be motivated to improve their health program just to keep up with the other school.[2] There is an additional problem in that the type of students who seek care from the clinic may already be different from nonclinic students in ways that cannot be predicted in advance or controlled for later.

3. The presence or absence of a school-based health clinic cannot be considered as a single variable affecting outcomes. Instead, the clinic is a multifaceted entity that is likely to affect students' behaviors in a number of ways, all of which vary by factors such as race, sex, income, community context, etc. Dr. Kirby's analysis, which extended over two years of clinic operations, failed to demonstrate that the clinics significantly (in the statistical sense) affected pregnancy and birth-control rates, and results pertaining to risk-taking behaviors (e.g., decreased smoking, drug use) were only significantly established at one or two sites. On the other hand, some of the process data, based on interviews, indicated that students found the clinic very helpful in providing contraceptive information and that for many low-income students, the clinic

was the only source of health care they received. From this perspective, the clinics did make a discernible difference in the quality of students' lives, a case of where the outcomes were important
in a behavioral sense, even if they were not statistically significant.

4. The most critical information concerning contraception and sexual activity cannot be collected across all schools on a survey form
without entailing enormous community opposition in certain
areas.[3] Most of the data collected by the Center for Population
Options was in large metropolitan areas where there apparently
is not the same level of community distrust as would be the case
in Florida. You will note that on the survey forms we have submitted for review, we have avoided asking questions concerning contraceptive use and level of sexual activity.[4] This information can
be obtained from interviews, but that would not yield a sufficiently large sample from which to do a statistical analysis. However, case study data can be used to draw analytical conclusions.
(project memo, June 28, 1991)

In a subsequent memo, we also raised two questions about outcomes
for the program personnel to consider:

This approach raises two questions which need to be addressed: (1) What indicators can be used to demonstrate improved student health and a reduction in teen pregnancy
rates? (2) What types of instruments are needed to collect this
information? With regard to improved student health, it was
suggested that the following indicators would provide useful information: a reduced absenteeism rate in schools, since fewer
children would need to be sent home for illnesses; an increase
in students' knowledge of healthy lifestyle behaviors as reflected in the reduction of certain problems recurring in the
health room; and a change in students' attitudes toward practicing healthy behaviors. The data on teenage pregnancy would
include the compilation of statistics indicating a reduction in
the number of births to teenage mothers and, concurrently, a
reduction in the rate of low-birth-weight babies to teenage
mothers, a reduction in the number of sexually transmitted diseases among teenagers, and an increased willingness of teenage
mothers to seek prenatal care. To collect data on several of
these outcomes, it was originally proposed that a pre- and posttest survey be administered to a random sample of students involved in these projects. However, several problems with this

approach were noted at the meeting. The most serious problem is that blanket permission from the Department of Education would need to be acquired for all participating schools in
order to avoid the problem of gaining approval from individual
school boards. It was decided that this issue would be discussed with appropriate education officials to see if this could
be arranged. A second related issue concerned the content of
the survey questions, and it was suggested that the data obtained from a recent risk assessment survey administered by
DOE might serve the purpose of this evaluation.[5] As for collecting data on children's health indicators, an important tool will
be the form used by schools to collect information in the
health room. The form originally proposed for this task will be
redesigned and given to all schools so that information collected across schools can be compared. The instrument for assessing children's attitudes toward healthy behaviors will also be
redesigned, one form for elementary students and one form
for secondary students. Existing forms available in the literature on children's health will be used when possible. (project
memo, August 5, 1991)

One indicator that we had wanted to keep in the evaluation design
was changes in students' attitudes toward risky behaviors as measured
through a pre- and posttest survey conducted six months apart. However,
for a number of reasons, we were only able to survey the students once
instead of twice; consequently, we suggested that this data be used as
baseline data for future evaluations. The program personnel were not
pleased when we informed them that we could not report on changes in
students' behavior as a result of programmatic activities, and they had
to settle for a detailed description of these activities, with the implied
assumption that some students may have been positively affected.[6]
The program staff had also wanted us to report on the program's
effectiveness with regard to pregnancy rates, dropout rates, injury rates,
and absenteeism. We struggled with this issue because we knew that all
four were very unstable due to differences across projects as to how this
information was compiled. At the beginning of the evaluation, we had
initially proposed that all projects use the same procedure for collecting
data on these indicators, but this proposal was rejected as being "too intrusive" on individual projects' autonomy. The program personnel had
also wanted us to collect data on all projects (99 of them); we compromised by collecting data on only the 47 projects that would be visited in
the 12 case studies. We argued that by going on-site, we would be able to

talk to people to learn how they kept statistics in these areas and that we would know how to interpret the information we received across projects.

Not surprisingly, the greatest variation occurred in the pregnancy data. One reason is that students were not required to report their pregnancies to school officials. Another problem was that, in many schools, the responsibility for keeping track of the number of girls who reported they were pregnant was often divided among different professionals: the school nurse, the school social worker, the guidance counselor, and/or the teacher in charge of the teen parent program. We spent hours in each school trying to verify our figures across these groups to make sure that the pregnancies were not being double-counted. To complicate the task further, many school personnel were reluctant to provide this information, since they suspected (no doubt rightly) that if their numbers were higher than the ones they reported on their original grant applications, this fact would be used by certain groups to argue that providing school health services increased student sexual activity. As the case studies indicated, the reality was that the numbers weren't changing—only the girls' willingness to seek help, since they now knew it was available. Ironically, some of the schools that reported an increase in pregnancy rates were located in districts that had a strict abstinence-based sexuality curriculum, while decreases were reported in schools that had a more liberal policy of presenting contraception options.

A third problem was that in many high-risk middle and high schools the student transfer rate could run as high as 70% in the course of a single semester. This meant that a girl would become pregnant while attending one school (perhaps one where no services were offered) and then transfer to one with services, where she would now report that she was pregnant. She could even transfer to another school within a few weeks and report being pregnant there. In these cases, it was impossible to establish which school (or schools) should be credited with the pregnancy, and short of tracking individual students (impossible for confidentiality reasons), there was no rational way to solve this problem.[7]

Because of the instability of the outcome data, we suggested that it be reported as descriptive information only and that no meaningful conclusions could be drawn. For reasons important to them, the program personnel requested that the data be reported out by specific schools, and, as expected, once the report was released, schools who were mentioned as having had an increase in pregnancy rates faced considerable protests from parent and community groups. By the same token, schools who reported a decrease were able to get considerable political mileage from it in terms of enhanced community support.

The final, and most contested, area of discussion was the recommendations. We limited ourselves as much as possible to making descriptive statements and hedged on drawing inferences that the program was the reason why certain outcomes occurred. A particular bone of contention was our refusal to recommend that the program be expanded to other schools, despite the need we saw expressed on our site visits (we did recommend that current projects should receive continued funding). We felt that a second evaluation should be conducted, using the baseline data we had collected, to document more conclusively the trends we saw as clearly emerging that the projects were making a difference in students' lives, if not directly in their risk behaviors.[8] We took this position because we believed that keeping the same projects constant would enable realistic comparisons to be made on where differences were occurring and that accountability to the larger public would be established. Although we believed strongly in the value of having these services available in schools (as evidenced by our choosing to write this book), we also believed that, if empirical data were to be used to drive decisions, more should not be claimed than what the data can support. The irony is that by choosing to conduct a process-oriented evaluation that was qualitative in nature, instead of setting up an evaluation design that was more scientifically oriented in terms of statistical controls, we were likely to be perceived by some colleagues in the academic world as having been compromised by the stakeholders' demands for continued involvement throughout the process.

Political Reception of the Report. Ironically, despite the agency's high level of concern about the form and content of the evaluation report and its potential positive or negative effect on the legislature's funding decision, the legislature showed little interest in the report when it was submitted to them in January 1993. The political and fiscal climate of the state had changed dramatically between 1989, when the program was enacted, and 1992, when the evaluation was completed. The state had been plunged into the worst depression it had experienced since the 1930s. Tax collections had fallen far behind estimates, which resulted in a series of funding cutbacks and withholdings of already appropriated funds. Between 1990 and 1992, almost $2 billion in appropriated funds were pulled back from state agencies. The legislators' attention was focused on funding existing programs and managing the short-term crisis. Furthermore, an increasingly conservative shift was making itself felt in the political arena, and all social and health programs were facing potential cutbacks. The progressive social service advocates were being forced into a more defensive posture, and simply maintaining current funding levels was considered a success. The key sponsor of the bill, Representative Lois Frankel, had resigned from the state legislature to run (unsuccessfully) for a congressional seat. A new Democratic governor, Lawton Chiles, had been elected, but his major social services priorities were in prenatal and early childhood programs.

The lack of interest shown in the evaluation report is ironic in that the ascending rhetoric of the 1990s has been that all governmental programs need to be regularly and rigorously monitored, and that only those with evidence of effectiveness will be maintained. But, in fact, a much older adage concerning governmental pathologies seems to have prevailed—once a program is established and funded, it disappears from the political landscape. Its proponents do not want to jeopardize its existence by drawing attention to it, and its opponents do not want to waste their time or political capital attacking a program that is already up and running throughout the state, one whose employees and beneficiaries could easily be mobilized in its defense (a good example of this latter case is described in Chapter 5, where a school board had to back down from closing the school clinic because of intense community opposition against this action).

Even more disheartening has been the almost complete disregard of even the most modest recommendation in the report, which was for the state agency to convene the local program personnel responsible for data collection and train them to establish a consistent and uniform set of definitions and protocols for collecting comparable data across sites on the key program indicators, such as pregnancy rates, dropout rates, and absenteeism. Our evaluation study had documented the methodological problems involved in collecting valid information across multiple sites on indicators such as pregnancy rates, and we recommended the need for statewide coordination and oversight. And since the evaluation study had established baseline data for only the initial full year of program operation and one year after that, subsequent data collection in the third, fourth, and fifth years was necessary to confirm or refute the initially positive findings of the first study. In the absence of ongoing data collection, though the state has funded the program for over five years, agency personnel still do not know if, and to what degree, the program has been successful in meetings its objectives. Nor have any promising practices or implementation models been confirmed that could then be adopted by other potential sites. On the other hand, as the case studies clearly indicated, there had been extensive local activity to refine and improve program delivery within the districts, and some individuals had attempted to evaluate the effectiveness of the services they provided. Overall, despite the many claims about the increasing professionalization and sophistication of state governments, simple "good practices," such as iterative program evaluation and policy reformulation, are clearly not happening often enough.

When we talked to Representative Lois Frankel three years later about the status of continued political support for funding school health services in Florida, she commented:

> A lot depends upon who get elected obviously. There's no question that across the country there are more conservative legislators elected. I think there is a risk that as you get some politicians more closely aligned with certain interest groups that poses a threat to school health clinics.

As one example of the kind of threat these services faced, we learned that in the 1995 legislative session a bill had been proposed that would have required parents to opt-in to receive school health services, including sex education (the current provision of HB 1739 specified that parents could opt-out from receiving services), and that the names would have been linked to the driver's license program so that children who were identified as coming from families who received school health services would pay an extra fee. Although this bill did not make it out of committee, the mere fact that it was proposed illustrates the kinds of continued attacks these services face in the political realm. Asking poor parents to request services can be a very effective means of reducing the demand, since these parents are the least likely to know that the services are available in the schools, and many of them are often not literate enough to read the consent forms that would have to be signed. Such a move would also place greater demands on school health personnel to conduct outreach efforts to make sure these parents were kept sufficiently informed of the services available. As for linking the names to the driver's license program, very few adolescents would choose to place health concerns over their need to drive; consequently, the numbers of high school students who would go to the health rooms for services would drop dramatically.

Returning to the Field

Even though we could not conclude that the program had a direct causal influence on reducing teenage pregnancies and/or high risk behaviors, what we did see from the visits we made in 1992 was how desperately these services were needed among a population for whom this program was their only access to basic health care and preventive services. Given that the conditions of children in Florida had only worsened in the three years after we finished the evaluation in 1992 (Florida Center for Children and Youth, 1994), we felt that by writing this book we could highlight and make visible the complex set of issues that have to be addressed if these services are to become a standard part of school life, not just in Florida but in other states as well. We were also intensely curious as to what had happened in the lives of project personnel we had come to know so well from our previous visits. The opportunity to return to the field is rare in an evaluation study, and because we wanted to write about the concerns we saw then that we could not describe in a formal report, we returned as independent researchers to three of the sites where disputes about ideological and intergovernmental issues in particular were most strongly featured.

We were fortunate in finding people willing to talk to us after a three-year lapse, in part because they were eager to speak about these issues to us since they had been aware of our sympathies from the time we came as evaluators. Although this return cannot in any way be judged part of a continued evaluation, to achieve a rough sense of comparability we did focus our questions on issues we had raised in our first set of visits. Throughout the descriptions, we contrast what we learned in 1992 to what we learned in 1995. To protect the identity of the sites, and the persons we interviewed, we have chosen to present what we call "blurred data." The descriptions of each site in terms of demographic data, as well as quotes and comments from our interviews and observations, are constructed from visits to several projects that shared similar characteristics. We emphasize that our purpose is not to single out any one school and/or district in terms of particular problems, but rather to argue strongly that the cultural, political, and social issues and concerns that surfaced in each case study site are precisely the ones likely to arise in places that share the same circumstances. In our return visit to each of the three sites, we talked to more than 20 people and also examined project documentation that people wanted to share.

Lessons learned from three distinctively different case studies are presented: one from Emerald County, a rural, southern conservative area; one from Silver County, a rural/suburban/urban metropolitan sprawl in one of the fastest-growing areas of the state; and one from Gold County, an urbanized, multicultural area that spanned the gamut from one of the wealthiest neighborhoods in the country to one where the poverty level rivaled that of an underdeveloped Third World economy.

The case study descriptions are organized in reference to the policy-making framework established at the beginning of this chapter. We specifically examine issues that were relevant with regard to the three categories identified as being barriers to implementation—ideological, intergovernmental, and professional—and explain how these challenges were addressed in the different sites and by multiple players. What will be evident in the case study descriptions is that not all categories applied across the board. For example, in Emerald County, which was characterized by the presence of several strong religious coalitions, the ideological issues took precedence. In contrast, the intergovernmental conflict among two powerful state agencies was the strongest element underlying problems in Gold County. These differences illustrate our point that any program's effects have to be viewed in context and that when assessing impact, this point must be kept in mind.

Chapter 3

"We Can Change Lives"

THE CASE OF EMERALD COUNTY

Emerald County is one of the more rural counties located on the northwest coast of Florida. Unlike many parts of Florida, which were more recently developed, its history dates back to the time of Tristan de Luna, a Spanish conquistador who established a colony in this area in 1515. This makes it one of the oldest sites in Florida, and it is arguably the region most southern in character, since both Alabama and Georgia are close by on the north and west sides. As one writer put it, "This is a place where Southern is spoken, where politicians quote the Bible, and where the attitude of my country, right or wrong, is writ" (Fiedler & Kempel, 1993, p. 323). It is also a place dominated by the military, due to the presence of several large naval bases that play a major role in the local economy. Emerald County is politically conservative, a site where abortion politics is highly contentious, and near the area where two physicians were murdered for performing abortions in a local clinic. Although registered Democrats outnumber Republicans by a two-to-one margin, the county voted Republican in the last gubernatorial and presidential elections. A life-long resident of the area, a woman who teaches at one of the local colleges, described the culture in these terms:

> Many people who live here have lived here their entire life—a lot of blue-collar workers who made a lot of money from their investment in land because waterfront property has gone up so much in value. It's a fairly wealthy community, although the education level may not be as high as other places. The business community, the education community, and the social communities are pretty tight; they work together, connect together.

Her comments suggest a community bound by family and tradition, an image borne out by the demographic data. Most of the residents are white (82%); 13% are African-American, 3% are Hispanic, and the remainder are classified as "other."[1] Ninety-seven percent of the residents are U.S.-born citizens; only 2% are immigrants. The median age is 32.5

years, with 12% of the population over age 65. Despite what our informant noted, the people are fairly well educated: Most residents are high school graduates (76.2%), and 18% have graduated from college. The poverty level is fairly low; 17% fall below the national standard. Most residents own their home (65%), and the median household income is $25,158, which is slightly below the national average. The picture that emerges of Emerald County is that of white, middle-class America, a place where people feel they live a fairly comfortable life in pleasant surroundings somewhat protected from the social problems besetting other parts of the country.[2]

But as is often the case with other comfortably ensconced communities, this sense of well-being masks fundamental divisions in how children will be educated and what types of services they need to become healthy and productive adults. As we shall see, this feeling also complicated the task of public health personnel and educators, who felt the residents underestimated the needs of many children who lacked basic medical and social services. Our informant was cognizant of this fact:

> There's a contradiction, well, there's two different kinds of people who live here. There's those people who have been here their entire life and then there's the military where a lot of people come and go. I think we're beginning to have a broader population, transients, who are coming in.

According to the school nurses we interviewed, the children of this transient population were the ones who were invisible to the larger community, but they typically required the most services. This fact became clear when we examined data on children's well-being in this county. Children under age 18 constituted 26% of the population, and based on 1990 census data, approximately 16% of children under the age of 18 were from poor families (Florida Center for Children and Youth, 1994). These figures are for the county as a whole, but in the schools where the health rooms were initially placed, the numbers were much higher. The teenage pregnancy rate for mothers under the age of 20 was 16%; the infant mortality rate was 9.3 births per 1,000.

PROJECT DESCRIPTIONS

In 1991–92, Emerald County received funding for two projects, both of which were based on the SHIP model. One was funded for $224,267 and was placed in five schools: three elementary schools, one middle school, and one high school. The second project was funded for $245,899 and was also placed in five schools: three elementary schools, one middle school, and one high school. The schools were characterized by high rates of teenage pregnancies and high numbers of low-income students who were considered "at risk," particularly in the African-American population. In 1992, the total enrollment in the schools served by these two projects was 9,111, and the standardized average cost per student for receiving services between the two projects was $43.93. Since the standardized cost per student across all 49 projects in the Supplemental School Health Program was $50.00, these two projects were less costly than some of the others in Florida (Emihovich & Herrington, 1993).

Descriptions of Initial Project Schools

As part of the grant application, each school had to submit a detailed profile of their student characteristics in terms of ethnicity, poverty level (calculated by the number of students who qualified for either free or reduced lunches based on federal guideline), number of pregnancies in the previous school year prior to their program application, dropout and absenteeism rates, a description of the three most common health problems, a description of the room where the health room would be housed, the type of health and social support services currently offered, and any other special programs offered on-site that would be linked to the new project. In most of the schools we visited in 1992, the majority of students came from families below the federal poverty line, even though all the schools were predominantly white. This fact underscored our informant's comments about the area's high transient population; many of these students came from families who moved to Florida from surrounding rural southern areas and other parts of the country during the 1980s to seek employment at the naval base or in tourist spots on the beaches. When the recession took place, these families were hard hit because they lacked health insurance and had few resources to support them while they sought new employment.

In the original project, each school had one nurse assigned to it, except for the three elementary schools, which shared a nurse on a "floater" basis. Six nurses were Caucasian, one was African-American, one was Hispanic, and all were women. Each nurse also had a health aide assigned to her to assist in the health room to provide the basic services (e.g., bandage cuts and burns, treat minor injuries, and call family members). Under the two models these schools used, the nurse's primary functions were to do classroom and community outreach through health presentations, counsel students on social and medical problems, and monitor students with chronic medical conditions. The emphasis was less on the health aspect of nursing and more on the educational and public health preventive modes. This shift in the nurses' role was somewhat disconcerting to the principals, several of whom expected the nurse to be, as one principal put it, "in the clinic all the time." The nurses, in turn, viewed routine clinical tasks as ones that could be easily handled by the health aide, and they preferred to work more directly with students on prevention issues.

Student Outreach

Without question, the most important reason for having a health room on-site in a school is to provide health or social services to students who would not otherwise receive them. In Emerald County, evidence of the need was clear, as indicated by the large numbers of students who began using the health rooms as soon as they were available. The school nurses used specific strategies to reach both the students and their parents to let them know that the new services were available in the schools. Several nurses made home visits when students were frequently absent, others held family workshops or health fairs, and all of them sent home flyers describing the new services. One view the nurses shared was a sense of injustice; while they were glad that their schools were receiving the services, they wished that the money could be spread out so that all schools could receive services, not just those with high-risk populations. Their view was shared by the school superintendent; he noted in his interview that the "need was so great nurses could work 24 hours a day in every school in the county." One of the female school board members, who was the most active supporter of health services in schools, agreed with his contention and noted that:

> I've been on the board seven years and we've needed this project for the past seven years. Students just don't feel comfortable with their parents anymore, but they do with the school. I hate to admit it but the nurses have told me that there are many parents in this town who would give their kids the wrong information anyway, because they just don't know any better. The kids are much better off hearing things from nurses than from their parents.

Not surprisingly, the middle and high school principals said that preventing teenage pregnancies was one of their main concerns. Both principals also felt that many of their students were not receiving basic health services, a feeling shared by the elementary principal. All three principals stressed the need for early intervention and for the schools to play an educational role in dealing with high-risk behaviors. The middle school principal was the most forceful proponent of this concept, in part because his school had both the highest percentage of poor students and the highest percentage of nonwhite students of all the schools in the program, and children in either of these categories were unlikely to have access to health services outside of the school health room.

In 1995, the students' needs for school-based health services had increased dramatically. All the school nurses reported that the number of students requiring medications had jumped over the last three years. It was not unusual in a school of 500 children for the nurse to have almost 20% of the student population receiving some kind of medication. The major reason for these increases was attributed to the inclusion movement, whereby children who formerly would have been sent to special schools were now part of the regular classroom. According to the nurses, teachers felt overwhelmed by the responsibility of caring for children who had previously been pulled out of the regular classroom, and they noted that many teachers were constantly requesting referrals for medications for hyperactivity and other attention problems.

IDEOLOGICAL ISSUES

The ideological issues that surfaced in the state legislature as it debated this program appeared in similar guises in the debates at the local level: What information should be given to kids; which health services should be offered in the school setting; and, most importantly, what is the role of the parents and the community in helping to make these decisions? Considerable controversy and confusion existed around what subjects could be broached in the classroom (particularly highly charged topics such as homosexuality, abortion, condoms, and gender-related violence). Likewise, the scope of services to be offered in the health room was controversial.

Controversial Content

The key question that faces all school-based health services is what kind of information about sexual matters the students receive, and from whom. Other researchers have suggested that because of the influence of the New Right, schools are increasingly reluctant to provide in-depth information on sexuality and related topics such as HIV/AIDS education

(Greenberg, 1992; Hennessy, 1992; Sedway, 1992; Trudell, 1993). We found considerable resistance, ambivalence, and confusion surrounding the issue of who would or should talk about what, a confusion that had increased in the time between our two visits. In our 1992 visit, an adherence to a basic conservatism that reflected underlying religious orientations was manifested in different ways. Official school board policy stated that abstinence was the only approved curriculum for pregnancy prevention. According to two school board members, the public health physician was prohibited by the school board from using the term *have sex* in his classroom presentations for middle-school students. When asked if they thought that this would create a rift between the doctor and the students in terms of their perception of him as being "out of touch with the reality of their lives," one board member replied:

> Most sixth- and seventh-grade kids don't know the meaning of *have sex*. But yes, the sixth-grade talk needs to be more explicit; we just haven't figured out how to approach this yet without upsetting parents and churches.

The board members' contention that sixth-graders don't know about sex contrasted sharply with national and state-level data indicating that by middle school significant proportions of students are already sexually active.[3]

Sexual Orientation. The school nurses exhibited a similar reluctance on our first visit to talk about some issues and expressed confusion over what was or was not policy and practice. While they talked freely about the issues they covered in health education classes, such as diet and basic health habits, they were notably reticent about several topics. When asked the question, "Are there any topics that aren't covered in the curriculum, for example, homosexuality," there was a long pause while all the nurses shifted nervously in their seats, and then one nurse blurted out, "Oh, we don't have any of that here." Her statement belied the fact that a controversy had arisen over the rising influx of gay tourists to the beaches, a fact that had always been known (and tolerated by the business sector), but was only now surfacing with the advent of more militant gays who were reluctant to downplay their identity.[4] While the other nurses disputed her statement, with one of the middle school nurses stating that she had counseled a gay male student and referred him to the school psychologist, the general feeling shared by all of them was that this issue didn't really belong in the health curriculum, but rather was one that a school psychologist should handle. One nurse summed up the group's reaction by saying, "We deal with sexuality problems by focusing on attitudes." Their reaction implied that homosexuality is a problem that simply requires counseling so students can develop a more appropriate (i.e., heterosexual) sexual orientation. Their statement also revealed their misunderstanding of other school personnel roles. Students' sexual orientation is not a problem school psychologists normally handle. Their primary function is to administer diagnostic tests to students to determine academic problems.

Three years later, we learned that this topic was still one that made most people uncomfortable and that there was continuing uncertainty and ambiguity about its place in the curriculum. Both the school board member and the nurses saw it as an issue that should be handled privately, but not as part of the continuum of human sexuality. In response to the question, "Does this [the issue of homosexuality] ever get discussed in the curriculum," the school board member replied:

> Well, when we give out curriculum on sex-role development, there's been some things that were controversial about—some of the things that they wanted to say I don't think ever really got spelled out in the curriculum. It's OK for a child to have two parents to be both the same sex. And that got to be a bit controversial. . . . And that's a touchy situation and I think it would probably not be dealt with in the classroom curriculum, but the teacher would probably talk with the child individually and that could be handled by the nurse.

The nurses agreed with the school board member's comments, and one nurse jokingly said in response to the same question, "Not even in Key West!" Their inability to talk about the issue of sexual orientation clearly bothered several of them, and a few admitted that they privately believed that the one or two suicides that had occurred in the local high schools were a result of students who could not find acceptance of their sexual orientation. This is an issue that is hotly debated in the literature on gay teens as well (Stover, 1994). When asked whether students could receive counseling or assistance after revealing that they were gay, one of the nursing coordinators replied:

> They could if they asked. Guidance counselors, or school nurses, or school psychologists, or school social workers could talk with them about it. Some have in the past, but it's only when the child refers himself.

Another nurse chimed in to say that "you wouldn't give a presentation about HIV and discuss, you know, that lesbians are at low risk for it." The fact that everyone in the room was very much aware of how this issue would be judged in the community was reflected in the coordinator's continued comments:

> There have been times when maybe two people might come to you privately and you could discuss with them, but you would be circumspect in what you are saying, you know, and how you are saying it, because when they leave there and go out and communicate this to parents and other people, then you would want to be sure that what you said could not be misconstrued.

Abortion. Another sensitive issue that could only be hinted at in many discussions was the question of abortion. On our first visit, one nurse admitted that at her high school she knew of five abortions that had taken place, one as result of a date rape. This information had been reported by the school district coordinator as part of the school's demographic profile when the county first applied for funding, although she admitted that "the principal wasn't happy about it." Several other nurses confirmed that they knew about other students in their school who had had abortions, a startling admission for them to make considering that several extreme, right-wing antiabortion groups maintained a strong presence in surrounding counties. The nurses told us that usually the girls would be tested off-campus if they suspected they were pregnant and that they would go to a private agency in the community for referrals on abortion services. As one nurse put it, "The guidance counselors will confirm a pregnancy case. Then all of a sudden, the girl is no longer pregnant." One particular agency kept statistics on abortions performed in the county, and during our first visit we learned that representatives had come to the high school life-management classes to discuss contraceptive options available through the agency. One nurse also pointed out that other girls sometimes served as informal peer counselors on where to obtain abortions. The school nurses acknowledged that although they could not discuss contraceptive options openly, even as part of the sex education curriculum, several did so privately with girls who sought them out.

This issue became even more contested when we returned in 1995 to conduct a follow-up interview with the nurses. By this time, a second physician had been murdered in a nearby county for performing abortions, and the school nurses were noticeably reluctant to discuss the topic.

One of the questions we asked was how the local community had reacted to the national attention it had received, and one nurse replied:

> I don't think—I don't think, in general, the community was
> pleased at all. Most of the comments that you would hear
> people say is, this gives us a bad name. We wished this didn't
> happen and why does this have to happen here. So in general
> most people were not happy with the violence issue. . . . There
> are people who work really hard that are antiabortion [she
> meant those groups who were very vocal in their opposition],
> and I think that even those people were against what hap-
> pened with the violence.

She noted that there was a strong contingent of people who supported women's right to choose and that the image this community had
in the national media of being made up of rabid abortion opponents was
overblown. In fact, as she noted, there was far more of a "live and let live"
attitude among local people than outsiders would imagine, primarily because a beach community attracted a greater proportion of people who
were more tolerant of diverse lifestyles. The nurses' primary concern
about the abortion debate was that because of the clinics' fear that they
would be bombed or their staff physically harmed, the girls' option to
obtain an abortion in the surrounding counties was becoming extremely
limited.

Condoms and Abstinence. Another issue that could not be discussed openly was the use of condoms to reduce students' risk of being
exposed to sexually transmitted diseases or HIV. This was as much true
in 1995 as it had been when we visited this school district three years
earlier. When we directly asked, "Are you allowed to talk about condom
use for STD prevention or AIDS prevention," one nurse flatly stated,
"You can't." However, the reality was more complicated because of the
advent of school-based management and advisory councils. As one of the
program coordinators explained:

> It depends upon the class that you're in and the school. Even
> within our own county, it depends upon what part of town that
> you're from, and you just have to learn what your principal
> and your faculty expect of you and God help you if you go be-
> yond that.

By 1995, the nurses had a more realistic view of the limitations miti-
gating against sex education in the school, especially since the idea that

promoting abstinence was the only acceptable way to approach teenage sexuality was in ascendance not only at the state level, but at the national level as well (Lindsay, 1995). The reason why was clear, as stated by one nurse:

> Our frustration was that we didn't really see any changes that we could make at the school. It was all the old, you know, teach abstinence, teach abstinence, abstinence, and we believe in abstinence, but we also felt that we have some sexually active teenagers out there that are at high risk and we wanted to be able to address that. But you know that in our community without community support we can't make a difference. Our hands are tied.

Now they felt that they could have much more impact by doing presentations in community settings instead of in the schools.

How free the nurses were to speak on this issue was reflected even in the interview. Although they were willing to talk while being taped, their deeper feelings about this issue came out only after the tape-recorder was turned off and our talk was now "off the record." One nurse talked about her experiences in another school health room in a large metropolitan school district where she was free to discuss condom use and contraceptives. As she put it, "We're not using condom models and showing them [students] how to put them on, and I know they've done that in other schools." When we asked if she was willing to do that in this school district, she laughed and said, "Yes I would, but I'm wild." The other nurses shook their heads and said that they could not risk alienating the community by raising these issues in the school, a position that had changed since our last visit, when we were told that people from outside agencies could come to the schools to discuss contraceptive options. However, the nurse who noted that community support was essential also commented that by taking these presentations out to the community and providing the "shakers of the community with objective facts about what is happening with the kids in our community," she felt they were beginning to educate the public about the complexity of the problem of teenage pregnancy and what role school-based health rooms could play in ameliorating it. In her words, "parents can question us directly about what we are doing instead of being taken down the road by some of these groups." She also noted parents always have the option to come to the school to review the materials being used in the classrooms, but that very few parents ever exercised this option.

Another difference that now existed to curtail the nurses' autonomy was that they were expected to use the human sexuality curriculum developed by the county school board instead of their own. Here, again, contextual differences played a significant part in determining how much the nurses could discuss. In some schools, nurses could go beyond the stated guidelines and provide more in-depth information. In other schools, they were not even allowed to cover all the topics approved by the school board.

Gender-Related Violence. A particular concern expressed by the nurses was reaching male students to educate them about their role in pregnancy prevention and violence against young women. Several nurses mentioned that they had conducted seminars on date rape and that they used local resources to refer young men to specific programs. When pressed on this issue, they admitted that the burden of pregnancy prevention still fell on the girls and that the message was still that it's their problem, not surprising in a "good old boy" culture where women's roles are still constrained.

Because of national statistics indicating that violence against women was increasing (U.S. Department of Justice, 1995), we raised this topic again on our second visit, but this time we framed the question more explicitly in terms of how the nurses helped girls deal with issues of sexual violence. Perhaps reflecting our concern, the nurses were far more vocal on this issue. One nurse described her experience this way:

> In the clinic I ask girls if they have ever been a victim of violence or date rape or do you throw things at your partner. It's kind of a case of—are you the abused or the abuser? I tell them that these things happen at our school. I spoke at a class about it where I knew that morning the kids told me that a girl had been beaten up at the bus stop by her boyfriend. . . . But that is an interesting topic about what they think is abuse and what is not abuse *(Interviewer: In what way?).* They don't think that it is abusive for some guy to ask where you are and who you are with. They find that as a form of flattery. This happens very often in the high school where a guy will slam his fist into a locker and the girls don't find that threatening or abusive. At least he hit the locker instead of them. They don't see the correlation between that threat and that voice—see my power.

Pregnancy Prevention. One nurse in a middle school was more successful in having both males and females realize both the consequences and responsibilities of teenage pregnancy through developing a program called "Sugar Babies." Students enrolled in an alternative education class were required to carry a 10-pound bag of sugar as their "child." The unique feature about this program was the amount of writing students had to do. They were required to keep medical charts, write letters to doctors about their child's medical problem (most students were assigned babies with medical problems to emphasize the problems of low-birth-weight infants, which are commonly associated with teenage mothers), and keep a daily log of their child's progress. She noted that between the writing assignments and dragging around a ten-pound bag all day long, most students ended the program feeling they never wanted to have children because it "was too much work."

When we asked at our second visit if they felt that the health rooms had had any effect on reducing the teenage pregnancy rate, we were surprised to learn that, as they put it, "statistically, the rate in this county has gone up." Most of them still felt that because the services were on-site, more girls were coming in to seek prenatal advice instead of dropping out of school. Consequently, the reported numbers were rising because more girls were identifying themselves as pregnant, not because more girls were sexually active. They also felt that because the abortion issue was so contested in the surrounding area the pregnancy rate was also going up because of the lack of abortion services.

In Emerald County, the pregnancy-prevention services in the schools were restricted by board policy to discussions of abstinence. No schools offered contraceptives or were permitted to refer students for contraceptive services. The state legislation specifically charged the school health program with the twin goals of reducing teenage pregnancy and improving students' health. However, it gave the local communities wide discretion regarding the mix of services that could be offered to pursue these goals.

It is clear that there are two issues at hand. One is the type of information that should be publicly available to young people; the other is the setting. In this community, contraceptive services and information were strictly restricted within the school but were available at the local county public health unit (CPHU). For example, Norplant was available to teenage girls at their public health unit without prior parental permission, and the local doctor said that the number of girls who requested it were steadily increasing. This fact was known to the high school students, since several students acknowledged in their interview that the CPHU was a "good place" to get contraceptives.

The school board member and school superintendent stated that they believed that the community did not want to acknowledge the extent of the teenage pregnancy problem. They felt that the lack of acknowledgment was partly due to the fact that because teenage pregnancy was often "hidden" from view, "people can't see the extent of the problem" and were unwilling to support any programs other than those concerned with drug and alcohol abuse, since these effects were more visible. The superintendent was very cognizant of the dilemma faced by the nurses: "We need an abstinence curriculum and a condom curriculum."

The adults' feelings about the value shifts occurring among adolescents concerning sexual behavior were mixed. One high school principal was distressed over the fact that not only did five girls declare they were pregnant at his school, but that "they seemed to be proud of it." Most of the CPHU personnel took a more sanguine view that since adolescent sexual activity was not easily controlled, it was essential for them to have access to safe and reliable contraceptives. At the same time, many respondents expressed a longing for a return to earlier values, when the only publicly acknowledged problem of students was whether they had a date for the prom. This longing for the past was especially prevalent among those over age 50, as revealed in one CPHU doctor's response. As one exception to the CPHU staff's willingness to accept current adolescent mores and focus on prevention, this medical doctor, an older man in his early 60s, stressed the role of values over behavior:

> It will take a generation to turn around behavior. Education is
> not the whole answer. What we need is a return to values. We
> shouldn't mix sex education information with promoting absti-
> nence. We should tell the young kids to abstain and provide
> the information about condoms and the rest later.

Student Health Issues

A second goal of the original legislation was to improve student health. It was our supposition that nonsexual health matters would be much less controversial than contraception and sexual practices. And on our first visit, this proved true. Little controversy existed except for problems related to the distribution of the student health survey. On our second visit, however, we learned to our surprise how culturally charged any health issue might be. In this case, a districtwide wellness program proved to be one of the more controversial issues. One nurse described how she had started a club for children who were overweight and how successful these children had been in losing weight through exercising and developing more healthy eating habits. Another nurse added:

> In my school, the parents contacted the principal because they
> felt that the children were being pointed out, singled out for

being fat, and rather than the principal dealing with it the
school board decided that we're not going to have that
[a weight club].

We were so taken aback at this reaction that we pursued the matter
further:

> (*Interviewer: They took away a program that really benefited children
> because they felt it singled them out?*)
>   That's the most touchiest issue you can send a letter home
> about if they [the children] fall out of that height and weight
> growth curve. You send home a letter saying your child's over
> the 95th percentile and they [parents] go wild. They'd rather
> you sent them a letter saying their child is blind.

Apparently the national obsession with weight and diet had carried
over into the schools, which was confirmed by the school health coordinator, who noted that "being fat is a real stigma because everywhere you
look somebody's always on a diet, or someone is saying this person is too
fat. People are really paranoid about gaining weight." This issue was also
sensitive for class and race reasons: Many low-income families, especially
African-Americans, ate food that was high in saturated fats and calories,
with little nutritional value. The nurses were extremely concerned about
this issue, not so much because of appearance but because poor diets lead
to health problems later in life (e.g., hypertension, heart disease, etc.).
While the district as a whole was trying to promote good eating habits
through a wellness campaign, this campaign was resisted by various
schools, depending upon the population they served.
    A second health issue mentioned by the nurses was a support group
for children who were diagnosed as having Attention Deficit Hyperactivity Disorder (ADHD). The purpose of the group was to teach the children
behavior management skills in the form of "replacement therapy" instead
of resorting to medications. One nurse wryly noted that while it was often
difficult to get teachers to send children to the health room for reasons
other than medical emergencies, "the teachers were very cooperative in
sending these kids." Parents of these children were also mentioned as
being the most active supporters of the health room; as one nurse said,
"It's the only parent meeting where I have a consistently good turnout."

Parent and Community Reactions

On our first visit, the three principals we interviewed felt that the
parents were extremely enthusiastic about the program and that they ac-

tively supported it. Their feeling about the community was more mixed in terms of whether there was positive support, especially from those who did not have children at the school. It was this concern for potential opposition that undergirded the decision of two principals not to participate in the survey. The middle school principal stressed the importance of having a committee advisory group that was aware of the school's problems and would act as advocates to the broader public. All three principals noted that their school board was very actively involved with the program and that most of the members were supportive of the idea of providing health services in schools. The high school principal again mentioned his concern with potential community opposition, a concern he said was rooted in the community's image of his school, which was very "negative." When pressed to give examples of what kinds of opposition he had encountered in the past, the principal only said that he was worried about it, even though no specific complaints had been lodged against the program. All three stressed the importance of having school board members actively involved in the program, even to the extent of becoming advocates in town meetings.

The school board member who was interviewed was very outspoken, and she candidly admitted that her views about expanding sex education in the curriculum beyond abstinence were not shared by all board members. She had been actively involved in developing the sex education curriculum and wryly noted that "sex education is the *big* issue; it surfaces in every election year." She saw the need for school health services as "urgent" and felt they should be expanded to include all areas of high need. She also felt the program's focus was not well understood by the public, since she saw the purpose of the health rooms and the nurses' activities as focusing primarily on prevention. Her view contrasted sharply with some of the other board members, who worried that the health rooms would become places where contraceptives would be distributed. One positive aspect that she saw happening was that as the public became more aware of the program, more schools were "asking to come on board."

Her statement was borne out by the interviews with a few parents. All of them were profoundly grateful that health services were now available, especially for those who had a child with a recurring medical problem such as asthma. On the touchy subject of sex education and the use of contraceptives, one mother said she would be "concerned but willing to have the nurse approach this topic" because she recognized the need for students to have more education about sexuality. Her willingness to have this nurse discuss this issue may be due in part to the fact that her daughter (then an eighth-grader) was almost raped in school, and the mother felt that the boys in particular needed more information on topics like date rape. Several of the parents felt that other parents' negative reactions occurred because they received biased information from television news and the media on the purpose of the clinics, but once they knew more about the program they would be willing to support it. Their feelings were confirmed by the CPHU coordinator, who noted:

> There has been some resentment from the parents of teens who think their kids are going to have access to birth control, or birth control pushed on them, but in general the community has been supportive and responsive to the program, especially parents who work because they can have the nurse tell them right away whether the kid is sick and what he might have and where to go to the doctor.

Dealing with the problem of taboo topics was not confined solely to curriculum development. During our first visit, one elementary and one high school principal were uncomfortable at being interviewed since their schools had not participated in the student health survey, even though all selected schools were expected to do so as a condition of receiving program funds.[5] The elementary principal said her school did not participate because the school nurse did not tell her it was necessary, even though a letter from the evaluation team stating that a survey would be conducted was sent to all principals. The high school principal was more candid, admitting that he did not want his school to participate because of the controversial nature of some of the questions dealing with adolescent sexuality. In both cases, the principals' reluctance was linked to their fear of community opposition once the details of the survey's content were known, even though the most controversial issue on the elementary school survey involved questions related to school violence and drug abuse.

One superintendent who characterized his school community as conservative believed that the community's positive response to the program, which included a school-based health room, was due to the active role the school system had taken in keeping the community informed of all upcoming policy and program decisions, seeking wide input prior to action, and keeping the community informed throughout the implementation stages. He emphasized that the schools never hid anything from the community or tried to downplay curricular activities regarding human sexuality.

When we returned in 1995, we learned that in some cases there was now an organized effort underway to pressure school board members not to support issues such as health services in the schools. Although none of the schools funded in this area offer services that are typical of other full-service schools, such as family-planning counseling and contraceptive devices (Dryfoos, 1994), certain pressure groups, especially those funded by religious coalitions, opposed other services that they felt infringed upon their value system. This issue came up in our conversation with the school board member about teenage pregnancy:

> The issue has been raised more because of the increased con-servatism. There's more data and statistics now that supports your offering some of those services. You know we have full ser-vice schools now. (*Interviewer: Full-service schools meaning what?*) Full-service schools means that the school is open from sunup to sundown and that services are provided to the parents and community as well. And some people have come before the board and questioned some of the programs that we have in there. Even though they are for adults, they are still ques-tioning them. . . . To me the legislature opened the door for that because the purpose of school advisory councils is to get your parents and community involved, and if a certain area thought they needed that type of service we should support them.

While some opposition had existed when the clinics were first opened in 1991, it was sporadic and localized in just a few schools. Now, three years later, the opposition was highly organized and maintained a visible presence at all school board meetings. It was chilling to hear a strong, forceful woman who prided herself on taking activist positions in support of children's services begin whispering in her office as she de-scribed how the "little ladies" come to the school board meetings to audiotape them and then later play edited portions on radio and cable television networks controlled by a parent religious organization.[6] This board member was furious because one of these taped excerpts made her appear to be opposed to a position she actually supported, a position this group supported as well. She also noted that because her position on the board had switched from a majority to a minority political affiliation, "it's a little more difficult for me to present some things, now that I don't have the support on the board."

One of the program coordinators believed that hypocrisy was ram-pant among some of the health room's opponents: "Many of these people who sound like religious zealots don't even put a foot inside the door of a church." Some of the nurses considered the churches to be advocates for the health rooms, rather than opponents. As one nurse described it:

Everybody thinks the churches are the ones that are saying, "No. No. You can't do this, you can't do that." I only think it is one element in the church. The churches are very community-minded, very concerned about the same issues. In south Florida [where she worked before coming to Emerald County] the clinic was housed in the church, and teens used to come there for birth control. They said, "Yes, you can have our building because we need this in our community." And if you need money or medicine, you call a church.[7]

As another nurse commented, "Teen pregnancy is a community wide problem, and churches are part of the community." Several of them noted that historically the church was the center of the community, and they felt that reconnecting the schools with the churches in a communitywide effort was one way to address the problem.

Both the board member's and the nurses' comments about the importance of understanding the community's values raised a much larger question that we posed to several of our informants: "Who is the community? Is there one *true* community?" For example, were the people who were the most opposed to establishing health rooms in schools representative of the community. One of the coordinators thoughtfully answered, "You have to talk with people other than those people who talk a lot." As one way of doing this, one of the other nurses then mentioned the needs assessment that had been done as part of creating the partnership between the schools and the public health office in which 1,500 families were surveyed by telephone to determine what the community's health needs were and what services were wanted in schools.[8]

INTERGOVERNMENTAL ISSUES

In earlier interviews with the school board members, no issues surfaced regarding personnel or budgeting problems between the state and local personnel. However, by 1995, the need for services, the availability of more programs, and public scrutiny had all increased. The school board, for example, was more actively involved with other community-based service organizations.

As a result of this program as well as Goal One of Florida's Blueprint

2000 plan (which required interagency coordination to meet the goal of having children arrive at school ready to learn), the school board in 1995 was establishing written contracts with numerous agencies such as the Child Welfare Board, the juvenile justice system, Children's Home Society, and various church groups that sponsored volunteer programs. The nurses noted that they were also coordinating more services through Healthy Start, a state-funded program initiated by Governor Lawton Chiles to increase the health and well-being of Florida's young children. The school nurses felt that the two programs complemented one another; however, the issue of accountability was raised regarding the two programs. Some of the nurses believed that the Healthy Start program was assuming some of the credit for reducing infant mortality rates that belonged to the school health program. As they pointed out, it was often because they recommended to the young mothers that they seek prenatal care that the girls enrolled in Healthy Start.

Also as a result of Blueprint 2000, each school now had a school advisory council (SAC) comprised of teachers, administrators, students, parents, and community members. This extra policy-making body in the schools further confused the issue of who sets policy and for whom because its presence increased the local autonomy of each school to make decisions that reflected the will of that particular community. Creating policy for the entire district was the role of the school board, and it was possible that some schools could establish policies that the board could not approve for the district as a whole.[9] One of the school board members noted there were further limitations in terms of services that could be provided by outside agencies. As this board member told us, "the way the policies are written, it ties the hands of some of the agencies in terms of the services that can be offered." For example, no school would be free to contract with Planned Parenthood to provide information on family-planning methods independent of any information that the school nurse provided. One of the school nurses also mentioned that the kind of sexuality curriculum that prevailed in individual schools depended a great deal on the particular composition of the SAC, who was active in school affairs, and what their beliefs were. One of the SAC members we interviewed felt strongly that if the schools were more free to use multiple prevention efforts, including discussion of contraceptive options, then "pregnancy rates would be reduced." However, he also believed that "due to the conservative nature of the community, they would be stopped." His final comment was that because of "philosophy and religious beliefs these types of health problems will only get worse. Everybody responsible for themselves is the mentality."

Outside Referrals

Another intergovernmental issue that was mentioned was the use of outside referrals, especially for medically fragile children in the classroom. The federal government's requirement that school districts provide educational services to all children regardless of the severity of disabilities had sorely strained the resources and knowledge of the schools' personnel. One of the benefits of having a school nurse available was that teachers received much-needed assistance in dealing with medically fragile children in the classroom. Coordinating the care of chronically ill children, however, was sometimes a problem. To locate children with problems, the nurses sent cards to the teachers that were to be sent home in order to register students with special medical needs. These cards needed to be updated every year, which was difficult to accomplish in schools with large transient populations. One principal told us, for example, that 70% of his school population turned over between September and May. Although problems with children who were "crack babies" had not really surfaced in any of the elementary schools, all the nurses anticipated this would become a major problem shortly, given the extent of the drug problem in the surrounding communities. One nurse also reported that she had to deal with a high school teacher who was averse to working with a student diagnosed with AIDS and that more intervention work needed to be done in this area to help teachers cope with this issue in class.

The lack of adequate social services in the community to which students could be referred was deemed a problem, as indicated with one nurse's comment:

> There is really nowhere to refer them to except the health department. Private services are not an option for most families, and social services agencies are almost nonexistent. The real deficit is that there is no place to go for professional counseling on sexual abuse and that service is greatly needed. The waiting lists for substance abuse is very long, and people have to be suicidal to get into care immediately.

Her statement was confirmed by one of the SAC board members, who noted that if these services didn't exist in schools, the only places where many children would receive health services was either through "the emergency room and HRS clinics."

Typical chronic problems that the nurses handled were children with diabetes, epilepsy, heart conditions, and mental problems due to family disruptions; potential suicides; and substance abuse cases. One worrisome problem that the CPHU doctor mentioned was the rising cancer rates among children in the community, since one nurse had in her school two students with brain tumors. There had been a report on this issue in the local newspaper, and it was suggested that the problem was linked to the local water supply having becoming more polluted. For this reason, the school project coordinator only drank water from a thermos she carried to school.

Although the nurses felt there was a lack of sufficient counseling services in the community, they maintained an extensive list of outside agencies where they could send students to receive basic medical services (e.g., vision screenings) not provided by the school health room. Each student's family was also asked to fill out a special medical problems card that was updated every year. Each nurse was expected to submit a detailed nursing care plan for students with chronic problems that was reviewed by their supervisor in the CPHU.

Principal Involvement

An issue that is repeatedly raised in the research literature on intergovernmental problems for improving services to children is that of shared personnel, or personnel who are employed in one agency but are practicing at another. In all projects involved in the Supplemental School Health Program, the school nurses were supervised by the CPHU project coordinator, not by the principals. The nurses freely admitted that in some schools this division of authority conflicted with their school principal's desire to control all staff in the school. In three of the schools we visited, a sore point was the principal's edict that nurses remain in the health room during school hours, while they often wanted to be in the halls meeting students or presenting talks in classrooms. As the CPHU coordinator put it, "Who handled the problems of sick kids before the nurses came?" The answer, of course, was that it was left to the secretarial staff in the main office to monitor problems and call family members to pick children up. It is also the case that in Florida every school is required to have two people trained in first aid and CPR procedures, although it was a requirement not well followed in many schools. The nurses recognized that they needed to learn how to say "no" diplomatically and to remember that "you're in their territory at school." Most of them said they made an effort to meet with the principal weekly to brief him or her on problems and to interact with other school personnel who were also concerned with children's welfare, such as the guidance counselor.

The principals' level of involvement with the program varied from school to school. Only the high school principal said he had been actively involved with the whole grant process, not surprising since the others were newly appointed at their school. He had designed the site for the clinic, purchased equipment, helped determine the program's goals and objectives, and taken a leadership role in securing additional funding. He had also established a good working relationship with the project coordinators, as had the middle school principal. The elementary principal had some concerns about the lack of time the nurse spent at her school, and she was less forthcoming about her involvement with the program.

On our second visit, we learned that principals also played a key role in determining how freely nurses could talk about sexual behaviors and pregnancy prevention apart from just abstinence. As one of the coordinators noted:

> One-on-one nurses can talk to girls regarding condom use or birth control. But the nurse can't present information to a whole class unless it is in a school where the principal is inclined to have that kind of presentation made. And his reaction is to what is said is based on the patrons in his community.

Interagency Coordination

Whenever two large bureaucratic cultures converge at the point of service delivery, flashpoints are bound to occur. When the project was first started, we were interested to learn how issues of power and control would be negotiated between two very different cultures, the state education department and the public health unit. For the most part, the two agencies seemed to work well together. Their commitment to the goals of the program appeared to unite them. However, rough edges did surface. One such flashpoint was the issue of who controlled the funds provided by HRS to manage the project. Before their interview began, several nurses appeared uncomfortable at having to talk to the "evaluator," a not uncommon reaction that evaluators often encounter in the field. In their case, their discomfort was compounded by the fact that because of local political disputes, the director of the HRS district office was holding up necessary monies for the project; the nurses knew this and weren't sure whether they would be asked to talk about it. The CPHU project coordinator was exasperated by his failure to advance funds when needed and to approve expenditures for nursing staff to attend training seminars. Ironically, she found the school district office far more cooperative than her own district office, joking that her relationship with the school district project coordinator was like "being married." All the school administrators who were interviewed stressed the positive relationship they enjoyed with most of the CPHU staff, especially the nurses and the project coordinator.

Full-Service Schools

When we first visited in 1992, none of the project schools viewed themselves as full-service schools, a label that we heard quite frequently on our second visit. Because the need for services had increased dramatically, facilitating coordination among all concerned parties was more necessary than ever. Although the school board member used the term freely, the project coordinator was more cautious: "They're called full-service schools but they're not yet full-service." We probed this issue further by asking her to specify what was meant by this term. In reference to the term's usage elsewhere regarding the dispensation of contraceptives and condoms, the coordinator was adamantly opposed to this possibility:

> We don't have that, and that service will not be a part of our
> full service. We have had letters from people in the community
> about that. We've had calls, and one lady called me and told
> me she was just simply furious. And I said, "Well, why? What's
> the problem?" And she said, "Well I just left the school and I
> had to carry sanitary protection to my granddaughter." And I
> said, "Well, I still don't understand what your problem is." And
> she said, "Well, you don't provide sanitary protection for girls
> but then you can provide condoms for boys."

Upon hearing this story, all the nurses laughed in recognition of the common dilemma of how to combat these rumors, and one nurse joked that "condoms are really sanitary protection for girls." Another nurse noted that this story illustrated her point that "the nurse has to be visible to the community and let them know what we're doing."

PROFESSIONAL ISSUES

One of the project's goals was to have nurses and teachers form a team in providing health information to students. Since this concept required two different professionals to work with each other, we were curious as to how this relationship worked. The general impression we gathered was that personality differences played a greater role in facilitating cooperation than did professional responsibilities. In most schools, the nurses were invited into health education, life-management, or occasionally science classes to give talks on high-risk behaviors or to provide more detailed medical information about a particular problem. This is a tricky area, since schools in Florida are mandated to cover health education for at least one semester in high school, and most of them already have health education teachers who teach in this area. The nurses found that this was the area of greatest conflict—that the health education teachers felt threatened by them. They also noted that they had to overcome stereotypes held by the teachers that the school nurse was there "only to take care of sick kids." Most of the nurses said they enjoyed the teaching aspect of their position but that their time in the classroom or in a workshop setting was circumscribed by the high turnover of health room aides.

One aspect the nurses enjoyed about their job was that they had considerable authority to develop their own curricula and programs, in the sense that they did not have to follow established state guidelines, as did the health education teachers. But the recurring theme that sex was not a topic for open discussion surfaced again. As one nurse put it:

> We have a lot of control over goals and methods in the health
> area, except what we can discuss with regard to sexuality. We
> are supposed to stress abstinence or refer students to the
> health department. We'd like to be more open; the way we do
> it, we go through the back door, and that's not the message we
> want to get across.

The nurses' feeling of autonomy was puzzling, since they did have to seek clearance from both the school principal and the CPHU coordinator in order to implement their programs. They were also required to inform the coordinator when they planned to be off school grounds, but this was a formality that was often not observed in practice. However, in comparing the demands of their job against those of the teachers, who were primarily confined to the classroom and who had to follow a state-mandated curriculum, they were more autonomous. The school nurse's relative freedom to move about the school and to develop curricula independent of state approval was resented at times by the teachers.

One of the more interesting developments we saw taking place was that the nurse's role was evolving more into that of a services broker, since the basic health functions were handled by the health technician and the teaching role in human sexuality classes was not that extensive. One of the areas where the high school nurses felt that they would be expanding their role in the future was in ensuring that teenage mothers received good prenatal and postnatal care through the federal nutritional program for women and their children (WIC).

IMPACT/SUMMARY

Although we made it clear during our second visit that we were not asking questions in the role of evaluators, we did play devil's advocate to see how people would respond to the question, "How do you know this program is making a difference?" From every person, this question evoked a passionate response. The nurses, who are the ones essentially on the front lines of the battle to improve health conditions among children who need these services, could barely contain their indignation that this program was not being fully funded so that all children in the county could receive the advantages of being in a school with a health room. The school nursing coordinator stated that she received calls daily from parents "wanting their children to be in these schools." She further stated that personnel from other county schools frequently called, describing all the problems that were present in their school and wanting to know when they would be eligible to have a nurse assigned to their school. As she said, "It has to make a difference for me to get those kind of calls." Another nurse pointed out that the nurse at a middle school diagnosed two brain tumors in children who otherwise would not have received care. Each nurse said she kept anecdotal records of similar stories (e.g., undiagnosed epilepsy) that were on file in the health room office. The program coordinator took a more developmental view of potential effects:

> Where I know they're making a difference is when they [the nurses] come back and tell me about situations that they've intervened with. And what I see happening is students developing a working relationship with these nurses. And they have to follow up and these children have some place where they can go for help.

Establishing Accountability

One nurse undertook a survey to see how schools handled the issue of giving medications to students who had them on file. In comparing project and nonproject schools, she discovered that two hours per day were devoted in nonproject schools to managing and dispensing student prescriptions. She reported that the staff in schools without the assistance of either a nurse or a health aide were "extremely frustrated because they felt these children were not their responsibility and they were not trained to deal with this issue." The other nurses listened sympathetically as she talked, and the feeling widely shared among all of them was that many students "fell between the cracks" and failed to receive medicine they needed to help them function well in school.

Hearing about other schools' frustration we asked, "Does it create hard feelings among schools that some have nurses and others don't? How do you deal with that?" The school coordinator admitted that many schools did resent not being "chosen" to receive additional funding and blamed her, even though schools had to apply on their own and the decision was made not at the local level but at the state level by HRS program managers. Here is where the lack of money made a difference; no additional funds were allocated in the 1995 budget to expand the program to counties that already had some schools funded, and because of recent political shifts, the emphasis was on the reduction of services to schools, not on the expansion of them.[10]

Meeting Children's Needs

Another way we approached the issue of accountability was to pose the question, "How do you respond to people who say: 'Why don't they take the money now devoted to these services and put it into basic education and let schools go back to just being schools, instead of places where health and social services are available?'" The universal response received to this question was the same: "Kids can't learn if they're not healthy." It was not only the nurses who believed this, but everyone else: the school board member, the principals, the teachers, and the parents. A second common response was that if these services were not available in schools, many children would have no way to get to them. People whose only image of Florida is that of sunny beaches crammed with tourists have no idea how rural and isolated many counties in the state are. In some areas of Emerald County, families have to drive 25 miles one way to receive any kind of medical services, assuming, of course, that they even have a car. Low income also plays a part, as one of the nurses heatedly stated:

Many parents work two jobs from sunup to sundown, and when they're off the health service place is closed. And many times they don't have the transportation and so they're too tired or they've got all these other childre they've got to care for and so these children go unse

Class differences were also a factor, as one nurse explained:

There might be situations where the parents would be willing
to get help but they don't know the resources that are available.
Digging through some of the systems is a nightmare. Imagine
if you have trouble as a nurse what it's like for these parents. I
have to cut through all of the red tape to get help for a child
who needs help right away where the parent has become totally frustrated because they have been trying to get help. But
if you've ever gone into some of these HRS agencies, you know
that they are not always the most considerate people and they
don't give these people the kinds of services they should
get. . . . A lot of times they need somebody who will just cut
through all that and get to what is needed.

The nurses' comments were echoed in a statement made by the principal of the middle school that had the highest percentage of low-income
children of all the project schools: "Politicians need to get out and see
what matters and what doesn't before they begin cutting funds." All three
principals felt the program was meeting their initial expectations in providing basic health services to students who had rarely had access to it
before. The middle school principal said he hoped to see decreases in the
teenage pregnancy rate and in drug abuse rates, and that students would
have a "greater awareness of basic health issues." Unfortunately, his
school was one of those where the pregnancy rate increased after the first
year of program operation. While this outcome occurred in other schools
as well, a fact the nurses attributed to more girls coming into the health
room to admit they were pregnant, it's an outcome that was a public relations disaster in a conservative community because it lent support to the
contention of fundamentalist groups that school-based health rooms increased sexual activity among students.

When asked the question, "What do you feel has been the greatest
benefit of this program?," all the nurses mentioned "just being there for
students." Several said they received the greatest satisfaction from helping students obtain needed resources, items that are taken for granted by
those with money or adequate health plans but that are major expenses
for families on tight budgets—items such as glasses, basic dental care,
and routine check-ups. They also noted that they became resources not
only for students and their families, but also for the school staff. It was
not uncommon for teachers to consult with the nurses on their medical
problems and to seek information on where to obtain assistance. One

nurse summed the feelings of all the others by saying, "My dream is that we can change lives, and save the state of Florida."

Summary

What did we learn about school-based health rooms from the experience of Emerald County? In a conservative area, perhaps the best outcome that can be initially achieved is simply to have the community accept the fact that the health rooms exist, even though their acceptance is largely based on the perception that the nurse's primary function is to dispense basic medical services and to refer students as necessary to the appropriate social services. The more socially contested issues centering around sex education and pregnancy prevention have to be kept on the back burner, even though there is a tacit understanding shared by everyone that some information is getting out to students, albeit through underground channels. Although the school board's official policy was to disapprove any information about pregnancy prevention except abstinence, unofficially schools could develop their own in-house policies that met with local community approval. In an area dominated by the presence of the military, it is perhaps not surprising that sex education in this school district is accomplished by the politics of stealth.

Chapter 4

"We Are the Child Lovers"

THE CASE OF SILVER COUNTY

A first impression of Silver County largely depends upon the direction from which it is approached. From one direction, the county embodies some of the tackiest aspects of American culture: strip malls, fast-food restaurants, used-car dealerships, and rundown motels that raucously vie for travelers' attention along several miles of a major highway that runs through the area. From another direction, a traveler is greeted by gently rolling hills, green pastures, and a vision of a countryside that everyone longs for in their dreams. The schizophrenic nature of the county is due to the population boom that has occurred in the last two decades: The influx of snowbirds from the North and Midwest jostle for land with the locals who have lived there all their life hunting and fishing in the lush backwoods. The rapid development first caught county officials unaware: As one county administrator put it, "The first six miles are a mess, but the other 45 are beautifully planned" (Fiedler & Kempel, 1993, p. 689). Although the new residents are usually older retirees, they don't necessarily vote conservatively. Currently, Democrats outnumber Republicans by a slight edge and the county voted for Clinton in the 1996 election.

The county demographics portray a place that is slowly aging (median age is 48 years, with 32% of the population over the age of 65), primarily white (94%), and lower-middle class with a median income of $21,480. African-Americans constitute only 2% of the population, Hispanics 3%, with less than 1% classified as "other." More than two-thirds of the residents are high school graduates, with only 9% holding a college degree. Eighty-one percent of the families own their homes, an indicator of a very stable population despite the rapid influx of new residents. People who come here bring their own wealth and don't require extensive public health services, since less than 12% fall below the poverty level. Given this profile of a relatively older, more settled population, the fact this county supports some of the most innovative school health clinics in the state comes as a real surprise.

Although the general population is reasonably well-off, the children of the backwoods areas are not. The rapid development of the county's outer areas left behind a lovely countryside where rusty trailers hide amidst the tall grasses. Based on 1990 census data, children under the age of 18 represented 18% of the population. Although only about 8% of the children under 18 lived in poverty, almost all of them were concentrated in the more rural areas of the county (Florida Center for Children and Youth, 1994). The teenage pregnancy rate for mothers under age 20 was 14%; the infant mortality rate was 5.9 births per 1,000.

PROJECT DESCRIPTIONS

In 1991–92, Silver County received funding for seven projects, six of which were locally designed and one which was a full-service model (this school was the only one that did not participate in the 1992 evaluation survey). The total amount of funding they received for these projects was $280,963. The high schools that qualified for receiving these funds were characterized by high rates of teenage pregnancies and high numbers of low-income students who were considered "at risk." In 1992, the total number of students served by these six projects was 10,145; the standardized average cost per student for receiving services among the six locally designed projects was $36.66, and the full-service project per-student cost was $45.65. Since the standardized cost per student across all 49 projects in the Supplemental School Health Program was $50.00, these projects were among the least costly in the state (Emihovich & Herrington, 1993).

Descriptions of Initial Project Schools

As part of the initial grant application, each school had to submit a detailed profile of their student characteristics in terms of ethnicity, poverty level (calculated by the number of students who qualified for either free or reduced lunches based on federal guidelines), number of pregnancies in the previous school year prior to their program application, dropout and absenteeism rates, a description of the three most common health problems, a description of the room where the clinic would be housed, the type of health and social support services currently offered, and any other special programs offered on-site that would be linked to the new project. Only high schools were involved in this project. Unlike the schools in Emerald County, only two of the six schools had a large number of students who came from families below the federal poverty line, and all the schools were predominantly white. This fact underscored the problem of differential rural poverty that was pervasive in this county: In certain areas the poverty rates were quite high, while in the rest of the county towns were undergoing rapid urbanization and becoming more prosperous. With one exception, the pregnancy rates at the high schools involved in this project were also higher than those we studied in either Emerald or Gold County.

Seven nurses worked in the program. Each school had one nurse assigned to it, and all of them were Caucasian females. The seventh one worked in a special teenage pregnancy program related to the project. Each nurse based at the school also had a health aide assigned to her to assist in the clinic to provide basic services (e.g., bandage cuts and burns, treat minor injuries, and call family members). Under the locally designed model that each school followed, the nurse's primary functions were to do classroom and community outreach through health presentations, counsel students on social and medical problems, and monitor students with chronic medical conditions. The emphasis was less on the health aspect of nursing and more on the educational and public health preventive modes. As was the case with Emerald County schools, where nurses followed a similar pattern, this role shift was not entirely welcomed by several of the high school principals. The nurses' attitude was that routine clinical tasks should be handled by the health aide, and they much preferred to work more directly with students on prevention issues. Unlike some of the other school districts involved in the Supplemental School Health Program, this district had a prior history of having nurses available in the schools.

Student Outreach

When we first visited in 1992, we asked about the ways in which the nurse reached out to the students. The response given at one high school was typical:

> (*Interviewer: What attempts have been made to reach students to learn about their problems?*)
> A needs assessment was done last year. We also used data from the Youth Risk Behavior Survey.[1] We also talk with students and teachers.

The nurses candidly admitted that some methods simply didn't work; the hot-line was a good example. As one nurse said, "We gave it our best try, but it was a bomb with the kids. Even though the kids requested it, they went to the nurse directly." Although the nurses relied on external data such as needs assessments to some extent, they also emphasized the importance of just "walking the halls" and meeting the students during lunch outside on the lawn. We discovered in interviews with students that many of them were reluctant to be seen going to the clinic and that some of the best conversations about intimate matters took place in unexpected settings. There was no doubt in many nurses' minds about the clinic's importance to students, as expressed in this heartfelt comment by one nurse in response to the question about whether the program was meeting students' needs:

> Yes, yes! It's overwhelming, the need is growing each day and there's not enough time. We can impact more students, more classes. It feels like a lot of girls have been saved due to getting their life back together and staying in school.

The students were also strongly supportive of the health clinic. When asked how they felt about the presence of a school health clinic, the typical responses we received were: "It's accessible and convenient; they provide professional-quality care; we're able to talk about family problems and our personal life; we don't worry about checking in or out; you can just drop in, no appointment is necessary; the health clinic can provide follow-through for problems." However, several students stated that they would not go to the clinic to discuss serious problems; for that, they would turn to their friends. As one student said, "The only person in a school you can trust is your friend." Many students felt that they didn't know the nurse well enough yet to confide in her; one girl explained, "In order to talk with someone you need a longer-term relationship to develop trust." The students did feel that the nurse would be more apt to listen and not give the standard textbook response that teachers or other school personnel were likely to give. One popular way students contacted the nurse in one high school was through the Ask-A-Nurse column that appeared each week in the local paper. The students would send questions in anonymously and the answers would appear the following week.

Once the clinic was firmly established in each school, the nurses found that they had to do very little outreach since the students either just came to them or they were referred by the teachers. As one nurse put it:

> I get a lot of referrals from the health aide and the teachers. The longer I have been here and the social worker both—we really know all the teachers and they're real good about referring if they see anything different. We have a school doctor three hours a week and students can just come in.

IDEOLOGICAL ISSUES

On our first visit in 1992, we asked about the kinds of topics the nurses felt that they were free to discuss with the students. Several of them mentioned that they could discuss birth-control options, but only after the girl had come to the clinic to request such information. One option the girls were told about was Norplant, which was available through the county public health unit. What was clear was that they could not discuss birth control as a topic in the health education class. One nurse jokingly referred to a ZIP group (Keep your Zipper Up) that she had started in her school. All the nurses agreed that stressing abstinence was their first choice, followed by a discussion that emphasized responsible decision making. As the nursing coordinator said, "We avoid issues that bring the conservative groups out." When we asked what those issues were, she replied, "No homosexuality, no abortion, no masturbation." She felt this policy was justified because no real opposition had surfaced thus far in the community.

Controversial Content

One of the issues that all the nurses had confronted was the problem of incest. Although most cases came from low-income families, the case that had the entire school district buzzing was one that involved a girl from a very prestigious family. The girl had first told her guidance counselor, and then it was reported to the authorities. The mother had had a history of psychiatric problems, and the father was an alcoholic. The father ultimately went to jail, and the nurse was left with the onerous task of helping the girl regain her composure, since the family blamed her, not the father. Two nurses mentioned that they knew of several girls involved in incestuous relationships and that there was a strong pattern of denial in all the families.

When we asked several student focus groups about what kinds of sexual issues were discussed, we learned that from their perspective not enough information was given on topics they really cared about—or that it was given too late. For example, they felt that a lecture on the problem of date rape, which often occurred on prom night, should be given to ninth-graders instead of to seniors. They also felt that this information, which was usually given by the school resource officer, put too much emphasis on legal issues and not enough on the emotional concerns of both males and females. The information they felt was most lacking was methods of preventing pregnancy, a view shared by the nurses, who wanted more freedom to provide this information.

Condoms and Abstinence. One of the biggest surprises of our return visit was to learn how much freedom the nurses had acquired in three years to discuss sexual topics that had previously been off-limits. The state legislators' willingness to give considerable flexibility to the local school districts and county public health units to determine the types of services that would be offered was apparent in contrasting the differences between Emerald County and Silver County. When one nurse mentioned that she taught birth-control methods in a life-management class, we recalled our interviews in Emerald County and asked if there were any restrictions on what she could talk about. She seemed to find this question amusing as she laughingly replied:

> No, none at all. (*Interviewer: Really? That's very surprising.*) I know, some districts, they can't even say the word *condom*. In our district—Now, on the back of the emergency card it says (*Reads from card*) "I give consent for my child to participate in the school health services program. This means my child will receive hearing, vision, dental, skin, height and weight, scoliosis and blood pressure screening at certain grade levels. In addition, the school nurse conducts classroom presentations and individual counseling. These presentations are on health issues such as drug abuse, abstinence, birth control, sexually transmitted diseases, weight control, AIDS, and seatbelt use. If I object to any of these health screenings or programs, I will notify the school in writing."

She noted that she keeps track of the names of students whose parent or guardian objects and contacts these students before going into a classroom. They are told they can spend class time in another room during the presentation. She mentioned that the life-management curriculum also contained a section on sexuality and that teachers routinely informed parents when these topics would be discussed. Apparently providing this waiver to parents was sufficient to allow the nurses to discuss topics they had been unable to raise on our last visit.

It was not just the fact that the nurses could discuss these issues that was a surprise, but also how much detail they could provide. But the details depended upon a nurse's comfort level. As one nurse said:

> I go into class and show all the products. We use overheads. I mean, I take the condom out of the package but I don't put it on. . . . I'm very conservative. It took me a while to even take it out of the package (*laughs*). You know, the first two years I

would just show the package about the pill, and we'd talk
about the side effects. And when it came to the condom, I
would show the package and we'd talk about the expiration
date, all the little facts you should know about condoms. And I
never really took it out because I had a little film that I showed
where a guy takes it out of the package and actually just puts it
on his hand, finger. And just shows about rolling it down. So I
felt that that got the message across. This year I've gotten a
little bit braver, you know, I actually take it out of the package
and I sort of unroll it and just show things about it. . . . The
sky's the limit in Silver County. We've never had a complaint.

We probed this issue further because it was unusual that the school
district had not experienced any complaints from either parents or community members. In other districts we had visited or had been mentioned in news reports, most schools had encountered people who pro-
tested the presence of school-based health clinics at board meetings or
other community forums.[2] The nurse we spoke to was genuinely puzzled
at our question as to why this district had not encountered these
problems:

I don't know why really. I guess the nursing coordinator helped
a lot. I just know she was a real advocate of it and our district
survey showed that our students, if they are telling the truth,
use condoms more than the national average. We're hoping
that they are, I kind of wonder but. . . . We've had more complaints about the breast exam and for testicular examinations
(*laughs*) from parents than about birth control.

The fact that these nurses were more able to discuss certain topics
than were the nurses in the other county did not mean that they were
free to discuss all sexually related issues. We were interested in learning
whether schools in this district were expected to emphasize abstinence as
well as to provide information about birth-control options. We raised this
issue with one of the school board members, a woman who had taken a
very activist stance regarding the nurses' freedom to discuss birth-control
options. She clearly recognized the dilemma that school boards faced in
managing the tension between two competing viewpoints:

We struggled with that, because we have Sex Respect in our
curriculum and it is an abstinence-only program. We put birth
control with it, and it is a kind of incongruent thing. And we re-

ally struggled, but we still feel strongly that the kids need that information. But we present it in saying—we say, we know you don't need that information today but when you do we may not be here. Or you may have a friend or you may have an older brother or sister or whatever. So you at least need to have that information.

Although the nurses were able to present several birth-control options to the students, one option that was rarely discussed was Norplant. When we first visited in 1992, Norplant was viewed as a positive contraceptive solution because the girls didn't have to think about using it, since it is surgically implanted. However, it had fallen out of favor over the past three years because girls had begun complaining about side effects, and also because it was seen as a way for girls to continue their sexual activities without being concerned about consequences. Condoms had risen in favor because they could both prevent pregnancy and reduce the spread of AIDS.

Date Rape and Sexual Violence. We also wanted to know if the issue of date rape or sexual violence against women was receiving more coverage in the human sexuality curriculum than it had in 1992. One nurse responded that it had:

I think date rape is covered. Last year one of the guidance counselors and I went to all the seventh-grade classes and did date rape for three days. That was real good.

Her comments suggested that the nurses were responsive to the students' complaints that some topics were discussed too late and should be covered earlier, in middle school. However, she really didn't elaborate on this issue, as did the nurse in Emerald County, leading us to believe that how much emphasis the issue received depended upon the feminist orientation of the nurse. This nurse was, by her admission, "very conservative," whereas the one in Emerald County was more attuned to how sexual violence was a part of the girls' daily experiences in ways they didn't fully comprehend.

Sexual Orientation. One topic that was off-limits in Emerald County was also not covered anywhere in Silver County, and that was the issue of adolescent sexual orientation. When we first visited this county and asked, "Are there any topics about sexuality you haven't covered?", most of the nurses said "no." However, several admitted that they personally felt uncomfortable with discussing homosexuality. When we asked what counseling services were available to gay students, one nurse commented, "It's not really a big issue. High school students are often bisexual in orientation, and the real focus is on AIDS prevention."

Three years later, the answers to our questions about this issue were still short and to the point. At one full-service school, the nurse stiffened at the question and said, "There isn't any discussion. I would be surprised if there were. There's nothing in the curriculum." When asked, "So what does an adolescent do who is aware that he or she has a different orientation than peers?," the nurse brusquely stated, "It's not a talked-about subject." Her behavior changed at this point in the interview, curtness replacing her initial warmth, as did her body posture, which became closed—changes suggesting to us that this was a topic best not pursued.

Facing such reticence, we approached the issue of handling sexual diversity from another perspective. We asked if human sexuality was ever presented in terms other than fear and prevention, if it was ever discussed as an aspect of life that was important, meaningful, or pleasurable. The nurse's first response was to tell us to interview the life-management teacher because "honestly, I don't know what all their curriculum is." She then gamely tackled the question by saying:

> I know it would be treated as a healthy activity. They talk about
> the birth of babies, and they really do go into a lot of different
> issues. And they used to use Sex Respect as their—well, they
> still use it because they have to since it's abstinence-based. And
> we definitely stress abstinence. In fact, when I go into birth con-
> trol I start with abstinence because it's 100% and we talk about
> that and then go from there.

Her response revealed that the idea of sexual activity as something that was pleasurable could not be raised with adolescents, since the main focus was on how to keep them from becoming sexually active, and if they were, to keep the girls from becoming pregnant. One of the school board members felt that discussions of sexuality in her district were framed from a positive perspective, rather than perspectives of fear or disease:

> Our curriculum has never been heavy on the guilt part. One
> lesson that we use in the tenth grade that I really like is talking
> about the ocean. How it's viewed as being beautiful and you
> see the waves and it's just so gorgeous. And then you go in for
> a swim and there's a sharp undertow. And if you really can't

swim and you get out over your head, that same beautiful
ocean that was so calm and idyllic will kill you. And then we re-
late that to sex. Yes, in the proper place it can be a wonderful,
beautiful thing but if you get over your head. . . . At least we
try to tell kids that sex feels good.

While it's not surprising that Floridians would select a water metaphor to illustrate the power of sexuality as a force of nature, we wondered
how many tenth-grade students would make the connection between the
"beautiful ocean that can kill you" and the frantic sexual coupling that
takes place in the back seat of a car.

Pregnancy Prevention. One of the reasons the school district requested funds for this program was to reduce what was perceived to be a
high rate of teenage pregnancies in the local high schools. This district
had a reputation for developing innovative programs to support teenage
mothers, since it was one of the first ones in the state to provide on-site
day-care service for teenage mothers so they could remain in school.
Ironically, the same school board that supported these services also refused to allow the nurses to have open discussions of birth-control methods in the health and life-management classes. The nursing coordinator
confided that her goal was to develop a full-service program at one of the
high schools that would include dispensing contraceptives. She noted
that she would need to proceed very cautiously to build community support for this idea, but that one advantage working in her favor was that
she had a predominantly female school board to work with, one of the
very few that existed in the state.

By 1995 the school board had experienced a major shift in policy
regarding the discussion of birth-control options, thanks in part to the
intensive lobbying done by the nursing coordinator, who took up the
cause of educating board members about the extent of the problem with
teenage pregnancies. In our interview with one of the school board members, a woman who had been actively involved with this program, we
raised the issue of why schools in this district appeared freer to discuss
some sexuality topics (e.g., condom use) than in other districts. Not surprisingly for an elected official, she told us that how the issues were presented made a considerable difference:

We have been extremely careful about materials. For example,
there was a health care agency that was showing a film with a
real penis. And this whole thing about the scrotum and all this.
And when I saw it I said "no." Obviously it was something I

had not previewed before. But it was a great relief to the parents because they believed then that I was trustworthy and so forth.[3] You just have to represent that very conservative viewpoint, and that has served us well. The program is not materials, the program is people who are well trained to be in the classroom to do the right thing.

She was also well aware of the tension of maintaining the delicate balance between providing students with sufficient birth-control information without appearing to condone sexual experimentation.

Another problem mentioned on our 1992 visit that all the nurses shared was reaching male students to discuss their responsibility in preventing pregnancies. One nurse said that every time she heard a boy talk about being a stud, she would confront him and ask, "Who are the studs having sex with?" She also tried to raise students' consciousness by pointing out to them differences in cultural perceptions regarding sexual behavior: Boys with many sexual partners were considered "studs," while girls were "sluts." The nurses were frustrated by their inability to reach the boys, since most of the visitors to the clinic were girls and they could not discuss sexual topics in class. One nurse mentioned that she was able to discuss these issues:

> There have been some attempts to get male students involved in various groups. I often talk about date rape and about having sex on prom night. I try to make all curriculum useful to boys and girls. For example, I teach about breast and testicular cancer.

By 1995 some of the nurses displayed a much more realistic attitude about their role in preventing pregnancies. As one nurse told us:

> I know one goal of the grant is to reduce teen pregnancies, but I feel those tendencies are developed well before high school. We can help with information about birth control, but they have pretty well decided before ninth grade whether they choose to be abstinent or not. That is a very tough battle.

The principal of one full-service school saw the problem of teenage pregnancy in terms of larger social issues:

> Education is the key, but not in and of itself. The problem is not that the kids don't know how *not* to get pregnant. They

want to get pregnant, and you can understand it when you
look at the profiles of their lives. Many of them live in some
small trailer, maybe there's a history of abuse and neglect. They
want someone to love them for the first time in their lives, but
they don't realize the responsibility that's involved.

He dryly noted that society has changed its mores about unwed pregnancies as well: "The scarlet letter of pregnancy no longer exists. Pregnancy is a badge of honor among some girls." He also blamed the media
for promoting sexuality on cable TV and soap operas, and he was quite
dismayed over the difference in sexual imagery between his childhood
and today's children:

When I was young, the most sexual exposure I got was when I
went into the back room of a mechanic's shop and saw a calen-
dar of Marilyn Monroe bending over. Kids are protected from
nothing these days. Four-year-olds can watch sex scenes on
cable.

On-Site Day Care. Questions regarding sexuality in the curriculum
as well as sexuality in the school were nowhere more visible than when
the issue of school-based child care was broached. One of the most striking images with regard to on-site day care came home to us when we
walked in the door of one of the high schools where it was now available.
As we came in, we saw a young girl wheeling around a six-seater wagon
filled with poster-child children between the ages of 12 and 24 months.
She told us that she brought the babies down to the office every day and
wheeled them around the hall so the students could talk to them. The
children were all adorable, and we wondered if making these young children so visible in the school would have the effect of making young, impressionable adolescent girls want one for their own, especially since child
care was so readily available. In asking the nurse, the principal, the social
worker, and a school board member for their opinion about this practice,
we received four different answers. The nurse was interviewed first, and
she was clearly uncomfortable with the idea that child care was available
on site:

I have to talk to the principal about this. I just heard a lot of
kids that don't like it because it's a high school. One student
even said, "Oh, this is their trophy for showing off." Well, it's
not fair to the baby, you know, but it's in a high school and it
makes it look real acceptable and all that. It's taken me awhile

to form an opinion. This is the only school that has it on-campus. The other two are removed from the school. And here, I mean I've had some girls say, "Oh, if I get pregnant I'll just put my baby in the school day care. It will be so easy." And I don't like that. Not that it's going to make them get pregnant or not. But it makes it OK. It just makes it OK.

The principal of the same school was more ambivalent about the issue, and he admitted he had struggled with it since he was also an ordained evangelical minister. We suspected that in his heart he would have liked to have seen the girls suffer more the consequences of having a baby out of wedlock. But what tipped the balance for him to approve having the on-site day care available was an incident that had taken place a few years back when he was working at another school. He had been called by the local sheriff, who informed him that a female student's baby was dead. She had gone to school and had left her boyfriend in charge of minding the baby. He had gone out for a few hours; while he was gone, the baby had become entangled in the bedclothes and smothered. The principal was the one who had to tell the girl that her child was dead, and obviously the incident had left a deep emotional scar. His voice trembled as he told us, "I don't ever want to tell another young girl that her baby is dead because she couldn't find child care while she went to school." He also saw the value of having day care available because:

It is a way to break the cycle, help the girls get an education and raise their self-esteem. We hope they will convey these values to their child and that it will help them realize that the rite of passage to adulthood is accepting responsibility for their child, not the act of childbirth.

In sharp contrast to the concerns raised by both the principal and the nurse, the social worker and a school board member strongly supported the idea of on-site day care and the practice of wheeling the children around the school. The social worker had this to say:

The children in the cart I don't mind. Those babies are protected, they're not in mom's arms, and there are usually two staff members, one pushing and one accompanying. I think that's important for the children who are in the program, toddlers, you know, that they understand that they're part of a school, they're on school grounds. And mom's going to school and this is the principal, and these are adults who can make a fuss over them. I don't mind that at all. I think there are people who would because they feel it makes teenage pregnancy and having a baby—glamorizes it. But babies can be found anywhere, in Wal-Marts, in grocery stores, in McDonalds.

When we probed her response further by asking her to respond to some critics' concern that the availability of on-site child care made pregnancy easier for girls because they didn't have to suffer the consequences of dropping out of school or finding adequate child care, she fielded the question easily:

It's a good point. Except that the baby's here. The baby already here is a fact of life. And rather than go through what my generation went through when you were banned from school, banned from education, probably a time in your life that you needed it most in order to begin to build a future. That was eliminated or you went out of state or something if your parents could afford that. Today this is a fact of life that's happening and life goes on. And school is a part of their life.

The social worker's view was shared by the school board member we interviewed. She also commented on an aspect that no one else had concerning the charge that the availability of on-site child care meant the girls didn't have to worry about the consequences of becoming pregnant:

You know, if Marlene [the nurse at the high school with child care] is correct, then her pregnancy rate should be twice that of any of our other high schools. And it isn't. It's remained just about like everybody else's. So I hear what she's saying and I know emotionally what she's saying. But I still have to say that these things are not what's going through a girl's mind when she's in the back seat of a car Saturday night deciding if she will or will not give up her virginity (*laughs*). She's not thinking, "Gee, I can just stay right at the high school if I get pregnant."

Student Health Issues

At the high school level, a nurse does not have to monitor students' chronic health problems as closely as she would with younger students. As one nurse noted, "Basically, these students are aware of their problems, but I check in regularly with them, refer them to the free clinic if necessary, and follow through as needed." Problems that might need monitoring included illnesses such as diabetes or epilepsy. Most of the high schools had developed programs to help students develop a more healthy lifestyle, such as the one described by this nurse:

> We've started a dating relationship group that's divided up by age groups. We've also started a weight group to talk about healthy lifestyles. We have support groups for kids with chronically ill parents and children with alcoholic parents. This is the largest problem in the school—dysfunctional families.

When we returned in 1995, the students' health needs were perceived as greater than ever. According to one nurse:

> I've been here four years now and we are seeing—the social worker and I are both feeling that students are coming to school with more problems . . . lots of single family homes. They're not getting—I don't know what they're not getting— there's lots of drugs. The teenage pregnancy rates are staying about the same. There's a lot more emotional and physical needs. We're both just pretty well swamped all the time.

The nurse's reaction was confirmed by the social worker. When asked about the typical problems she encountered, she had this to say:

> All kinds of problems. From kids who run away, to kids who teachers are concerned about, to kids who need to talk about something. Truants, that's one of the drug symptoms, all kinds of things.

We also interviewed one of the school board members on this point, and she carefully assessed the issue:

> We still have pregnant teens. We still have kids who need health care. I think we have answered some problems in making health care more available to kids through school. . . .
> Many of our bad areas are moving toward health care on-site. And so that's made a difference, you know, in just making a lot of the things that we spent a lot of time not there anymore. So that part is good. I see that the problems of children overall are growing more serious. (*Interviewer: In what ways?*) Violence; we had two boys arrested at one of our high schools last week

because they had murdered their neighbor across the street. We had another group of boys who murdered an older man and his mother in a home. That kind of thing. Our expulsion rate is so much higher than it was even five years ago. So those kinds of problems are definitely worse.

Her comments echoed the comments of others that while the clinics had been successful in addressing some of children's basic health needs, the kinds of problems the nurses and social workers were now seeing were so much more intractable and rooted in a social pathology that was difficult to attack at the school level. We can attest to the fact that these kinds of problems were not as visible on our first visit; then we heard much more about the need to provide basic health services. In just three years we heard testimony that indicated that schools need to broaden their mission to reach children who are in crisis over social and emotional issues, not because they can't afford a physical or a pair of glasses.

Parent and Community Reactions

Unlike in Emerald County, the provision of health services in school clinics was never really a controversial issue even from the beginning of the funding period. This was confirmed in our interview with the school superintendent when we first visited in 1992. As he noted, everyone in the community considered the issues of student health and teenage pregnancy "very important," and he pointed out that the Youth Risk Behavior Survey administered the year before by the Centers for Disease Control evoked no objections from parents. The school principals had a similar reaction. As one principal commented:

I have not had any negative complaints. Parents are not comfortable with sex education and don't understand AIDS, therefore they are relieved that the school is taking over for them. If it were not for the health services, there would be no information, only misinformation. The entire program has been open to parents and the community.

One of the parents we interviewed on our first visit gave almost the same response as the principal. She agreed that the issues of health and teenage pregnancy were "important issues to be covered in school" and that the clinic was "another resource that may make students more comfortable to talk with parents." She also noted that "pregnant students were more stabilized and aware of options available to them because of the program." She was well aware that few options existed for students in the community to keep them out of trouble; "there's not a lot of community support for children—no social activities. There's not even school-sponsored dances." She concluded by saying:

> Any education is well worth the time spent on it even if it is controversial. Only education will change behavior. Schools are reluctant to take on the role of families, but they need to because of dysfunctional families. It's not the ideal, but it's necessary.

We suspect that one reason the advent of the clinics provoked little reaction was that this district had a tradition of having nurses available in the schools, and this project was seen by many people in the community as just a logical extension of the nurses' role. The nurses used various strategies to reach parents and community support groups concerning students' health promotion. According to one nurse:

> The parent newsletter contained an article about the program. It gave the nurses' phone number. I often talk with the school advisory board. There was also an article in the Silver County newspaper. There's also individual parent contact. Some students put on a show for the school board on AIDS prevention. It's more difficult to get parents involved at the high school level.

The nursing coordinator said that her staff and she had engaged in considerable "public relations efforts—parent letters, a health fair," and even the "local medical association had pledged support." Her long-term goal was to have "physicians eventually adopt a school." The superintendent also made a point of keeping the school board well informed of what plans and events were taking place in the clinics. He mentioned that during board meetings:

> Twenty percent of the reporting time goes to the assistant superintendent in charge of human services. The grant reporting would be handled during this time. The school board is given written materials prior to meetings, and monthly workshops are held where all subjects are covered.

When we returned in 1995, we found that community support was still strong, but it was also evident that it remained high because the program personnel took great pains not to create waves by discussing controversial issues that had come up in other school health rooms. As the principal of one school noted, the school's policy was to promote abstinence first, but also to provide information about birth-control options. Even though he was at a full-service school, the policy was not to dispense condoms, contraceptives, or prescriptions for contraceptives because "we are sensitive to the values of the individual home and we serve the community." However, he recognized that community involvement also meant that everyone in the community had an obligation to become involved with health services in schools:

> It takes a whole village to raise a child. Schools are on the firing line, but the churches, the community, the Chamber of Commerce, all need to play a part. Corporate America has to face up to its responsibility. They promote smoking, wine coolers to entice kids to drink. They can't evade their responsibility. It's so obvious I can't see why they don't see it.

The social worker also felt that community support was solid but that it had to be developed over time. As she told us:

> In the beginning, when we first came, the big issues were— what did we talk about? We talked about birth control. Oh boy, and there were people who said, "No, my child will not be served by the full-service school." But I think that it became a forum for people to say, you know, we'll take care of our babies at home. We don't want you doing that. In fact, we'll let you teach, but don't teach about this and that. So I think in the beginning there was a fear. There was also a fear of lines and lines of sick and indigent people flooding my doors and sitting in all the seats. So there were fears, natural fears and apprehensions people had. That passed, I believe. I believe that if we started—I think the nurse probably told you that we have pregnancy tests here, and she probably told you that parents sign a form. But the fact that this is here and we haven't had anyone picketing around the school saying, "how dare you have those pregnancy tests there." I think that's an indication that we are serving the broader needs of the community.

What she was alluding to was the fact that over a period of three years in this community, people had recognized the fact that teenage pregnancy was a major social problem, and they understood the need for providing school-based services, either to help reduce it or to keep teen-age mothers in school.

The school board member had a more pragmatic perspective on why so little opposition had surfaced. In response to our question about the extent of community support for school health services, she bluntly stated:

> I guess if we had to rely on the community we probably
> wouldn't have them, because I'm not sure they even know the
> services are there unless they access them directly. The people
> who vote aren't the ones who are utilizing them. That's because
> the people who vote generally take their children to their own
> health care. So, I'm not even sure they know these things are
> available.

Her comments led us to believe that school-based health services for mainly poor children are tolerated in a community as long as middle-class people don't see that their interests are being compromised. The exception is the group of middle-class people who oppose these services from an ideological or religious standpoint, not because they stand to lose some tangible benefit that they would gain if the clinics were not funded. Because opposition of this kind had been so visible in Emerald County, we asked if any school districts in this county had encountered cases of people monitoring school board meetings closely. She answered this question immediately:

> Yes, we do have that. It's a very tiny group. It's called the Chris-
> tian Coalition for Excellence in Education and that is a nation-
> wide group. . . . The actual attendance is probably less than 10
> people. But the church group that these people go to—they
> can always tap into them for phone calls to the board. We do
> have this lady who comes to 95% of our board meetings and
> tapes them. She edits her own tape and on her spots on her
> TV show on free cable puts it on. Whatever she wants. Nobody
> ever sees it anyway and, besides, the quality of the tape is
> terrible.

In telling us about the board's experiences with this group, the point she made was that their opposition was not confined to health issues, but that it extended to all aspects of the teaching and learning process. She contended that it was absolutely vital for schools to "monitor the temper-ature" of their community and to take the time to present policy changes to parents and community before taking action. We think that this pulse-taking was precisely why this district did not experience intense opposition to school-based health services—because the nursing coordinator and others had taken time to build community support prior to securing the grant funds. As the coordinator told us in her interview: "We went slowly. We educated parents along the way. We did teacher in-service training." When school personnel just implemented a new policy without laying sufficient groundwork, as was the case in one school district with a new grading policy, then over 3,000 parents signed a petition against it. As the board member said, "There's a lesson to be learned here."

She further noted that while the community may not have been aware of the day-to-day health services provided by the clinics, people were very much aware of the sexuality curriculum. When we asked how people felt about it, she smiled and said:

> We're very comfortable with that. I do not see much change, interestingly enough, even though I see nationwide more conservative views. I've had no calls for five years, and then I had two calls one year, and maybe three the next year. So yes, there's a tiny little increase in concern, but it's very very small.

INTERGOVERNMENTAL ISSUES

Because full-service schools typically serve as the primary site for a multitude of educational, health, and social service programs in a small area, turf wars can easily develop. As we talked about this issue with the social worker, she reeled off a dizzying array of programs that were available in her full-service school, all with their unique way of operating in terms of policies and procedures. She pointed out that personnel from different programs have to be able to adapt their protocols to meet the circumstances of the students' needs, rather than rigidly adhering to policies that may work back in the agency, but which no longer work when they are co-located in a school.

Interagency Collaboration

The cooperation in this district between the school system and the public health unit appeared to be very smooth. The superintendent maintained direct contact with other agencies in the community through the formation of a multiagency coordinating council that met four times yearly to "keep all lines of communication open." His comments were echoed by the county public health administrator, who noted that "we're happy with the relationship, especially with the school nurse coordinator." He further noted that "basically money is given to the school district to run the project." The nursing coordinator mentioned that the county was focused on "collaborative decision making" and that a "wellness committee" had been set up to develop lesson plans.

Cooperation, however, was not freely obtained in all cases. As he wryly noted, "I had to work very closely with the county medical association to overcome their initial concern that school-based health services would drain business away." He felt very clearly that the most innovative aspect of the clinics was the open access to health services:

> Having the clinics on-site at school means that it doesn't require students to leave campus, which is essential. Otherwise, these kids will not get services. For example, some asthmatic students can be kept in school because health services are available on-site. Approximately 35% of children in Silver County are uninsured for health care. It's a heavy service economy, and many jobs do not include health benefits. For a number of reasons, school-age children are not readily processed through Medicaid. An attempt to get the clinics to be more family-oriented would be an advantage for those without another clinic or doctor to go to. They would have somebody to talk to.

When asked his assessment of whether the clinics would be successful in either improving student health or reducing the teenage pregnancy rate, he thoughtfully answered:

> It's not the long-term answer to medical care, but as long as the state does not have universal access to health care, school-based services are absolutely the way to go. Health problems are interrelated with all social services.

The social worker we interviewed in one school noted that interagency collaboration was very important, especially at a full-service school. She noted that when the program was first started at this school, initially the health department was not clear as to how to interface with schools, and they hired a person to be a liaison between the school and the health department. One of the problems that immediately ensued was that this person, as the social worker delicately described it, "had her own agenda, which included being very antiabortion. There were a lot of problems with that." This position was not funded the following year, and the school's real need was more for eligibility personnel (people who could certify students as eligible for Medicaid), since the school was in an isolated area, and students and family members found it difficult to go into town to receive services. The response from the health department was to assign to the school a counseling psychologist, who had very little understanding of how schools worked. According to the social worker, he alienated many teachers by pulling students from class for counseling sessions, instead of scheduling them in advance with teachers. The social worker said that she followed a policy of doing group sessions after school, since few students had any periods free when they were not involved in academic activities. By doing this, she lent credence to the school personnel's belief that the primary business of schools was to provide an education, not health or social services.

The man was finally replaced because of complaints from the district, but the whole experience gave the social worker new insight into the need for training people to learn how to work in a collaborative situation. In her words:

> But it was while all this was happening that I realized training, setting up the collaboration is very important, because you can have people with their own agendas who can come in, or their own *idea* about what needs to happen, and they're not really working as an agent for their agency to serve their clients.

Outside Referrals

When asked about the kinds of referrals that were routinely made, one nurse replied, "A multitude. The difficulty is with the waiting list. There's no problem with obtaining cooperation." Typical agencies to whom referrals or calls upon for services were made were: the Lions Club for vision care and free eyeglasses; the county public health department for treatment of sexually transmitted diseases and birth-control prescriptions; the state department of health and human services for food stamps; private mental health clinics; and the Mom's program.

The kinds of referrals the nurses made in 1992 were basically unchanged in 1995. At one school, most of the nurse's referrals were to the county public health department. Because this school now had a social worker, she dealt with most of the mental health issues and with family dynamics. One of the questions we posed to her was the extent to which the kinds of problems she encountered daily could be redressed by the various agencies to which she made referrals. In other words, how much collaboration can occur among different agencies to solve problems that are multifaceted in nature and often quite intractable? To her credit, she gave us a straight answer:

> Well, I think they need to be put on the table as problems. And I think, you're talking about interagency collaboration. (*Interviewer: Yes.*) OK. What I thought was interesting at the beginning when full-service schools first started—I went to the conferences and they were really neat and I enjoyed them. One of the big subjects was interagency collaboration. What we need to do now is have that intermediate link that can help schools and agencies interface. It's nothing mystical. There are skills and steps that can be taken to do this. And there may need to be certain changes. Each may not keep its own integrity. There may be because of this combining a modification, so that when in collaboration, while you're each doing your own thing, you have a way to meet and make certain modifications so that you can service clients.

We pursued this topic by asking her which group she thought should take the lead in making collaboration happen, the school or the state department of health and human services. She replied thoughtfully:

> I think HRS is the authority as far as mental health, substance abuse services, and all of that goes. I think that it would be a good idea for them to have the technology, the awareness of the technology. I think in order for it to happen, it needs to come from both.

One of the organizational changes that had taken place over three years was that the clinics that were initially funded in 1991–92 by grants through HRS were now funded as a line item in the general school revenue. This change meant that while the school districts had more direct control over the money, instead of the county public health unit, interagency collaboration in terms of billing for services was still complicated. One principal commented that "you can't dictate to other agencies," and this was particularly the case when the billing for services was done through Medicaid.

Full-Service Schools

When we visited in 1992, the idea of a full-service school was only held dear by the nursing coordinator, who mentioned that one high school was "struggling to become a 'real' full-service school by pulling the community into the school. The community is not used to going to schools for these services." On our second visit in 1995, the situation was completely changed. Two of the high schools that had been funded in 1991–92 were now considered full-service clinics. However, they still faced some restrictions in terms of providing contraceptives and family planning on-site. In one school we visited, we asked the nurse if the physician could write birth-control prescriptions. She replied:

> We don't do any family planning. She only sees illnesses. We write prescriptions for antibiotics, something simple, nothing major. For anything major, we refer to the health department and I can get information. We didn't get into pregnancy testing; now that's something a little different. . . . But you know, you have to have permission. The parents on the first day of school, they sign a permission about the services we provide and if they circle pregnancy testing, I don't do it. 'Cause the parents don't want that. I'm very conservative and that's fine. . . . As far as family planning, I do not give out condoms, which I could sometimes. I've had students come here and ask, "Could you give me some?" And they have no money and they probably won't go to the health department where they could get them free. Those are the people I wish I could help out, but I would get fired if I did.

One nurse commented that she thought she could get fired by overstepping the boundaries by giving out condoms. We felt this was indicative of the fact that the school district was still not entirely comfortable with its role as a provider of social and health services as well as education. The principal of one of the full-service schools stated that "first and foremost we are an educational institution." Although he supported the concept because "adolescents need to know these services are available here," he felt "we have to keep these issues in perspective. It's very difficult to work with multiple agencies in a school."

When we first visited in 1992, a social worker was not based full-time in any school but was part of a traveling team that also included a nurse and school psychologist. On our return visit, we learned that both full-service schools had a full-time social worker available and that the primary task for each one was to deal with counseling issues. We also learned from one of the school board members that the two schools did not offer equivalent services because they were funded from two different sources. One school was funded from the health and human services funds; the other school was funded from the state Department of Education funds. The difference was that one full-service school was primarily oriented to providing health and social services, while the other school offered a broader array of educational services (including an afterschool program for children up to sixth grade). Students at this school received their medical care either through private physicians or through the health department.

Principal Involvement

All of the principals we talked to on our first visit were very supportive of having a clinic on site. The reaction of one man spoke for them all.[4] When asked, "How important are the issues of student health and teenage pregnancy in your school?," he replied, "It's critical. Teenage pregnancy leads to dropping out, etc. The most important thing is prevention." All of them felt that the nurses were working well with the teachers and other school personnel, and that they were especially helpful in dealing with parents.

Although the principal is the person who is held responsible for all matters taking place in the school, he was not perceived as the one who made the final decisions concerning clinic issues. This was clear in one nurse's comments:

> The nursing coordinator is the final authority, although she gives pretty much the go-ahead because the baseline relationship was already established. Approval and review are handled informally and preemptively. Principal approval is a given.

The reason why the principal's authority could in effect be bypassed by the nurses was because of the high degree of trust and esteem in which the nursing coordinator was held by virtually everyone in the county. She was widely acknowledged to be the driving force behind putting nurses into the schools long before other school districts in Florida had them, and she played a pivotal role in securing the grant funds to expand school health services. A transplanted northerner who had lived in the county for over 20 years, she was a strong and forceful advocate for children's needs and, more importantly, knew how to translate her convictions into political activism.

As was the case in 1992, principals were still strongly supportive of school clinics, even as they acknowledged some of the difficulties in managing them. One principal that we talked to spent almost an hour out of a busy schedule discussing the impact of the clinic in his school. In his words:

We have a responsibility to protect our kids. That's why they go
to these militia. These groups take them in and make them feel
someone cares about them. We need to do whatever we can to
protect kids from aberrant influences.

PROFESSIONAL ISSUES

The nurses felt that they had established a good working rapport
with the teachers, even with those who taught health education classes,
where the nurses' presence might have been perceived as a threat. When
asked, "Has there been any team teaching?", one nurse responded, "I
taught life management with the social worker." The nurses also mentioned that teachers were more likely to refer students with problems and
to let them know when particular students needed assistance. As the nursing coordinator commented, a good working relationship with the school
staff was essential; "all nurses feel that they have it, and there is no way
they could do without it."

With regard to sexuality, there was a clear-cut division of labor maintained between the nurse and the social worker in one full-service school.
Although the social worker's job was to handle counseling issues, she told
us that she only discussed sexual behavior in the context of relationships
and that all other matters (pregnancy prevention, STDs, AIDS, etc) were
handled by the nurse. Even date rape, which we would have thought
could be discussed as part of male/female relations, was viewed as belong-
ing to the nurse's role. The social worker did mention that she was
concerned about the lack of students who discussed the issue of sexual
orientation, since she quoted statistics to us on the linkage between cases
of teenage suicide and conflicted sexual desires. She commented that she
had seen evidence that some kids were willing to express their differences:

> Through what we would call our counterculture in school,
> freaks, couples walking hand in hand, usually females, I've
> never seen males, but I'm thinking it may be a posture that
> they're assuming. Flamboyant, you know, just trying things out.

She also told us about a suicide case in the school several years ago.
Had she been in the school at the time, she said she would have investigated it further, since a conflict over sexual orientation seemed to be one
of the precipitating factors. When we raised this issue with one of the
school board members, she agreed that the issue had been silenced in

most classrooms, but she defended her district as being aware of the problem:

> We do have in our media a couple of videos that address that. But whether they're checked out I don't know. I think the nurses are available for counseling, and our guidance counselors are very sensitive to this issue. And we do know there are youngsters out there who are struggling.

IMPACT/SUMMARY

When we came in 1992, we usually ended our interviews by asking people about their expectations for this program and their wish list of resources. The nursing coordinator commented that she would like to see "mass messages" about prevention go out and to be able to use a mass media approach, such as a teacher team, that would write teenage pregnancy objectives into the curriculum. She also wanted to have nurses in middle school, with a physician easily available. One of the parent's expectation was that more information would be provided about date rape, teaching girls "refusal skills" and more parenting education. A principal noted that the program should be funded at a higher level to pay for a social worker and a psychologist because they needed an entire team. As he stated:

> The kids' attendance level is poor, their social skills are so poor. They can't cope, the social pressures are tremendous. There's an increase in violence within school, to other kids, to the teacher.

What was most significant about our return visit was our realization that many of these expectations had been fulfilled, a rarity in a state-funded, bureaucratically managed program. Two of the schools had been designated as full-service schools, which meant they had a full array of professionals on staff to deal with problems. The nurses were able to develop a curriculum that was much more inclusive about sexuality than the one they had to use when we had visited three years earlier.

The one area that was still unchanged and, in fact, was under attack by the current legislature, was the issue of funding. Most of the schools felt they could use more funds because the needs were steadily growing each day. But what worried most of the people we interviewed was that the services could be eliminated because of recent political attacks regarding services for low-income people. The principal of one full-service school was especially concerned:

> Well, I'm a Republican but I'm about ready to turn in my
> party card. I disagree with the position of slicing services to
> those in need. We need to invest in these kids. With a society as
> rich as this one, there's no excuse not to invest in these kids.
> We will have a grim future if we don't.

ESTABLISHING ACCOUNTABILITY

We posed the same question as we did in Emerald County: "How do you know this program is making a difference?" In 1992, the answers were couched not in the language of hard data, but in the emotions and feelings of the people involved. One nurse believed that "students have changed their unprotected sexual behavior." The superintendent believed the program would make a difference but also that the "fear of AIDS will have an impact." The students took perhaps a more realistic view of the clinic's effect in changing behavior. Several students just shrugged their shoulders over this question and these comments were elicited: "People do whatever they want. Something has to happen to you before you learn. Some kids have to learn the hard way." They suggested that high school students should become mentors to middle school students.

In 1995, after the program had been operational for almost four years, some systematic attempts were made to collect empirical data on the program's outcomes in the form of student attitude questionnaires. The school district administered their own version of the Centers for Disease Control Youth Risk Behavior Survey that had been conducted in 1990, and they found that condom use, at least through self-report, was higher than the national average.[5] It was also the case that during our visit, several schools were participating in another state funded program evaluation study.[6] But in our conversation with one nurse, it was clear that she did not know how to respond to the issue of accountability:

> I don't know how we're going to justify this, keep track of it.
> We do keep track how many kids are sent home for illnesses.
> We give them Tylenol or something, and maybe they stay in
> school. Or we call their parent and they go home. I wish we

could say we are making a real big difference there, but we
keep them comfortable while they are here. (*Laughs and shakes
her head.*) I don't know. I just don't know.

She mentioned that the program personnel kept track of documents
related to health room activities, such as antismoking or drug-prevention
workshops and presentations. Some of the nurses at the other schools
kept newspaper clippings or pictures of students engaged in health-related activities, such as a seatbelt or Students Against Drunk Driving campaign. She admitted that most of her information was anecdotal in nature
and that it was very difficult to keep track of information other than student health records.

One of the social workers we interviewed agreed that accountability
was the primary concern of the taxpayers, but instead of citing statistics
pertaining to her school, she framed the issue from the broader social
perspective of being concerned with children's welfare:

We're trying to look at pregnancy rates and hopefully, if this exists, then that will decline. But we really need to open it up
and look at the bigger picture. I know at the beginning of this
movement we were looking to knock out teenage pregnancies.
(*Interviewer: Right. That was part of the intent of the original legislation.*) But there's been change, there's been a shift, so it's not
the first pregnancy, but it's the second, third additional pregnancies. That's what we're looking to do. You may not have
been able to catch—the kids who are most at risk are not the
first-born of teenagers, although they may not have lots of advantages, but it's the second- and third-borns who are throw-
away children.

Not surprisingly, the school board member was the most concerned
with the issue of accountability, since she faced this issue daily from the
taxpayers. Her response was honest and to the point:

That is where health education and health services is the very
weakest. We've got to measure what we're doing. Of course,
the best instrument we have available to us is the CDC Risk
Survey. But these stupid counties in Florida, many of them will
not allow it to be given to the children because of the provocative questions. And that's wrong. I think funding should absolutely stop until people are willing to evaluate their programs.
Because you are throwing money away if you are not going to
evaluate it.

Meeting Children's Needs

Another question we asked to address the same issue was, "Why should we put this money into schools? Why shouldn't we just put the services in the community and let schools be schools?" The nurse at one of the full-service schools had a ready answer:

> Because they are coming to school with so many problems they can't learn. It's just different. We feel kind of frustrated this year because it's overwhelming. The drug thing is really big and that's a battle. I think they're using a lot of marijuana, smoking more . . . then they get suspended and get behind. Next year one of my goals is to do more on drugs. . . . It's a change in society and I feel really frustrated this year for the first time.

Although the principal at her school also felt frustrated at times, particularly with regard to students' ingratitude ("they think the services were always here and don't realize what it was like to live without them"), he also saw that school-based health services were filling a tremendous need in the community:

> I'd love to go back to the "good old days," but this is the hand that we've been dealt. The services are here, and the kids can reach them. If they were somewhere else in the community, there would be problems with transportation for many students. Also, the nurses know the kids well and the kids know they will keep the information confidential. There's a level of trust you can't find in these other places, where no one knows who you are. Because of the clinic, the school is now perceived as a more sensitive place.

The social worker in this same school also had a quick answer to the critics on this issue:

> Well, the services don't make the kids different. The services are a reaction from society to changes in the society which are reflected in the institutions. And yes, the primary purpose of the educational institutions is learning, teaching, knowledge, and all that. We're finding that students are challenged by many factors outside the school that reflect in the school. I can just tune into terms and give you any number of kids who have

problems right across the board. . . . So I believe that the schools seem to be the one common area that kids have. They may not see parents for days on end. But we know that there are 180 days a year where they all have something in common for six hours. It's the one commonality that pulls all kids in because legally they have to be in school until age 16. So this is the place. I feel it's the only place. That's where all kids come.

When asked this same question, a school board member sighed and rolled her eyes, since her constituents often asked it as well:

That's been an argument forever. I can remember someone saying that very thing to a group of teachers at a meeting probably 15 years ago when we were just a little country community. And this woman said, "Listen, when this child comes to me and he's hungry, I have to feed him before I can teach him. And if his clothes are sopping wet, I have to get him dry clothes before he'll learn any math." You know, the problems are not going to go away, and if you don't deal with them you will never be able to educate the child. Because they will not be ready to learn.

Over and over again we heard the same concept echoed in different voices. Children are coming to school with greater needs that are unmet within their family configuration, and schools become the first line of defense. And if the schools cannot pick up the slack, in a place where children spend as much as seven hours per day, there are virtually no other centrally located societal institutions that can meet these needs.

A final question we asked was related to the future of health services in schools. At the time of our second visit, several legislators had already threatened to cut funding for continuation of the program or to impose restrictive conditions.[7] When we posed this question to one of the nurses, she responded in a hesitant manner that she was not sure how much financial support was required to maintain the program, and she was unclear as to whether there would be sufficient community support to keep the services available if the state funds were cut. The social worker felt at first that the services were not at risk, and she was surprised to hear that the state was in the process of contracting services for Medicaid clients out to private HMOs, who could then choose not to cover the health or social services provided to children in school. Once apprised of this fact, she quickly changed her mind about the future of school-based services:

As a social worker, I'm alarmed about that. It's already happening in hospitals, where they are pushing social workers out. I noticed that at the last conference on full-service schools, I was not even invited to that. I see that we really need to keep the concept of system alive because we're dealing with a whole person and a whole environment. We need to keep a healthy respect for the other disciplines and the collaboration among them.

She reiterated the need to build strong school/community coalitions to keep these services visible in schools. She recalled an occasion when the clinic first opened and the principal received a lengthy letter slipped under his door in a brown envelope. Part of the letter contained a description of a book chapter that "attacks the child lovers," but as the social worker commented:

It used child lover like you would use _____ lover, any kind of person of whom bigots say, Oh the bleeding heart, the _____ lover, whatever. The child lover! And this is a reason for slippage in the community, a slippage of morals and all of that. And he showed me the letter. My belief is that it came from a faculty member. This is kind of the Bible Belt. I'm a New Yorker. I felt that the staff had to accept the concept of the full-service school. See, that's the system awareness. That's something that I think we've made some really good strides in. Rather than being a social worker who should be condemned and cast out, in any full-service school we are the child lovers.

The school board member was worried about the lack of funds to maintain the program, let alone expand it. She had heard that in neighboring counties schools had already cut their nursing staffs by as much as 50%. She commented about what she had told the staff in one full-service school:

And what I try to tell these people is, you're frills. A school psychologist is a frill. A school social worker is a frill. A guidance counselor is a frill. Because you're not directly linked to the classroom. And you can't measure what you do. You can't stand forever on the budget and say, I saved one child.

She felt that an upcoming school board election would be a pivotal one in terms of determining the future of local school health services because some conservative groups were expected to make a strong push to elect someone who shared their views that these services should not be available in schools. Her final comments reflected her belief that being an advocate for health services was not enough:

> All programs have to be able to validate their worth. I had a gentleman tell me in one of our meetings that it's not enough to tell me you have a good program. That will not wash anymore. You have got to give me hard data.

Summary

The picture that emerged of Silver County on our return visit differed considerably from the one we painted of Emerald County. In Silver County, the community was far more tolerant of sexual issues that could be discussed by school personnel, primarily because it lacked a strong nucleus of people who shared a common set of religious beliefs centered on opposition to any discussions of sexuality in schools and concomitant health services. Personnel in this county also emphasized the need for building community consensus prior to taking any new actions.

We also realized the importance of having someone in the community who was willing to take on a leadership role in actively promoting the concept of school-linked health services. In this case that person was clearly the nursing coordinator, who promoted the concept and actively campaigned to gather community support. She intensively lobbied for these services, and she became politically savvy as to how to forge a community consensus that the services were needed. As a result, Silver County is far ahead of other counties in the state in providing care and, as our limited cost-effectiveness data indicated, at a cost substantially lower than those at other projects. Whether these services will result in lowering the county's high teenage pregnancy rate is yet to be determined.

Despite the ambivalence expressed by the principal and school nurse at one full-service school about family planning and on-site child care, an ambivalence that reflects their underlying conservative values, virtually all of the people we talked to cared deeply about the students' problems and searched for ways to improve their lives. It's a sad commentary on American culture when the word *child lover* can be used pejoratively to describe people who care about children's welfare, and it raises alarming concerns about the future of public policies designed to improve poor children's access to health and social services.

Chapter 5

"We Are Making a Difference in Children's Lives"

THE CASE OF GOLD COUNTY

Gold County has been described as a place where "fairy tales collide with reality" (Fiedler & Kempel, 1993, p. 669). Home to some of the wealthiest and most beautiful seashore residences in America, it is also a place where families live in impoverished areas that rival those of any Third World country. The economic boom of the last 30 years passed many of its citizens by, but it is a county that continues to draw new immigrants daily from all parts of the world, especially the Caribbean and Central and South America. As a result, the demographics of the county are slowly shifting to a nonwhite majority, a trend that is expected to accelerate in the next century. Based on the 1990 census, 79% of the population was white, 12% were black, 8% were Hispanic, and 1% were classified as "other." However, in the schools we visited both in 1992 and 1995, there was already a rich mix of cultural backgrounds present, since the "other" now included a growing Southeast Asian population as well. One principal told us that in her school there were at least 21 different languages spoken, a mini–United Nations that bore little resemblance to the world predominantly white retirees expected when they moved here. Although the county is heavily populated by retired snowbirds from the Northeast and Midwest (24.4% of the county is over 65), because of the growth surge in children under 18, the population is also fairly young, with a median age of 40 years. Due to the presence of extremely rich families on the coast, the median income was the highest of all the counties we visited, $32,534. The people are well educated (79% are high school graduates, 22% are college graduates) and fairly liberal, since Democrats held a slight voting edge and the county voted for Clinton in 1996. Like many other counties in Florida, the political climate has shifted somewhat to the right; in the 1994 gubernatorial election, the Democratic candidate barely carried it.

The fairy tale environment for adults mirrored an increasingly grim reality for children, especially those who were poor. In 1992 children un-

115

der the age of 18 constituted 20% of the county population, and of these children, 20% lived in poverty (Florida Center for Children and Youth, 1994). The pregnancy rate for females under the age of 20 was 10.5%; the infant mortality rate was 11.3 births per 1,000. On all indicators that suggested a deterioration of social conditions (child abuse cases, deaths, incidents of violence, juvenile justice referrals, etc.), the numbers steadily increased even in the period between the time we visited in 1992 and our return in 1995. Although the clinics were initially placed in schools where children were likely to require the most services, several political shifts that have taken place over the last three years (described later in this chapter) have lessened the possibility that these services would be received by those most in need.

PROJECT DESCRIPTIONS

At the time we conducted the evaluation in this county in 1992, there were two projects funded: One was a full-service school in the school district where virtually all the students were either African-American or Hispanic; the other was based on the SHIP model, with services provided through a feeder system of an elementary, middle, and high school. The full-service school project was initially funded in 1990–91 for $78,303, and the monies were requested to support a full-time nurse, an aide, and a health teacher. Funds were later added in the next funding cycle to support the services of a physician who worked on-site three days a week. This project was one of three in Florida that could be described as a school-based clinic in the way that term is used in the literature on school health services (Dryfoos, 1994). The purpose was to provide a full range of health services through a health clinic (including the dispensation of contraceptive prescriptions) that was located in a portable unit on school grounds. The nurse at this school was a white female who was a long-term resident of this area; the health aide was black. The physician who came to the school three days a week was a Hispanic female from a Cuban background.

The second project, funded for $87,997, was placed in a feeder pattern (elementary, middle, and high school) of schools where children were deemed at risk on a number of indicators. The high school was allowed to conduct pregnancy tests but not to provide contraceptive prescriptions. Because these three schools served a large number of children who were not native English speakers, the nurse who served both the elementary and middle school population was a black female from a Jamaican background; the nurse at the high school was a black female from a Haitian background. The health aide at the elementary school was a black female who spoke Creole, while the health aides at the middle and high school were white females. In 1992, the total enrollment in the schools served by these two projects was 4,598, and the standardized average cost per student for receiving services at the full-service school was $82.04, while the cost at the SHIP schools was $43.29.

Descriptions of Initial Project Schools

As part of the initial grant application, each school had to submit a detailed profile of their student characteristics in terms of ethnicity, poverty level (calculated by the number of students who qualified for either free or reduced lunches based on federal guidelines), number of pregnancies in the previous school year prior to their program application, dropout and absenteeism rates, a description of the three most common health problems, a description of the room where the clinic would be housed, the type of health and social support services currently offered, and any other special programs offered on-site that would be linked to the new project. Our 1992 data indicated that both high schools had large numbers of students who came from families below the federal poverty line, but only one high school was predominantly white. One high school was located in the middle of farming country, and the population was comprised of children of the migrant workers who picked sugar cane and vegetables in the surrounding fields. This high school also had the highest teenage pregnancy rate of all the schools participating in this program that we studied.

Under the SHIP model for one project, the nurses' primary responsibilities were to engage in classroom and community outreach through health presentations, to counsel students on social and medical problems, and to monitor students with chronic medical conditions. The emphasis was less on the health-related aspects of nursing, and more on the educational and public health preventive modes. However, because of the large number of immigrant children in these schools, the nurses spent a disproportionate amount of time just handling basic immunizations, an activity that significantly reduced their opportunities to make classroom presentations or do outreach activities with parents. The task was often complicated by cultural differences: Many of the Haitian parents did not want their children to receive shots because, to quote one nurse, "they felt that they were the mark of the devil." The Jamaican nurse told us that one way she reached out to parents was through meeting them at the community market on the weekends, where she passed out literature and answered their questions.

Student Outreach

When we visited in 1992 there was no question that the services were desperately needed by the children in these schools. As soon as the clinics became operational, they were filled daily with children who came for a variety of reasons. At the elementary level children came to receive basic health care in the form of vision and hearing screenings, immunizations, treatment for minor injuries, and physicals. As one principal noted, many of the children in her school were undocumented aliens who did not want to qualify themselves to receive health services through the county public health system because they were afraid of being identified and deported. She admitted to having mixed feelings about their use of the school health clinic:

> On one hand the schools can reach more people to provide re-
> sources, and children can be protected. On the other hand,
> these families become too dependent on schools to provide
> medical services and they don't seek access to other resources
> in the community.

The principal at the middle school was less concerned about the stu-dents' lack of access to outside resources because he felt strongly that these clinics should become a necessary part of school life in high-risk areas. He felt that the "clinic helps students who lack basic health care," and he further noted that these clinics served "a necessary function be-cause of family breakdown and lack of community resources." His view was shared by the principal at one of the high schools. An African-American woman who spoke with quiet dignity and immense care about the students in her school, she came across as a very passionate advocate of health services in schools. She spoke with pride about her attempts to encourage parents to sign up for extended services such as pregnancy testing and contraceptive prescriptions by taking the permission forms directly into the churches and the grocery stores.

All the nurses felt that the teachers were more than cooperative in referring children to the clinic. In most cases the nurses did not have to make presentations to classrooms to secure the teachers' cooperation. In fact, at the middle school the teachers commented on the difference in just one year of having the nurse available to help "direct kids to the appropriate medical resources." The students at this school were deeply appreciative of the nurse's presence, as evidenced in three of the letters the nurse showed us while we toured the clinic. As might be expected, a clear gender difference emerged in terms of their concerns, but not in gratitude for having the nurse there. One girl wrote:

Dear School Nerse [*sic*]: I am 15 years old. I think you should have a sit in twice a month. One day for girls and one day for boys. Also, help educate the students on safe sex and proper manners toward their health. Some children just don't understand. Can you also make it possible for us to see you in extreme emergencies when teachers don't understand? Thanks for taking the time to listen.

In a similar fashion another girl wrote:

Dear School Nurse: I be really glad you are here to take care of us. What we need in this clinic is really good support. We need someone who can take our temperature. We need someone who can give us medication. Things like asperns [*sic*] for headache or stomache [*sic*]. Also prescriptions can be taken. Also we need someone who really be there to take care. Thank you for your concern.

Both girls' letters stressed the importance of having someone who would listen to students, and they were written from the perspective of students who saw themselves positioned within the larger school community. In contrast, the boys saw the nurse more as a source of information necessary for personal development, especially by those who played sports. In his letter, an eighth-grade boy made this typical request:

Dear School Nurse: I play a lot of sports in this school and I'm always sore after practice. I would like to know if you can get some medicine muscle rub or something would relieve this pain. It would do a great deal of work and help us a lot after practice every day. Thank you for your understanding.

When we returned in 1995, we learned that the students' need for services was greater than ever. At the elementary school, the school nurse (a white woman had now replaced the Jamaican nurse, although the Haitian health aide was still there) spoke about the endless stream of children who came to the clinic to receive basic health care. Even during our interview, we were interrupted numerous times so that she could handle children's minor complaints. In just three years, the school population had shifted from being predominantly white (62%) to predominantly black (85%), with more than half of these children coming from Haiti, where many of them had never seen a doctor. She noted that without her health aide, she could not have coped with the transition, since as she put it:

I have one health support specialist, she speaks Creole, she's from Haiti. That's a great help. More so than the language translation I think is understanding, the authenticity, cultural things, and trying to make progress with treatment plans and case management. It's that sometimes not understanding I try to do what I think would be the right way, and it works out for their culture that it's totally unacceptable . . . you need to approach it from a different way.

When we asked for an example, she replied immediately:

For instance, the ringworm treatment, which means they are excluded from school until it is cured. They must go to the doctor and get oral medication for it. I've had lots of times we'll send them home with the form letters stapled to their shirt; they'll stay out a week and they've never gone to the doctor. Or, they'll go to the doctor and they never got the medicine filled because they don't think it's anything to be worried about so they keep them out long enough and then bring them back to school. I have to exclude them, and a lot of times it's like you have to approach it from . . . not threatening, but you need to take a real firm stand that this is what you have to do with it. . . . Resourcewise we use a lot of social workers, and they'll do home visits for us. For instance, our Creole-speaking one is a very, very tall man, so when he goes to the house, they're much more likely to comply with our request than if my little health support specialist, who's like, 5'1", were to explain it to them that they have to have it. So it's a different way of approaching things. I find that it helps tremendously having somebody that understands the culture. I guess that's what I'm trying to say.

Although we were not able to visit the middle school, we did talk to the nurse at the full-service high school. We learned that while the students' needs were as great as they had been three years ago, the school's ability to provide treatment was complicated by a change in state policy with regard to families receiving Medicaid assistance. Because this policy change impacted all schools in this district, we discuss this issue in greater detail in the next section. In contrast to the previous two chapters, we begin with a discussion of intergovernmental issues because trends occurring in this county paralleled those that were occurring at the state and national levels regarding health care policies for poor and working-class families with no health insurance.

INTERGOVERNMENTAL ISSUES

The first issue is one that was first brought to our attention by an official in the state capital, an issue that did not exist at the time of our visit in 1992. That issue was the transfer of Medicaid patients to private HMOs to receive basic health services. Because of this policy, which was coordinated at the state level (but had not yet impacted all counties, which is why we did not hear about it in the other two we visited), a serious breakdown has occurred in the collaborative working arrangement between the school districts and the county public health unit. We had noted in our 1992 evaluation report that these two agencies had worked very effectively together, but that arrangement was jeopardized by this new policy; consequently, the negative impact on children's ability to receive needed health services within their school was enormous.

Privatization of Health Care

We first heard about this issue at the state level prior to our return visit to Gold County when we interviewed a high-ranking official who worked in one of the agencies that promoted health services in schools. She was a very forceful advocate of school health services because, as she put it:

> Schools have a captive audience of children with a wide range of problems who require support services just to stay in school. For example, many parents work, or they are underinsured, or the services are not as accessible in other parts of the community. What people don't realize is that this program no longer serves just the needs of the poor. Parents can't leave their jobs to give medications, for example. And having a nurse available can be a matter of life or death for some children.

When we asked her how she envisioned the future of these services in schools, she mentioned this problem:

> School-based services won't survive because of the direction of managed care. HMOs will take over, but they will be located in places where kids can't get to, or if they provide them on-site at the school, not all kids will be covered. If there are 20 HMOs operating in one school, who will coordinate the care?

She noted that as a result of the 1994 state elections, Florida had already begun contracting with HMOs to serve Medicaid patients because this contractual arrangement reduced state costs. This policy change meant that the state department of health and human services, the agency that managed the school health services program, could no longer bill the federal government for services provided to kids who were on HMOs unless a prior arrangement had been worked out with that particular HMO. We did not fully understand the implications of this policy until we went to Gold County and asked both the nursing coordinator and the school health liaison for their thoughts as to what impact this new policy would have on children's health. From their answers, we quickly learned how detrimental the policy was proving to be. The nursing coordinator spoke first in response to our question about what had changed since our visit in 1992:

> The one big difference is the HMO piece. Some children have been assigned to an HMO and the HMO gets the dollars to serve them. So we [the SSHP (Supplemental School Health Project) staff] no longer serve them. And there has been no waiver written at the state level for school health to be able to do services and bill the HMO. *(Interviewer: I see. So these kids come to the clinic and you find out that they're on this HMO, do you have to tell them you can't see them?)* Right. We can't give them immunizations and we can't give them physicals. Now during an emergency, a sore throat or whatever, we would do the assessment and send them to the HMO. But essentially, the number of kids who've been served through the clinic has dropped.

According to the school health liaison, many of the children's parents didn't know they had been assigned to an HMO. As she put it, several companies had engaged in "alleged solicitation" of poor families to get them to sign up by offering incentives, rewards, and so forth to join a particular company. The parents were then unpleasantly surprised to learn that as a result, their children were no longer eligible to receive health services at the school but instead had to travel to the HMO office, which was often located miles from the child's school or home. Both the coordinator and the school liaison felt the change had a particularly strong impact on pregnancy-prevention efforts, since many of the girls who came to the clinic to receive information about family-planning options could no longer be seen by the nurse.

This same situation existed at the full-service high school that we visited. The nurse stated that because the majority of students in her school were assigned to one of several Medicaid HMO providers, she was no longer able to provide the most effective care to students who came to the clinic. The end result was that she saw fewer students, and because the school was located in a remote area, her role shifted to coordinating care with the HMO providers. She described some of the problems to us:

> Some of the private providers for the students out here are in another county, or as much as 60 miles or more away from here. So that presents a problem . . . trying to get the families to comply with our health requirements [e.g., basic immunizations and physicals so new students could enter school] plus if they're sick and we [SSHP project staff] have problems in having to get them to their private provider. The majority of our patients or our families do not realize that they have been placed on an HMO. And then trying to get the providers to go ahead and see them in a timely manner is another problem, even if they are in the local area.

Interagency Conflicts

A second issue that had now emerged was the intense competition for limited public funds. On our first visit we had noted in our report that the public health unit and the school district had developed a close working relationship as exemplified in the friendship between the school liaison, who was employed by the school district, and the nursing coordinator, who was employed by the county public health unit. By 1995, with the competition for state funds intensifying between two state agencies, this collaborative arrangement had largely broken down. School administrators began to resent the money put into the schools for health services when their budgets were too strapped to purchase books or computer equipment. By the time we arrived to conduct our interviews, it was clear that an intense struggle over the funding of school health services had emerged between several schools and the county public health unit.

This struggle was clearly manifested in the decision by one of the school districts that had been involved in the state program to pull out of the program and contract with a local hospital to have them create eight to ten full-service schools. When we asked why the district would want to do this, the nursing coordinator replied:

> I think there's two issues. One, the area superintendent that was over this feels that a lot of the issues that surface are directly related to the health department piece, abortion, condom use, and they have no control over us, what we can do. . . . (*Interviewer: I see.*) They would have control of what is

delivered, they think, if it was someone who was contracting directly with them. They also see that it is politically more acceptable to the board to have people coming in that don't cost them anything, delivering services.

The nursing coordinator was referring to the fact that when schools received SSHP funds from the state department of health and rehabilitative services, the administrators often felt they had ceded control over controversial curriculum issues to the county public health unit, since that was the agency through which funds were channeled, and to whom the nurses, and the nursing coordinator, were accountable. In contrast, they felt by entering into cooperative agreements with private providers, they could maintain control and reduce costs.

Both the nursing coordinator and the school liaison were concerned because apparently the school that had pulled out of the SSHP program had adapted a model of interagency collaboration that the public health unit had carefully worked out with a school in a neighboring district. However, the area administrator had borrowed this model without fully understanding the complexity of the contractual arrangements that ensue when a public school seeks to develop a relationship with a private vendor who is not subject to state control. As the nursing coordinator explained it to us:

> What they didn't realize is that we have stood behind School X every step of the way, and when issues would come up, we would be needed to help solve the issues. . . . And that at any given moment they can lose that if the hospital no longer chooses to stay there, whereas we are legislated to be their partner.

In other words, when the program to bring health services to schools is managed through the state department of health and human services, school administrators experience a trade-off between loss of control (since the regulations come from a state agency other than the Department of Education) and continuity of care (personnel at the public health unit are mandated to provide services). The nursing coordinator was so concerned that she had the medical director send a letter to the school disavowing any liability if the hospital pulled out and left the school without any health services at all. She took this action because of the bad experience another school in the area had had with a private vendor. This school had pulled out of the state program and had contracted with an out-of-state private company to provide health services, only to find three months later that the company found the task of providing health services too complex and consequently terminated the contract.

These two issues illustrate the downside of privatization of public services. In the case of families on Medicaid assistance who were shifted to private HMOs, the cost savings have to be balanced against the very difficult problems these same families face in seeking health care. The irony is that while we documented in our 1992 evaluation report that the students who had the highest constellation of risk factors were also the same ones who were the most likely to go to the school health clinic, these same students in 1995 are now the most likely to be denied care in school since they have been placed on private HMOs. To middle-class bureaucrats, traveling 60 miles to seek health care perhaps does not seem excessive, but for poor people in a rural area with no car and no public transportation, the distance is insurmountable. In the final analysis, health costs are likely to rise since the students will not receive treatment for medical problems until the effects become so visible they cannot be ignored.

It was at this full-service school that we learned of the most dramatic effects of having a health clinic on school grounds—the teenage pregnancy rate dropped 73% in one year after the clinic opened.[1] We suspect that the steep decline was due in part to having a doctor available on-site to write birth-control prescriptions, a belief that was substantiated when we learned that the doctor was no longer available and that the pregnancy rate had doubled in the last year. Although the nurse told us on our return visit that she could still engage in preventive activities with these students, the fact that the girls could pick up their prescription right after they had been given information about birth control no doubt was a powerful motivator in ensuring they would seek protection.

The trend emanating from the state level to have schools move to site-based management was particularly strong in south Florida, which made it easy for schools to seek out private vendors to provide health services. As the nursing coordinator said, one reason may have been that school administrators felt they would have more control over the curriculum content concerning sex education, an area where the public health personnel maintained a fairly liberal stance. However, they also ran the risk of having these private vendors pull out once they realized the difficulties of providing services to schools where the students' needs were overwhelming. In contrast, over the three years the state program had been in operation, the experience gained by public health personnel and cooperating school officials in coordinating health and social services for children was invaluable. As the school health liaison proudly told us, "We're the ones that are out in the trenches! And we know what's happening! We've got our finger on the pulse of everything."[2]

Principal Involvement

When we first visited in 1992, all three principals we interviewed actively supported the idea of having health services available in the school, but their feelings about community support were mixed. Two of the principals (at the elementary and middle school) felt that most of the parents in their district lacked sufficient knowledge of the program to have either a positive or negative image of a school clinic. Neither one had done extensive work themselves to build community support, in part because they had not faced the organized opposition that was more characteristic of other sites we had visited. However, the elementary school principal did videotape one of her teachers who spoke Creole in teaching parents how to fill out the appropriate school forms.

In contrast, the principal of the full-service school felt that building community support was an important part of her job, so she had made an active effort to inform parents of the availability of school services. She felt it was especially critical at her school since parents were required to fill out a form that authorized the physician to provide all services, including family-planning ones such as writing birth-control prescriptions. As we noted before, she actively sought out parents by taking these forms into the churches and the grocery stores, instead of just sending them home with students. Her strong support of this program was rooted in her belief that these services were desperately needed at the school, where 95% of the students received some form of public assistance. She closed her interview by saying: "These kids need all the special attention they can get to do something with their lives."

Of the three principals, only the middle school principal had experienced a conflict of authority regarding the supervision of the school nurse's activities. He felt that she was "sermonizing" too much to parents, and he was concerned as to how she represented the school. He felt frustrated by the fact that the school nurse was not really accountable to the school and that he would have to ask the nursing supervisor to intervene when he thought the nurse's behavior was inappropriate. The other two principals felt they had developed a comfortable working relationship with the public health personnel, and they felt the division of authority between the two organizations was clearly delineated enough that they had not experienced any problems.

Upon our return in 1995, we were only able to interview the principal of the full-service high school again. In contrast to our interview with her three years earlier, when she was more relaxed, in this interview she appeared more on edge. We attributed this change to the intense battle the community had recently won to keep the school clinic open against a campaign that had been carried out by a member of the school board to close it (see the section "Parent and Community Reactions" for more details). Although her commitment to the concept of school-based health services had not lessened, we felt she was more on guard against possible threats as to how her actions could be misinterpreted, even from well-meaning researchers who supported the concept as well. She had continued her policy of not restricting what the nurse could say to students about family-planning issues, and she felt that she still had the support of the community to do so. To maintain that support, she met with community groups once a month at the local churches to brief them on the services being offered at the school. Her primary concern was that because of the new policy of sending students who were on Medicaid assistance to private HMO providers, many students were not receiving the same level of care, since they could not come to the clinic. As she told us, "If you don't take care of the entire child, you are doing a disservice to the whole generation." We learned later that she was planning to retire soon, and our impression was that of a woman who had become weary of the struggle to maintain health services for a student population whose needs only increased year after year.

IDEOLOGICAL ISSUES

Unlike in school districts of the other two counties we visited, sexuality and health issues were strongly interrelated with race and class differences, in part, we believe, because the project schools in this district had higher concentrations of poor, nonwhite children. Although the school districts were equally conservative in terms of what the school boards (a majority of whose members were white middle-class to upper-middle class people) believed was appropriate to discuss in the classroom, the cultural differences so visible in the schools meant the nurses felt compelled to raise issues that would serve the students' interests.

Even in our visit in 1992, it was apparent that the nurses believed they had more freedom to discuss sexual issues that other districts could not address. The Jamaican nurse at one of the middle schools told us that she experienced no "real taboos" in what she could discuss privately with students. Her principal confirmed this in his interview, and he stated that parents would only be notified if a student asked about family-planning matters *and* if the student gave consent. Otherwise, he left these discussions to the nurse's discretion. He followed this policy because he felt that many students' parents were not knowledgeable about family-planning options. A Haitian nurse at one of the high schools also said she was free to discuss contraceptive options with students in private. Although neither nurse was able to raise these issues in classroom discussions, the fact that they could do so in their office was a marked departure from the stories we heard from nurses in the other districts we visited.

Controversial Content

Differences among the three sites were clearly evident in which issues could or could not be discussed and which issues became the most salient. While some topics remained constant in terms of being excluded from the curriculum (e.g., homosexuality), others received more or less emphasis depending upon the project staff's interests (e.g., gender-related violence).

Sexual Orientation. We had noted in our discussion of sexuality in the other two case studies that adolescent homosexuality remained a taboo topic across all schools. While an open discussion of this issue was still not sanctioned in schools in this area any more than it was in the other places we visited, there seemed to be a greater tolerance among the students for peer behavior that deviated from mainstream sexual orientation. We heard an example of this when we asked the nursing coordinator whether there was any discussion of ways of dealing with students who manifested an alternative sexual preference. She sighed and said flatly: "No." She then elaborated on her answer:

> They [the nurses] describe it. They give it a definition. There is a group that held hearings last summer to get them funded. Every time they surface there's some trouble with the same group of people that were behind our plan being pulled [referring to the attempt by religious coalitions to have the full-service school shut down]. But they're making headway. And they are in the community. Now at one high school I had a transvestite and he's flagrant.

We were surprised at this answer and pursued it further:

> *(Interviewer: He's in the school?)* Oh yeah. My aide [the health technician at the school] came in one day and she said, "I have

to pray today because I was really bad. He came in and I was having a really bad day, and he was flipping his fingernails and his lipstick in my face, and I told him to go to the bathroom to wash his face so he was a boy again." She just couldn't deal with him as a girl. *(Interviewer: How does he survive the peer culture?)* Well, that's the point. The kids are much more pragmatic about this than the adults. He's got his little group of followers, and they're very aware that there are gay students. And that there are alternative lifestyles. It's the adults who've been disturbed by it.[3]

We followed up this issue by asking whether there was any discussion of human sexuality in the context of pleasure and desire, instead of the emphasis on fear and disease. The school health liaison told us that the human sexuality curriculum approved by the school board concentrated on "just the facts, ma'am." Furthermore, although the curriculum had been approved by the school board, not all schools were aware that it had, and as a result, they refused to use it and created their own, which in many cases was far more conservative.

Sexual Exploitation. While in neither of our two visits did we hear anyone speak forcefully about the issue of gender-related violence (e.g., date rape) as much as we did in the other sites we visited, we did turn up evidence of a very disturbing pattern of sexual exploitation of middle school girls by older men. When we first visited in 1992, this issue was not openly discussed in these terms. Both the nurses and the principals at the middle and high schools we visited expressed their concern over the rising level of sexual activity among middle school girls. The principal at one high school did mention that she felt that some of the pregnancies in the feeder middle school (which did not participate in this program) were due to "girls taking money from older men." We noted these comments and used them as additional evidence in support of our finding on the student health survey that 33% of the middle school students sampled ($N = 345$) across all twelve sites were already sexually active (Emihovich & Herrington, 1993).

When we returned in 1995, the two nurses at the middle and high school as well as the assistant high school principal now made a direct connection between the exploitation of young girls by older men and the rising number of AIDS cases. The nurse at the high school commented on this in relation to the problem of providing students with timely information about sex:

I feel like a lot of this counseling and education, especially family planning, needs to be started in the middle schools. Because by the time they get to high school, it's almost too late.
They're already sexually active, a majority of them. And whenever you're talking to them and you get a sexual history on
them, some of them started in the fifth grade, but especially
with sixth and seventh grade. . . . Most of their partners are
older men. And it's a recent trend, older men wanting these
younger girls. Whenever you ask the students why you think
these older men want these younger girls, it's because they say
the younger girls are not diseased. This is their feeling about
it. And, of course, the older men have the cars, the jewelry,
money, and these little middle school girls are attracted by
that.

We heard an almost identical story from the nurse at the middle
school:

I just told the fifth grade the other day that in the three years
that I've been here that anyone who has been pregnant has
been pregnant by an 18- to 25-year-old. . . . What we're finding
is that the men are using these young girls because they feel
pretty safe that they are not going to have AIDS. So they're getting to younger and younger girls. But the girls think they are
truly in love with them, that's the very sad part, they don't see
the scenario. . . . The girls are definitely ripe and ready and
some definitely want to be pregnant because of that affection
bond. [For] some it's not . . . ignorance, I have to say that. Any
of the eighth-graders we've counseled that have been sexually
active, it's not that they didn't know about precautions—it's
that they choose not to use it.

The assistant high school principal commented that "the younger
the girl, the older the male who fathered the child" and then added an
interesting twist to this issue when he noted that the males no longer
seem to pay a price for their involvement in a pregnancy. He wondered
aloud what had happened to statutory rape convictions and whether
there was a connection between the rising rate of teenage pregnancies
among girls under age 16 and the lack of convictions in this area.[4]

Pregnancy Prevention. When we visited this area in 1992, all the
nurses told us that they were actively involved in making classroom pre-

sentations related to pregnancy prevention. As was the case at the other sites we visited, their freedom to discuss family-planning options in detail depended upon the cooperation of the principal and local community mores. What made this site unique was that it had one of only a few full-service schools in the state where a family physician was available three days a week to see students and to prescribe contraceptives. We interviewed the doctor, a Cuban-born woman who was very dedicated to serving adolescents' health needs, and learned that she believed strongly in the value of providing students with access to safe and reliable contraceptives. She was particularly concerned about the high rate of sexually transmitted diseases that she saw in the clinic, and she told us that she emphasized the idea that "there is no such thing as safe sex" because she was worried about AIDS prevention. Her belief that teenage pregnancy rates could be reduced if students had easier access to contraceptive options was validated by the fact that this high school experienced the sharpest decline in the teenage pregnancy rate among all the project schools (Emihovich & Herrington, 1993).

Upon our return visit in 1995, we learned that although the official school board policy was to place greater emphasis on abstinence as a primary means of birth control, the nurses were still free to provide information about contraceptives at the high school level. The nurse at the full-service high school discussed her methods:

> We stress abstinence as the only method of being 100%. But we also go into the other methods and the importance of them if they are going to be sexually active. Plus condoms because of the AIDS issue. We tell them, "If you're still sexually active what are you doing? Are you using some type of birth control? Are you using the condoms every time? Remember that nothing is 100% safe. You really need to know your partner." So we really do stress prevention, especially with sexually transmitted diseases and AIDS. And I think this is what cut down our pregnancy rate to start with from us doing the education counseling about AIDS, sexually transmitted diseases more than the family planning. Plus we go into some of the social aspects like "What do you want to do with your life? Do you want to go to college? If you do have a baby, what are you going to do with it? Who's going to take care of it?" We try to make them see that there's more out there and they can wait.

We gathered from the nurse's remarks that she firmly believed that the educational and counseling efforts that were done in the classroom had helped decrease the pregnancy rate at her school as much as the availability of the doctor who was on hand to write birth-control prescriptions. When we inquired about interviewing the doctor, we learned that she was no longer on staff. In her place the school had had a succession of local doctors (mostly pediatricians) who had stopped writing the prescriptions because, as the nurse explained, "Most of your pediatricians do not feel comfortable doing gynecological exams and Pap smears and writing prescriptions for birth control." As a result, the students in this school had lost the services of a caring and committed physician who believed not only in prevention efforts but also in the value of providing better access to contraceptives. At the time of our visit, the clinic was without the services of any doctor, since the health department could not afford to spare one for the school clinic because of a shortage in its own department.

We recalled the dramatic drop in the pregnancy rate this school had experienced three years ago and asked if it was still declining. The nurse told us it had stayed low for one year and then for some reason it had doubled between the 1993 and 1994 school years. We asked her if she felt that one reason was that a doctor was no longer writing birth-control prescriptions on-site. She demurred and said that the physician never wrote that many prescriptions in the first place (a fact disputed by the doctor, who had told us in 1992 that 70% of the girls she saw asked for birth-control pills). The nurse stated that quite a few of the girls who were counted as pregnant in the 1994–95 school year were ninth graders who came from a middle school where there were no health services, and that many of these girls seemed to lack basic information about their reproductive system. While we concur that premature sexual activity among middle school students was undoubtedly a contributing factor, we suspect the increase can also be attributed to two other factors: the fact that many girls now have to obtain family-planning services from a private HMO provider instead of through the school clinic, and that for those girls who are still eligible to receive services through the school clinic there has been a diminution of contraceptive services.

Student Health Issues

The student health issues that were prevalent on our visit in 1992 were similar to those common in other sites across the state: helping students achieve weight control, raising self-esteem, dealing with head lice, and preventing abuse, both sexual and physical. At one elementary school where there was a large number of immigrant children from Haiti, the nurse mentioned that she had several cases of children who were beaten as part of physical punishment, and she believed that it was a cultural norm among some of these parents to use force when disciplining their children. To her credit, she recognized that the problem of dealing with this issue was far more complicated than just reporting parents to the appropriate authorities. As she explained it to us:

> I have spoken to the pastor that has the Haitian church here because what I see when I go to the middle school is that apparently in Haiti physical discipline is a very acceptable means of discipline and there's a lot of locking horns here. So that's what I feel that we take away, but we don't give them any other parenting skills, and at the middle school I've run into tremendous problems where parents don't even want to deal with them anymore because they don't feel they have any control over them. What happens by middle school is that the kids are smart enough to call the state department hot-line on child abuse. I've had parents put on probation, parents taken overnight to jail for things I might have been inclined to discipline my child for. . . . Does it mean it solves the problem? I don't think so. Unless you replace what parents use for discipline with another skill. And that's where we fall short. But they [the parents] feel very threatened by the state, especially since many of them are not legal aliens, and yet they don't know any other way to punish their children so they stop doing it. Then I'm gonna have 12-year-olds pregnant in middle school unless the parents get control. It's very sad, and the support services are just not there.

This woman clearly recognized the problem of removing one form of culturally sanctioned punishment from parents without providing them with a viable alternative, but she felt trapped by the fact that she was mandated to call the state health office if she found any evidence of possible child abuse. Although her job called for her to engage in parent outreach efforts, the reality was that she was so overwhelmed in providing for children's basic health needs in the clinic she had no time to focus on these activities. Even as we spoke to her in her office, we were interrupted five times by children requiring assistance and two parents who had questions about the immunization form sent home by the school.

Several problems occurred here that were not so common in the other areas, and these problems again reflected underlying cultural differences among the student population. One problem was the extremely high number of students who required basic immunizations before they could be enrolled in school. On our visit in 1992, the Jamaican nurse who divided her time between an elementary and middle school told us that she could literally spend all her time administering shots and still have children waiting for them by the end of the year, since her caseload was approximately 2,000 children for both schools combined. Both schools had a substantial number of children who came from countries in South America, as well as from the highlands of Mexico and the Caribbean islands. Many of these children had never been seen by any medical personnel in their lives, and the nurses in this program found that they had to both provide the immunizations and engage in extensive parent education in order to help parents understand why the shots were necessary. The nurse at the elementary school we visited in 1995 had a large number of Haitian children, and she described some of her parent education efforts centering around basic health and child abuse concerns:

> I try putting things in newsletters. When we do immunizations, we do health education that way. The letters we send home for any of the illnesses explain what the illness is, what we suspect it is, because we really don't diagnose it. Organized parent classes, we really haven't done that.

We did wonder about the usefulness of sending reading material home to parents who may not have been literate in either their first or second language. When we interviewed the principal of this school on our visit in 1992, she mentioned then that more than 14 different languages were spoken among the children and that she had eight ESL (English as Second Language) teachers. However, it was not clear to us whether the teachers were used to help disseminate information from the clinic, a situation that had not changed upon our visit in 1995, even though the percentage of minority children had only increased during the three years since then.

Another problem that surfaced in our first visit at one of the high schools was that one student had been diagnosed as a tuberculosis carrier. At that time, the school administrators were very reluctant to allow public health officials to conduct more extensive testing because of the negative publicity such testing provoked in the general community. How cases like this were to be handled was constantly contested between the schools and the public health personnel, since the schools were sensitive to the issue of community relations while the public health people were concerned about the threat of a possible epidemic. The compromise reached was that the nurses would discreetly carry out the testing program while the school staff focused on informing only the parents whose children were at risk.

When we returned in 1995, we asked if TB testing was still a controversial issue. We learned that the nursing coordinator had instituted a program of testing all children in kindergarten, sixth grade, and ninth grade, and that the school officials had become more cooperative in working with the health department on this issue. However, new concerns had arisen over the testing of school staff, especially since there were frequently a high number of positives identified.[5] The nursing coordinator admitted that she had made a tactical mistake in not placing the number of positives in the computer database, although her reason for not doing so was well intended. As she told us:

> I probably made a mistake. I asked that it just go on the computer that the test was done. Because I felt that if it went in as a positive and the secretary pulling up the health screen saw it as a positive, and there was nothing on the record [meaning that the school had not been identified or the circumstances under which the testing had been conducted], it would be a nightmare issue. When secretaries see that, they tend to hyperventilate and create pandemonium.

The problem both she and the school health liaison faced was that the state had now asked for each school to identify the number of positives from both students and staff that turned up from the testing program. As a result, she had to ask all the nurses to backtrack in their records to compile the data. What they were discovering was that at many schools the numbers were quite high. The nursing coordinator told us that "depending upon the school, there can be more than 50 kids who are positive. I was just starting to compile and I took one school yesterday—there were 36 positives that the nurse had identified." When we asked if these cases were associated with any particular cluster of risk factors, the school liaison answered promptly:

> Third world and poverty. Because so many people are coming in. . . . I mean first it was the Indochinese came in with TB, it was an epidemic in Indochina. Now it's probably the Guatemalans and the Haitian populations that haven't had preventive health services.

The nurse at the middle school informed us that about 30% of her children had tested positive and that ensuring that they complied with the treatment (which lasted nine months) was one of the major headaches of her job.

Parent and Community Reactions

During our visit in 1992, we had interviewed several parents at the elementary and middle school. All the parents we spoke to were extremely supportive of having nurses available in the school. At the elementary level, the parents saw the nurse as someone who could treat children's basic health needs, provide medication so parents would not have to leave work to come to school to administer it, and coordinate the delivery of services for more complex health problems. As for the educational aspects of the nurse's job in terms of providing information about health-related issues (including prevention and sex education), they felt that this information was best disseminated by a person with a medical background. The parents at the middle school basically agreed with these parents, although they added the proviso that a positive reception to presentations on human sexuality would depend upon the type of information being provided.

The project coordinators viewed community outreach as one of their central roles, and we learned that they had done extensive networking with community agencies and had set up an interagency council to monitor the delivery of various health and social services among different groups. This council was still in operation when we returned in 1995, and one of its members noted that while there was basic community support for school-based health services, she felt it was not as strong as it could be. As she noted, "Student health is important to the community, but if it was very important there would be more funding. Children would have universal access if it was very important, and they do not." She also commented that most of the support was focused on children receiving basic care (e.g., immunizations), not on the more socially contested areas such as sex education and pregnancy-prevention services. She wryly noted that the "state department doesn't advertise its services, and most people aren't very aware." The biggest surprise for new residents from out of state was that there were not nurses in every school, as was the case in schools up north.

Because at our other two sites we had encountered instances of an organized religious coalition speaking out in school board meetings in opposition to school-based health services, we asked several people if this phenomenon had occurred in this area. We found that several months prior to our visit there had been a strong attempt by certain members of one school board to remove services completely from the full-service school. We talked first with Representative Lois Frankel, since she had been one of the chief architects of the bill to provide health services in schools in the state legislature:

> Well, there was an attempt, we think, by . . . well, there were some parents who tried to do that. . . . But in the end the school board backed up the program. I think there are certain agendas some groups would like to eliminate in schools like school-based health clinics.

To learn more about what actually happened at this school, we spoke to the nurse, who provided a more detailed story about why the school board backed down:

> *(Interviewer: We understand there was an attempt to close down this clinic by the school board. Can you tell us what happened here?)*
> I think the school board, what they said was they didn't re-alize we were providing family-planning services. And they wanted to close us down because of it. And the parents and some of the people from the community went to the school board and spoke up and said, "We knew what they were doing, we signed the consent form, it was notarized, we knew what was offered and we wanted it offered. It wasn't that they were doing something that we didn't know about it." So the commu-nity backed us, so they kept it. The only thing is we went ahead and changed our consent forms to spell out a little more about the family-planning service.
> *(Interviewer: Now why do you think this issue came up with the school board, because when we were here in 1992 you were already do-ing this, in fact you were doing more. [At that time the doctor at the clinic was writing birth-control prescriptions, which was no longer the case after 1993.] So why all of a sudden did they say, "Gee, we didn't know they were doing that!")*
> One of the school board members, I don't think she likes clinics in the school, I don't even think she likes nurses in the school. She thinks kids should not be sexually active, which ac-tually they shouldn't be, but she thinks the only thing they have to do is say "no," that it's not a big issue with kids. . . . Kids shouldn't get pregnant, kids shouldn't have sex, basically that was it. But she's got to stop and realize that if they want to become sexually active, that it's hard for them sometimes to say "no." Especially with their hormones going out of whack, it's hard enough for adults, much less for kids.

(Interviewer: So really, it was motivated by this one person.)
I think so. Personally, that's my opinion.
(Interviewer: She must have gotten support, though, from other people . . .)
Oh yes, all of her followers and all of her supporters. . . . They rounded them up and bused them in to the school board meeting to speak up against us. That we should be closed down and all that bunch of stuff. But then we only had two of our parents to get up and speak, and that's all it took.
(Interviewer: Now these parents . . . you serve primarily an African-American and Hispanic community?)
Correct. The majority of them.
(Interviewer: So that's very encouraging to hear that those parents took an activist role in keeping the service here.)
Yes, because I think a lot of our parents were teenagers when they had their children. And I think our parents realize the problems they had in raising their kids, and how hard it is to be a teen parent. And I don't think our parents really want their children to become parents like they did. They want things better for their kids than they had to go through. I've lived out here for 30 years so a lot of the students that I'm seeing, I knew their mother back before they were ever born. So they come and talk, and they know what they've gone through, and they know some of the hardships they've had . . . they know better. They've said they want better for their kids, and I guess we all do, really. And if that means that they're going to be sexually active, then they want them protected.

We describe this incident in detail because it illustrates several key patterns that will be discussed in greater detail in the next chapter. First, it demonstrates that there was organized opposition to the idea of school-based health clinics across the state, since we had heard similar stories from the other districts. In most cases it was grounded in a fear that the clinics would be providing family-planning services that would encourage or sanction teenagers to become sexually active. However, as our visits in both 1992 and 1995 documented, this fear was misplaced, since none of the health rooms breached community standards in providing more information than the community was willing to tolerate, and the primary focus of almost all health rooms was on meeting students' basic health needs. In fact, a valid claim could be made that the nurses were not able to give sufficient information about pregnancy prevention and sexually transmitted diseases given the overwhelming problems they faced in their student populations.

Second, this incident demonstrates the importance of establishing a strong base of community support for school-based health services. As we noted earlier, the principal of this school had actively sought out parents to obtain their permission, and she encouraged the nurse (who was a highly regarded local resident) to make presentations about the need for school-based health services to community groups such as the Rotary Club, women's groups, and so forth. Consequently, when the program at the school came under attack by people outside the school district, the principal and the nurse were able to mobilize this support. To some extent, we feel that community support was also linked to the widely shared perception among the residents that the needs of their children were often not considered as important as other priorities in the school district. In our interview with the principal and assistant principal, both of whom were African-Americans, the assistant principal directly commented upon this issue by stating that "most politicians are middle class—they don't know about the needs of poor children." The principal added her thoughts on this issue: "I think that any child at this school who needs services ought to be able to get them." We also learned on our 1995 visit that when plans were made for a new school that was just recently built, the nurse made sure that space was reserved for clinic facilities that would be housed directly in the school (instead of a portable unit on school grounds), and the local taxpayers did not object to the extra cost.

Finally, an important aspect that cannot be overlooked was that this was a successful attempt by minority community members to control the kind of health services their children would receive in the face of opposition from predominantly white religious groups. We asked the nursing coordinator if she had noticed this type of community activism in other schools in the area and she replied that she had:

> Things have changed tremendously since you were here four years ago. The children's services council has sponsored neighborhood initiatives. . . . And they have activated many of the communities and have got the grassroots starting to look at what they need and demand what they need, not what we think they need. And they are going after it, and they are going after the funding.
> *(Interviewer: That's wonderful.)*
> We probably saw it best illustrated in one of our middle schools. We were proposing to take one of our middle schools that's closing and turn it into a neighborhood service school concept. I'd say it's the first time in the decade that I've been here that the audience was predominately black males, and not middle-class white females. And they were pretty much saying,

"This is what we want," and there were black females there, too. . . . And that was the first time I've seen the community at the table. They are beginning to say, "We have to take responsibility and the rest of you sit back and wait till we tell you what we want." It's really an exciting time.

Her only concern was that because of the increased competition for decreasing dollars, the various groups would not pull together but instead would separate into factions and argue among themselves. She had seen evidence that this could occur within black groups, where the local African-Americans resented the intrusion of the Haitian population, who seemed more politically savvy, and the Hispanic population was segmented by groups bounded by national borders such as those from Guatemala, Nicaragua, Cuba, and South American countries.

PROFESSIONAL ISSUES

On our first visit in 1992 we had interviewed school staff in three project schools: elementary, middle, and high school. What had impressed us then was the high level of support they offered to the nurses and to the idea of school-based health services.[6] At the elementary school the group we met with (the areas represented were prekindergarten, English as a second language, physical education, guidance, special education, and speech pathology) overwhelmingly supported the addition of a nurse to the school. Their comments included the following reactions: "she helped reduce discipline problems due to poor health reasons," "she helped parents obtain services through the system," "she took care of accident reports," "she was invaluable in making referrals," and "she made parents aware of the need to get medical services." Their responses suggested that they perceived the nurse as part of a team to provide children with the necessary services so they could be successful in school. They also felt that the nurse was invaluable for making class presentations on drug and alcohol abuse, areas in which the teachers did not feel knowledgeable. Their primary concern was that, on several occasions, the nurse had been pulled away from the school to work in the public health clinic because of personnel shortages and that the potential conflict between the school and public health clinic's needs had to be resolved in the future.

The reaction of school staff at the middle and high school were similar. Not surprisingly, the special education teacher at each school worked very closely with the nurse in resolving discipline problems that were due to emotional handicaps. Both saw the nurse as someone who could expedite referrals through the state department that handled abuse cases. They also appreciated the fact that she was willing to make home visits. One teacher at the middle school commented that "because we have so many children from Third World countries, the best aspect is that she is right there to meet their needs." She noted that many parents didn't have transportation to the public health clinic and that many students would have no one else to attend to their health needs. The guidance counselor at the high school where there was a full-service clinic made this comment:

> It was a very wise use of funds to put the clinic here. Very few of our students have access to medical care. I don't see a conflict between what the nurse does and I do because the students go to the clinic for medical problems and I handle personal problems.

One reason why the school staff felt so positively about the program may have been due to the close relationship that existed at that time between the nursing coordinator and the school health liaison. Their plan was to have nurses be considered as part of a team that offered comprehensive health and social services on-site. The plan was apparently successful because in all three project schools we heard repeated references to the team concept.

When we returned in 1995, we were unable to interview many of these people again. Given the conflicts that had now arisen between some of the local schools and the health office with regard to the coordination of school health services and the competition for funds, we wondered if the same level of support would still be evident. We asked the nursing coordinator and the school health liaison about this matter and learned that cooperation in many schools had broken down because personnel were preoccupied with turf. The school health liaison that we had met three years ago had been replaced, and the one we interviewed was on her way out. There were now so many different agencies providing services in the various schools, some of which were connected with the original grant program and some which were funded from other sources, that the nursing coordinator could no longer keep track of all the services. She talked about the need to build coalitions, while saying at the same time that "everybody sees it as more work, instead of just a coordination of work." The school health liaison commented that some of the program specialists in the schools were "extremely territorial" with their things, such as materials, new program ideas, curriculum, assessment tools, and so forth, yet they expected the public health personnel to bail them out if they ran into problems providing services. The movement toward decentralization of authority that freed schools to contract with outside providers has led to a situation in which a dizzying array of programs can be offered at any one school, but there is no longer anyone who is coordinating the overall scope of activities so as to avoid costly duplication of services.

IMPACT/SUMMARY

As we did in the other two sites, we asked questions related to accountability. Our first question, "How do you respond to the comment that schools should just be schools, and that these health services should be offered somewhere else?," led to answers that were almost identical to those we heard elsewhere. The school health liaison answered first:

> They can't learn if they're not well. We just got back from a conference where we heard from a former superintendent of schools who went out on a limb. He decided to use his dollars that he had for other programs [e.g., from the Chapter I funds] and pump them all into health services. His premise was that a totally healthy child, physically and mentally, was going to do well on tests and in school. And in one year's time he proved that. And he showed the statistics that he had from the improvement of the overall well-being of the child. . . . That's something we've been saying all along—you have to have a well child in order for them to succeed.

The nursing coordinator then told us how one school administrator in the central office had wanted to pull the program out of two high schools. The coordinator told us what happened when she learned that a representative from the office was coming to hear why the program should not be pulled. She asked the two principals to be present at the meeting even though, as she said:

> And I didn't know what to tell them, because I didn't know what would save my grant. So they just kind of showed up and the question the administrator asked of them was, "Has this program had any impact on your absentee rate?" And both principals, without hesitation, said, "Absolutely. Our absentee rate has changed." And they had the figures to back them up.

And the other thing . . . one principal said quite clearly, "Don't take the health services away. You cannot imagine the difference in the schools."

Meeting Children's Needs

Perhaps because they were closer to witnessing the everyday needs of children for these services, the two nurses had an even more forceful reaction to the idea that the services should not be available in schools. The nurse at the elementary school had these thoughts:

> The reason the schools have evolved into what we're becoming, and why we're still evolving into it, is that these services are not being provided anymore in the households, in the community. It's that in order for the child to learn, they can't learn if they're starving to death. You can't function if you're not eating. Think of what your self-esteem is like if nobody will sit near you because you smell so bad that everybody makes fun of you and ostracizes you. To me, as much as it would be great to say in the 1950s, "Oh, it was wonderful with two-parent households with a mother who stayed home all day and did these things," that's not the reality today. In most cases it's a one-parent household, and if there's a two-parent household both parents are out working, and they're just not there. . . . Yeah, it would be great to say that our schools should just educate, but you can't educate if the child's not ready to be educated. They're not if they're hungry, or dirty, or unclothed, or pregnant, or they're not in school because they are sick all the time . . . if they're not in school they're not going to learn.

The nurse at the high school offered a more pragmatic response:

> I think one of the biggest things is that students that have no other means of health care and they rely on the school nurse or the school clinic to help provide, or at least direct them, refer them and help them go about it. Yesterday I had the father of a student come in, and the student was having some problems that needed to be seen right away. The father had nothing. He had never been through the health care system, no Medicaid, no insurance, no nothing. And he wasn't even working now. So we called and made arrangements for him to go to the health care department. . . . But a lot of times it's a lot

cheaper actually on the taxpayers if we provide the service, or
we refer them to the health department, or to somewhere they
can get some financial help and pay their rate, rather than end-
ing up in the emergency room every time they get sick. And
the same way with your pregnancy, it's a lot cheaper to prevent
a pregnancy than to raise a child for 18 years on Medicaid.

Establishing Accountability

We also asked about accountability in terms of whether there was any
way to prove that this program was having a positive impact on such factors as absenteeism, dropout prevention, reduction of teenage pregnancies, and so forth. All of the people we spoke to acknowledged the need
for establishing accountability, but several formidable barriers existed
that made it difficult to determine any kind of effect. One barrier was the
unwillingness of school officials to participate in data-collection efforts
that could be viewed by the general public as controversial. We had encountered this problem ourselves when we conducted a formal evaluation
in 1992 and found that several schools had refused to participate in the
survey of secondary students' (grades 7–12) risk behaviors such as drug
and alcohol consumption and sexual activity (Emihovich & Herrington,
1993). At that time, both the elementary and middle school project
schools had not participated in the statewide survey we conducted, although Gold County officials had developed and administered their
own version.

On our return visit, we asked if any further data collection had taken
place, and we learned from the nursing coordinator that this issue was
still problematic. The nursing coordinator mentioned that they were in
the process of creating a comprehensive database on children's services so
they could track where children had been referred. However, we pointed
out to her that this information was simply an indicator of services provided; it didn't provide any information about the *effectiveness* of those
services. When we asked again, "How do you know you're making a difference?," she responded quickly:

When I was writing the new grant proposal I asked my staff
[nurses and school health liaisons] that question, because there
were some people there who had been involved in this program from the beginning. And they had three things that they
said. Number one was that they felt they had had an impact on
the violent behavior that was starting to show up in the
schools. When kids got into trouble, before they went to the office, they went to the nurses and they were able to diffuse them

and talk them down and make a real impact there. And another thing was that they had pretty much identified the kids
that had care systems, and the kids who could be plugged into
care systems, and they now identified groups that didn't have
access to anything, and that was an area they were going to
need help with. Before that we had no clue who these kids
were. They were just statistics without a name or face. And the
third thing was they felt that the students had reached the
point of trust where they would come in alone or in small
groups and ask the key questions . . . about AIDS, about birth
control, about STDs . . . that they could feel free to ask this,
even though we may not be able to be free to go to the classroom and deliver it at the level we want to. . . . The kids have
gotten comfortable enough that they were able to come in and
they got the response they wanted and they would tell more
kids . . . they were making major inroads that way. In the elementary school, the one thing they felt they had identified
[was] some of the behaviors that were leading to problems in
the middle school and they wanted to build in a prevention
piece there. . . . So yes, we have made a difference.

She continued by saying that each school was unique in terms of its
level of commitment from both the community and the school personnel,
and that some of the effects from this program would not show up until
several years later. She agreed that having longitudinal data available on
changes in students' attitudes toward their health habits and risk behaviors would be extremely useful, but she noted that although the medical
director had supported the continued administration of the survey to
track this information, the schools would not cooperate because they
were concerned about parent and community opposition. Concerning
the one outcome that was central to the reason why this program was
funded in the first place, teenage pregnancy rates, she admitted that this
rate varied from school to school. In some places it had decreased, but in
others it had increased substantially.

When we asked the same question of the two school nurses, the high
school nurse felt that the program had had a positive impact on several
indicators, such as pregnancy rate, absentee rate, and the dropout rate,
although she didn't keep any records to substantiate this belief. As she
told us:

Well, not only does the pregnancy rate go down, but also our
students stay in school better—there's less absentees. I don't
know if the dropout rate has anything to do with it, but the

dropout rate is down compared to what it was before. And I'm sure that if students are in better health and feel better about themselves, then they'll want to learn and they'll be able to learn better.

As we noted earlier, the pregnancy rate in her school had doubled the previous year, a change she attributed to the lack of services at the feeder middle school. We believe that the loss of a physician who was able to write birth-control prescriptions had a much greater negative impact than the school officials were willing to acknowledge.

The nurse at the elementary school had the most emotional reaction to this question. Her voice trembled and she appeared on the verge of tears as she spoke:

> How do I know we're making a difference? We probably won't know until further down the road. I do see healthier kids, happier kids in a lot of instances. Teachers feel we're making an impact, that translates to lots of times, "Thanks for doing that," because otherwise it falls on them and if you've got 30 kids in the classroom, there's no way you can devote the same amount of time. . . . It's like, as far as statistics, I don't know if you'd be able to see that, I'd have to say. I know with our principal they're always talking about test scores and increasing them . . . you have to understand that we're not dealing with a white middle-income household who come to school to learn. The kids come to school sometimes because there's nobody at home, so they don't get their breakfast . . . they come to school to eat, they come to school to hang out to be somewhere with other people as opposed to being by themselves. For some kids, we're the only safe environment in their entire lives. It's the only place for six hours where they can feel they're not threatened by other people in their families. I don't know if it's measurable, but I feel we're making a difference in children's lives.

Summary

The events in Gold County are a harbinger of what is likely to happen if the U. S. Congress further decentralizes welfare benefits by making them state responsibilities and funding them in the form of block grants. A likely scenario is that the states will choose to use private providers and channel the funds through them, without sufficient safeguards to hold these providers accountable to standards of minimal care for poor people. Although bureaucratic agencies such as county public health units have been accused of being insensitive to clients' needs, the fact remains that the personnel are accustomed to working with poor, mostly nonwhite clients, and they are more familiar with the kinds of problems these clients often bring to the clinic. It's also the case that the personnel themselves are more likely to be nonwhite. If the funds are channeled through private providers, class and race differences in terms of staffing and awareness of people's needs are likely to be magnified, to the detriment of the people being served.

The fact that one community was able to save family-planning services at one high school is an encouraging sign of how parents (especially from low-income, minority groups) can take control of their children's health and welfare. But as one state health coordinator told us, the process of building community awareness requires that "communities be saturated with information and that parents be involved in discussions to search for solutions." This process is time-consuming, and it must be considered as an essential component when developing plans for implementing school health services in an area where they have not previously been offered. Although the needs may be self-evident to the professionals who work with children on a daily basis, they may not be so evident to parents who are not knowledgeable about broader health issues within the community. Lacking this knowledge, these parents are vulnerable to oppositional claims made by groups motivated by a fear that parents' rights are being eroded or that the school health clinics are promoting behaviors inimical to traditional family values. The events in Gold County demonstrated that professionals can indeed make a difference in children's lives if they take the time to create community networks that support their actions.

Chapter 6

School Health Services and Community Values

THE DISCOURSES OF DISSENT

> Without an understanding of the seamy side of sexuality, there is no understanding of politics.
> —Norman O. Brown, *Love's Body*

The ongoing ideological skirmishes in post–Cold War America to define the soul of America, which Hunter (1991) termed the "culture wars," have directed attention to both schools and health care. A growing cleavage exists between those who believe that an effective education, one necessary for preparation for an information-based economy, requires complex, critical, and problem-solving intellectual development and those who, increasingly suspicious of educators, insist that schooling should restrict itself to the transmission of factual knowledge and the development of the analytical skills of computation and communication. Similarly, the status of health care in this country is in a state of virtual upheaval, shifting from a fee-for-service basis to a corporate, bureaucratic model. The basic issues of who should receive services, who should pay for them, and how they should be delivered remain unresolved (Larson, 1992). Is health care a public responsibility to be assumed by all citizens, or should access to and quality of care be contingent on other factors, such as the ability to pay or the avoidance of risky behaviors?

CULTURE WARS IN SCHOOLS AND SOCIETY

The behaviors and situations we described in the three case studies embodied two themes that will be elaborated on in this chapter. The first is that the issue of situating health services in schools is emblematic of the struggle over which groups have the moral and political authority to define the value structure for American society. As Hunter (1991) argues, cultural conflict is defined by "political and social hostility rooted in different systems of moral authority" (p. 42). He believes that these conflicts, though not clearly articulated, are expressed in two polarizing tendencies: the impulse toward orthodoxy and the impulse toward progressivism. The first impulse is characterized by the "commitment on the part of adherents to an external, definable, and transcendent authority," while the second is characterized by the "tendency to resymbolize historical faiths according to the prevailing assumptions of contemporary life" (pp. 44–45). Viewing the three counties through Hunter's lens, we found that Emerald County was characterized primarily by a fundamentalist culture that embodied a strong adherence to a traditional Christian code of morality and reliance on a higher authority, Gold County could be described as a rapidly changing progressive culture that was being transformed almost daily by the diversity of the people moving into the area, and Silver County was characterized by the struggle to balance competing elements of both the fundamentalist tradition and the progressive ideas brought in by new residents.

Polarization of America

The polarization of American society has not gone unremarked by cultural anthropologists and journalists. Appadurai (1991) noted that the factionalization of group identity is becoming a standard feature of cultures around the world and suggested that some "brute facts" we must face include the "changing social, territorial, and cultural reproduction of group identity. As groups migrate, regroup in new locations, reconstruct their histories, and reconfigure their ethnic 'projects' or goals, . . . the landscapes of group identity all over the world are changing" (p. 190). Katz (1995) substantiated his comment by noting that:

> Our communal and civic open spaces—courts, workplaces, Congress, Academe—are no longer places where issues are settled, but battlegrounds on which the most pressing conflicts will never be resolved. America is no longer a one nation indivisible, if it ever was, but a land peopled by many bitterly divided tribes. (p. 130)

Both the polarizing tendencies and political splintering of community support were clearly visible in our case studies. The ideological divisions within school districts ran deep, and the state legislators chose to side-step them by allowing each area to develop a program that met community needs. One of the questions that concerned us was the nature of community and which groups held the most sway in determining school policies that affected the community as a whole. From both sets of interviews (1992 and 1995) we learned that project personnel had to balance the competing concerns of a number of groups who varied in their level of support for these services. In each county different strategies were employed to make ideological compromises: Emerald County used the politics of stealth by putting information undercover, Silver County worked within existing bureaucratic structures by having the public health nursing coordinator work actively with the school board, and Gold County mobilized parent and community support across a diverse coalition.

Contested Discourses

The second thematic issue is that these cultural conflicts are to an increasing degree class- and race-based, a difficult fact to reconcile with American notions of social equality (Magnet, 1993). One point the cases stressed is that there were no hiding places from diversity in terms of race, gender, or class issues; it is an acknowledged fact of life in modern American times that we saw replicated in various forms across the three sites. One obvious way in which ideological differences were manifested was over the contested use of language—the use of the word *clinic* versus *health room* in describing where the services took place. In two of the case studies, people always described them as clinics, but in one case study we kept the word *health room,* as used in the bill's original language. We also noted that many of the informants used the metaphor of war to describe how they were engaged in a "battle" to keep people aware of children's needs that were being met through the provision of school-based services.

We see both these themes played out in terms of what we call the discourses of dissent, following Gee's (1991) notion that discourses are "a socially acceptable association among ways of using language, of thinking, feeling, believing, valuing, and of acting that can be used to identify oneself as a member of a socially meaningful group or social network" (p. 143). Gee suggested that discourses embody several important points, two of which are central to this analysis: (1) Discourses are inherently ideological, and "crucially involve a set of values and viewpoints about the relationships between people and the distribution of social goods"; and (2) because discourses are closely linked to the distribution of social power and hierarchical structure in society, "control over certain Discourses can lead to the acquisition of social goods (money, power, status) in a society" (p. 144). In effect, we suggest that with an issue as complex as placing health and social services in schools, there are multiple discourses constantly in play: the discourse of sexuality, the discourse of health, the discourse of politics, the discourse of care, and the discourse of morality.

DISCOURSE OF SEXUALITY

More than any other discourse, the discourse of sexuality brought people face to face with their deepest discomfort and shame about the body, a discomfort intensified by the fact that this discourse was centered around the behavior of adolescents. The focus on adolescents' behavior in terms of what Dryfoos (1994) called the "new morbidities" such as premature and promiscuous sexual activity, sexually transmitted diseases, and teenage pregnancy, more than any other focus, has made adults uncomfortable about the world their children are entering. As Esman (1990) noted, American culture has always viewed adolescent sexuality in terms of shame and guilt. Yet this sense of shame was not always the case. Foucault traces the emergence of a new cultural code regarding sexuality to the beginning of the nineteenth century. Prior to that, a much more sexually open code was in effect, even for children:

> At the beginning of the seventeenth century a certain frankness was still common, it would seem. Sexual practices had little need of secrecy; words were said without undue reticence, and things were done without too much concealment; one had a tolerant familiarity with the illicit. Codes regulating the coarse, the obscene and the indecent were quite lax compared to those of the nineteenth century. It was a time of direct gestures, shameless discourse, and open transgressions, when anatomies were shown and intermingled at will, and knowing children hung about amid the laughter of adults; it was a period when bodies made a display of themselves. (Foucault, 1978, p. 3)

Contrary to prevailing beliefs, significant changes in American sexual mores occurred in the early decades of the twentieth century, not in the 1960s, as popular culture would have us believe. Seidman (1992) characterized the history of American sexuality as a struggle over two broadly conceived sexual ideologies: (1) libertarian sexual ideology, where sex is joyous, an act of self-expression or pleasure, and legitimate in all adult consensual social exchanges, and (2) sexual romanticism, which emphasizes the affirmation of sex as a joyous act while recognizing its dangers—disease, sexual objectification, violence, and so forth. While the liberalization and eroticization of American sexual culture took place prior to World War I, Seidman (1992) noted two features of postmodern culture that contribute to an understanding of contemporary sexual values: (1) "A defense of sexual choice, variation, and pleasure gained mass social support at least among the middle class"; and (2) "A challenge to heterosexual, romantic, and marital norms that was helped by the sexual radicals . . . and trends within feminist and gay communities" (p. 45). In the projects we observed, these conflicting ideologies, intended to refer to adult behavior, also influenced notions of an appropriate sexual curriculum that could be disseminated to adolescents.

Sexuality Curriculum

In sharp contrast to the "shameless discourse" of earlier times, people that we met in the case studies were so careful with their speech. The irony, of course, is that adolescents today are showered with frank and explicit discussions of sexual activity and other sexual deviance daily on television. Multiple partners, cross-generational pairings, ratings of sexual proficiency, masturbation, and premature ejaculation are topics raised repeatedly, and often irresponsibly, on situation comedies and talk shows. Pipher (1996) noted that:

> Plato said that education is teaching children to find pleasure in the right things. This generation has been educated by the media to find pleasure in many wrong things—alcohol, casual sex, violence, and consumption. . . . The decision to have sex can be as casual as the decision to see a movie, and as meaningful. Many young adults have had dozens of sexual partners and no real relationships. There is lots of shacking up and getting laid, and not much sexual joy. (pp. 179–180)

The bold voices are the least responsible ones. And those who are best informed and seriously committed to helping young people cross the divide into adulthood feel they must censor and minimize their comments. Everyone spoke of sexual issues as "these issues"; few people were willing to name them directly, except for the nursing coordinator in Silver County. Rather than affirming the joyous aspects of sexuality, the emphasis was consistently placed upon the risks. For example, the curriculum guide used in Emerald County focused entirely on abstinence and the dangers of teenage pregnancy; no mention was ever made of sexuality as a healthy part of human emotions. One of our informants, a professor at a local college, said that when he taught a human development course to graduate students and discussed sexuality in terms of pleasure and desire, students hung on his words "as if they were hearing it for the first time." He was often called upon to work with full-service schools in the area, and he confirmed the statement made by many people that "the only acceptable public sex education program is abstinence."

But this county was not alone in its discomfort. The emphasis on abstinence in sex education curricula is a national, not a local, phenomenon (Lindsay, 1995). Trudell (1993) noted that two approaches characterized classroom instruction about sexuality: abstinence-only and abstinence-based. She described the first approach as one dominated by the Religious Right, where the curricula, such as *Sex Respect* and *Teen Aid*, focused on the following issues: the dangers of sexual arousal; negative consequences of premarital intercourse; risks of contraception and abortion; limited information about anatomy and physiology; biased and inaccurate information about sexually transmitted diseases, abortion, and sexual response; and virtually no information about contraception (beyond inflated risks), safer sex, or homosexuality. In contrast, abstinence-based programs incorporated a focus on abstinence while they provided adolescents who were already sexually active with information about contraception and prevention of sexually transmitted diseases. While these programs offered "information on sexual and reproductive anatomy and physiology, and more limited information about contraception, they generally avoided more controversial topics such as sexual pleasure, masturbation, homosexuality and abortion" (Trudell, 1993, p. 6). Carlson (1992) noted that the sexuality curriculum has always been marked by conflicting ideologies, which he identified as follows: (1) a traditionalist ideology, characterized by an emphasis on sexual sin and sickness; (2) a progressive ideology characterized by the concept of ensuring sexual "adjustment" and secular state management of sexual "problems"; (3) a radical Freudian ideology characterized by nonrepressive sexuality within a postcapitalist society; and (4) a libertarian ideology characterized by sexual diversity and individual sexual rights.

Both Trudell's distinction and examples of Carlson's first two ideologies were mirrored in our case studies; the sex education curricula in Emerald County drew heavily from programs like *Teen Aid*, while in both Silver County and Gold County the nurses were freer to discuss some contraceptive options. Ironically, the curriculum guide in Emerald County referred to the success of a health clinic in another county in reducing teenage pregnancies without being fully cognizant of the fact that the physician there was openly allowed to prescribe contraceptives and the nurses could refer students to family-planning clinics. In both these sites, however, any reference to sexual behaviors had to be couched in language that reflected biological or medical concerns (e.g., onset of puberty, what happens during ejaculation, menstrual cycles, etc.). As Weeks (1985) noted, "Findings of sex research and theorizing have been allowable when they have been compatible with an acceptable discourse, usually that of medicine" (p. 78). Whatley (1992) commented that because of the influence of the Christian Right, self-censorship among sexuality educators was common, but she argued forcefully that "progressive sexuality educators cannot cede the whole territory of sexuality education to the Right" (p. 83).[1] The dilemma for these educators was to find an acceptable discourse that acknowledged the importance of developing attitudes that encouraged tolerance toward a diversity of sexual behaviors based on the shared beliefs of a broad segment of the community, while instilling a sense of responsibility among impressionable adolescents. Sexuality educators must also resolve the inherent tension between the goals of reducing teenage pregnancy by promoting greater access to contraceptive options and reducing sexual activity. Many conservatives believe that the same strategies used to reduce teenage pregnancy (e.g., sex education, contraceptive availability) also serve to increase sexual activity.

Brooks-Gunn and Paikoff (1993, p. 181) respond to the question of what constitutes adolescent sexual well-being by offering a definition that includes four developmental challenges: (1) positive feelings about one's body and the acquisition of secondary sexual characteristics; (2) feelings of sexual arousal and desire; (3) the engagement in sexual behaviors; and (4) for those teenagers who are engaging in sexual intercourse, the practice of safe sex. Haffner (1994) suggested that an appropriate sex education curriculum that embodied these criteria would contain the following components: (1) accurate information about human sexuality; (2) an opportunity for adolescents to explore and assess their attitudes and feelings about sexual matters; (3) an emphasis on communication skills, including decision-making processes, assertiveness training, and peer-refusal skills; and (4) a focus on helping adolescents exercise responsibility in sexual behaviors, including the use of contraceptives and measures to prevent sexually transmitted diseases. Based on these criteria, the projects we visited focused primarily on the first one, paid little attention to the next two criteria, and addressed the last criteria depending upon the context of sanctioned community values. Their failure to do so has serious consequences, since S. S. Brown and Eisenberg (1995) cited research which demonstrated that:

> Sexual activity in adolescents can be postponed and the use of contraceptives can be increased once sexual activity has begun by comprehensive education that includes several messages simultaneously: the value of abstinence at young ages especially, the importance of good communication between the sexes and with parents regarding a range of interpersonal topics including sexual behavior and contraception, skills for resisting pressure to be sexually active, and the proper use of contraception once sexual activity has begun. (p. 12)

Gendered Perspectives

Discourses about sexuality cannot be examined in the absence of gender issues such as male dominance and sexual coercion, and the father's role in teenage pregnancy. As one example, the issue of date rape brought into focus the complexity of providing sex education in schools in the absence of discussing the broader social and political context in which adolescent sexuality emerged. As Gregor (1990) commented:

> The inherent asymmetry of sexual coercion creates two radically different male and female worlds. A woman who matures in a society where coercion is prevalent will come to see herself as simultaneously sexual and vulnerable. A male's self-concept will also reflect an alternately aggressive and protective relationship to women. Ultimately, in this setting, gender relationships will be eroticized in ways that intertwine sexuality, interpersonal control, and community level politics. (p. 477)

Sexual Control. Gregor's comments echoed the statement made by one of the nurses in Emerald County that "girls don't see the violence and control underlying the boys' concern that they should be faithful." Sears (1992a) cites several studies to suggest that both the curriculum and the textbooks reflect a distorted view of the female sexual experience:

> History teaches us . . . that female sexuality has been subject to varying degrees of power and social control, from legal and cultural proscriptions to enforced pregnancy to genital mutilation. . . . Although the textbook authors do discuss sexual violence and provide some good analyses of its social antecedents, they generally fail to incorporate these insights throughout the text. So we are left with the impression, in one section, that women are socialized for passivity and men for aggressiveness, but by the next chapter, they are equally participating sexual partners. This contradiction raises the larger issue: can sexuality in this society be free from power relations? (Goettsch, quoted in Sears, 1992a, p. 21)

Apart from the one nurse in Emerald County who correctly understood the linkage between sexual violence and power, none of our informants made any reference to date rape in these terms. In most districts we visited, middle and high school students were shown the obligatory film about date rape, but we encountered no cases where the nurses stated that the showing of the film was followed by a discussion of this issue in terms of sexual control over women.

With one exception (that of the school nurses in Silver County), few of the project staff ever alluded to the presence of sexual desire, whether by males or females, although the ignoring of this topic impacts more negatively on girls than it does on boys. A cultural taboo, one that is shared by many adolescents, exists on speaking openly about female sexual desire. As Brooks-Gunn and Paikoff (1993) noted:

Sexual desire is seen as paramount for boys and is ignored for girls, as seen in the phrase, "boys do the action/girls get the blame." Girls' desires are almost never discussed, only the consequences of their sexuality, specifically pregnancy. By pretending that female desire does not exist, girls are given few strategies for incorporating it into their lives or for planning how to handle it. (p. 187)

The issue of sexual control over women cannot be discussed in the absence of male voices. A serious problem that many nurses faced across all the schools in our three case study sites (as well as in all 12 sites we visited in 1992) was how to attract males into the clinic. In our 1993 evaluation study we learned that adolescent females were more likely to visit the health room than were boys, a finding confirmed by other national studies (Brindis, 1991) as well as by our subsequent visit in 1995. These visits were significant because if any discussions of sexuality were to take place, it would most likely be in the privacy of the nurse's or social worker's office. Most of the students were aware that these conversations could be kept confidential, and the project staff reported that girls were more willing to talk about their problems with boys when they were alone.

Another critical issue was that of sexual exploitation. The nurses also commented in every site we visited that the male partner in a pregnancy, particularly if the girl was under age 15, was likely to be older and out of high school. This fact has been acknowledged by other researchers (Males, 1993) as well as recently noted in the media (Gleick, 1996a; Navarro, 1996), where it has been reported that among teenage mothers aged 11 to 15, more than half the fathers are post–high school adult men. In Gold County, both African-American and Haitian informants lamented the fact that middle school girls were particularly susceptible to the blandishments of older men because they provided the girls with either emotional support or material goods that the girls lacked at home.

Social Constructions of Teenage Mothers. Nowhere are the discourses more conflicted than over the social construction of the teenage mother. Every day, it seems, we are presented with new statistics on the alarming rise in the number of teenage mothers, especially among Caucasian girls. A closer examination of these statistics reveals a much more complex picture, one that is more reassuring in terms of the extent of the "problem" but also one that is more troubling in what it reveals about the lack of caring adults who are concerned about adolescents' health and well-being. First, the problem of teenage pregnancy needs to be recast by locating it within social, historical, and political contexts (Lawson & Rhode, 1993). From a public policy perspective, the issue is not so much that teenagers are giving birth but that the rates are rising among unmarried teenagers who presumably will require public assistance to support their children. Related to this issue are concerns that teenage mothers are more likely to have low-birth-weight infants who exhibit a variety of problems and that pregnancy is a major reason why many girls fail to complete high school. In a comprehensive review of teenage pregnancy, Burdell (1995) presented persuasive evidence suggesting that not all teenage mothers necessarily ended up on welfare,[2] that "early pregnancy is not inherently detrimental to infant survival but is correlated with socioeconomic circumstances that are damaging to the infant's and mother's health, regardless of age," and that "most female dropouts left school before they became pregnant and that teens who got pregnant while still in school were not particularly likely to drop out" (p. 172). While admittedly both groups can manipulate statistics to serve social and political agendas, in that liberals see a problem that requires greater expenditures for social services while conservatives see it as further evidence of society's breakdown in moral values, the slowly emerging consensus is that teenage pregnancy is a multifaceted issue where one of the most critical aspects is being overlooked.

The striking omission, and one that is at the heart of the debate, is the representation of the teenage mother. Burdell (1995) opts for a critical feminist perspective, agreeing with Nathanson (1991) that "current debates about teen pregnancy are historically linked to the social control of female sexuality" (p. 176). Schools by their very political nature are unable to assume the task of allowing adolescent females to articulate viewpoints that violate conventional standards, a point strongly asserted by Fine (1992):

> The historic silencing within public schools of conversations about sexuality, contraception, and abortion, as well as the absence of a discourse of desire—in the form of comprehensive sex education, school-based health clinics, and viable life options via vocational training and placement—all combine to exacerbate the vulnerability of young women whom schools, and the critics of sex education and SBHC's, claim to protect. (p. 49)[3]

Burdell (1995) suggests that three general assumptions characterize school programs for teenage mothers: (1) the assumption of an "inherent conflict between the private domestic role of motherhood, separate from the public role of wage work, and high school education" (p. 199), as reflected in programs that emphasize child care and effective parenting practices; (2) the assumption of "a need to retreat from the conflicting values of medicalized discourses of those promoting special programs and the discourses of morality often used to challenge these practices"

(p. 200); and (3) the assumption on "the part of school personnel that the primary need is to render pregnant and parenting students and special programs for them invisible" (p. 200), which is based on the need to "maintain a separation from 'politics', contentious issues of sexuality and the prejudices of community members" (p. 200). Burdell based her critique not only on a review of literature across the education, medical, policy analysis, and social service fields, but also on her ethnographic study of the life histories of five school women whom she followed through pregnancy, childbirth, and the first nine months of child rearing.

We concur that Burdell's perspective fits the case of Emerald County, where project personnel maintained silence on all aspects of sexuality except medical ones, and to some extent the case of Silver County, where separate programs were established for teenage mothers that were heavily focused on parenting practices to help the girls become "good mothers." However, our experiences in Silver County contradicted Burdell's third assumption that schools engage in a concerted effort to keep these programs invisible. The project personnel were proud of the fact that their county pioneered the use of an in-house day-care program for teenage mothers, and it was widely known within the community that these services were available. If anything, some school personnel felt that the program was too visible and feared that it would tempt girls into having children because they knew they could remain in school and have a place to care for them. The nursing coordinator who set up the program scoffed at this belief, as she trenchantly noted in her interview: "These things are not what's going through a girl's mind when she's in the back seat of a car Saturday night deciding if she will or will not give up her virginity (*laughs*). She's not thinking, 'Gee, I can just stay right at the high school if I get pregnant.'"

While Burdell and others (Phoenix, 1991) correctly assert that a missing voice in these debates is that of the teenage mother herself, researchers who have taken the time to hear these voices have concluded that the image of an adolescent girl free to choose the sexual autonomy historically ceded to males, which may include the choice to have a child, is wildly at variance with the developmental needs of most adolescent females. Judith Musick, a developmental psychologist, analyzed dozens of qualitative data sets from the Ounce of Prevention Fund that included interviews and journal entries from several hundred adolescent girls from all ethnic backgrounds and social classes, ranging in age from 14 to 18 years. Her first point is that use of the word *choice* to describe the girls' behavior is already problematic. She draws upon Ellwood's (1988) work on rational choice models as an inadequate means of explaining out-of-wedlock pregnancy in stating that:

> When referring to a teen's engaging in unprotected sexual relations as
> an unwise choice, I do not mean that she has rationally chosen this
> course of behavior. Rather, I see her behavior as stemming from com-
> pelling social (external) and psychological (internal) forces which pro-
> mote unprotected sexual activity and premature child rearing. (Musick,
> 1993, p. 33)

Her primary conclusion is that intervention or sex education programs that fail to take into account adolescent girls' developmental needs
for intimacy, self-esteem, achievement, coping skills, and protection from
predatory males will fail, particularly in the case of poor and/or minority
girls who have few resources to call upon in a struggle to achieve a viable
adult identity. As Musick (1993) noted:

> For many poor adolescent girls, early motherhood is attractive because
> it promises to resolve issues of identity, intimacy, and achievement bet-
> ter than anything else in their experience. Motherhood settles certain
> fundamental questions about who the girl is and whom she relates to,
> what she does and what she can do well. (p. 124)

Musick's assertions were validated in our interviews, as well as with
the first author's evaluation of a teenage pregnancy-prevention program
for early adolescents (Emihovich & Davis, 1994). Over and over again in
all three counties, we heard poignant stories from nurses as to how proud
the girls were of their babies and details about the horrifying circumstances of their lives that led many girls to "choose" pregnancy as a way
out. Conflicted relationships with men was another oft-repeated theme.
In Gold County, the comments of the nurses and the two school administrators about the sexual exploitation of middle school girls underscored
Musick's (1993) point that "for a sizable group of adolescent mothers,
contemporary social and sexual relations with males may be reenact-
ments of patterns established earlier in life: lessons of victimization
learned all too well" (p. 91). Although the evidence strongly suggests that
girls who begin sexual activity before the age of 14 are likely to be co-
erced, the voluntary continuation of this activity in later years may reflect
the girl's deep sense of shame and lack of self-worth that can only be
reclaimed by the attentions of another male.

Critical theorists of teenage pregnancy such as Burdell (1995) are
right to point out that these constructions of teenage mothers as vulnerable, as needing protection from a hostile and uncaring environment,
should be framed within class and race differences. Despite this contention, in no school did we hear about discourse practices that allowed
adolescent girls to challenge prevailing notions of their sexuality in male

terms, to resist images that viewed them simultaneously as temptress and victim, and to construct alternative identities that did not revolve around traditional roles of wife and/or mother. What is needed is an approach that takes into account adolescent girls' developmental needs at different ages and according to life circumstances, while acknowledging Burdell's (1995) point that "more work is needed that can unpack the effects on pregnant teens of school, race, class, popular culture, ideological constructions of women's rights, and normalizing technologies of science" (p. 202).

Silenced Voices: Adolescent Homosexuals

While gender issues regarding sexuality may have been given short shrift, the silence surrounding the issue of adolescent homosexuality was deafening. No school that we visited in either 1992 or 1995 reported any discussion of the issue of homosexuality as an alternative sexual orientation. If the issue came up at all, it was either within a medical context of nurses' discussion of how AIDS is transmitted or within a context of fear, as was the case in one high school where the nurses mentioned that because of the periodic influx of gay visitors to the beaches, school officials feared the spread of AIDS among young boys by men looking for "safe" partners. This silencing is not unique to Florida; Harbeck (1992) noted that "the paucity of literature, intervention, and understanding in this area is a national disgrace" (pp. 1–2). The seriousness of the problem is emphasized by a 1989 report from the U. S. Department of Health and Human Services suggesting that 30% of all teenagers who commit suicide are gay and that gay teenagers are two to three times more likely to commit suicide (Stover, 1994).

Establishing a discourse about this issue is enormously complicated for school health personnel. The nurses and social workers were often sensitive to the fact that homosexual students were present in the school population, and we heard poignant stories about their inability to respond to these students' needs without jeopardizing the acceptance of the entire program. Although they also mentioned incidents where presumably gay students were called names by other students, they felt that high school students were more tolerant of alternative sexual choices than were the adults in the community. Parental and community opposition is rooted in stereotyped concepts of homosexuality as a lifestyle "choice" (rather than being genetically determined, as suggested by the growing biomedical literature), parental anxiety over a son or daughter's failure to conform to mainstream sexual behaviors, religious beliefs that view homosexuality as an "abomination," and the prevailing myth that homosexuals prey on children to look for safe partners against the spread of AIDS. Nor is the community the only group at fault. We suspected that many of the school health personnel were unable to raise this issue because they shared these beliefs with the surrounding community. Sears (1992b) noted that school staffs' expressed willingness to address homosexual issues in a supportive way is "highly correlated with their attitudes about homosexuality and their feelings toward lesbians and gay men" (p. 69).

The discourse of heterosexuality as the only "normal" option is so strongly embedded in most social institutions that school health personnel face a painful choice. They can choose to ignore the question of adolescent homosexuality and thus condemn many of these students to a life that most of us would find unimaginable, based on one student's comment:

> We could keep the truth to ourselves, and become totally isolated from everyone else. Or we could lie to the others, and become alienated from ourselves. Either way we lost. (Nickel, 1992, p. 4)

Or they can attempt to locate discussion of this issue within the continuum of human sexuality through the use of curriculum materials that address this issue in a nonjudgmental way. Trudell (1993) mentioned the development of PROJECT 10, an example of a low-cost, school-based program about homosexuality that focused on counseling, intervention, and education, which had considerable positive impact on most students in the Los Angeles School District. After its implementation the general student population showed

> greater acceptance of and sensitivity to diversity and sexual orientation. Gay, lesbian, and bisexual participants reported feeling better about themselves as well as greater social acceptance, interpersonal connections, academic success, and safer sexual practices. (Trudell, 1993, p. 185)

While these outcomes would be desired by the school health personnel in many of the projects we visited, our clear impression is that at present, given the constraints most school health personnel face, their choice is to maintain silence in favor of meeting more pressing student health needs related to teenage pregnancy prevention and basic health care.

AIDS Education

The most recent statistics on the incidence of new HIV infections is that one out of four cases are estimated to occur among people under the age of 20 (*Youth and HIV/AIDS*, 1996). Despite these alarming predictions, none of the projects had made AIDS education a high priority. In most cases, discussion of AIDS was folded into discussions of prevention of other sexually transmitted diseases. Most of the project personnel were extremely reluctant to acknowledge that they had any HIV cases in their schools, in part for confidentiality reasons and from fears of creating a community backlash.[4] No testing was done at any school; a student who came in and requested information about where to get tested was referred to the county public health department.

A complicating factor for all the projects we visited was that discussion of the most effective means of AIDS prevention cannot really be disentangled from discussions of condom use, and here the discourses were marked by conflicting perspectives. As Gamson (1993) noted, condoms are "a disease preventive that also happens to block conception, and a conception preventive that happens to block viruses" (p. 312). He also noted that condom use is framed by two competing self-interests within society: (1) monitoring and protecting public health, and (2) monitoring and protecting the sexual morality of its citizens (1993, p. 315).

These dual interests complicated the mention of their use in classroom discussions. In Emerald County, where the emphasis was on an abstinence-only model of preventing pregnancy, the nurses stated they could not even mention condom use as a way of preventing the spread of AIDS. In the other two sites, the nurses could discuss condom use, but only in the context of AIDS prevention. However, they freely admitted that students could obtain them from the health rooms.[5]

The opposition the schools expected they would face in even discussing condoms was more imagined than real, judging from national polls, where in 1992 it was reported that 68% of adults favored the distribution of condoms in their local public schools ("School Poll," 1992). However, 25% qualified their support by stating that schools should require parental consent. In the sites where condoms were discussed, school personnel were careful to send home letters indicating to parents the nature of the health services being provided to students, both in the health rooms and in classrooms. These same letters also gave parents an opportunity to have their children opt-out of any services they didn't want them to receive.

This lack of attention to the dangers of HIV infection is disturbing, because the message that is promulgated in schools is that only certain groups are at risk. As Cummings (1993) noted, "AIDS narratives might equally be called pedagogies. One of the lessons they teach us is the distinction between 'us' and 'them'" (p. 354). Many nurses admitted that the only way in which homosexuality was referred at all was in the context of discussing the spread of AIDS, thus reinforcing the perception that AIDS was a "gay disease." In schools where high drug use within the community was known to be a factor, school staff might also mention the risks involved with intravenous drug use. Yet in the interviews we conducted with middle and high school students in our 1992 visit, in response to the question, "What other kinds of information would you like the nurse to talk about?," almost all the students stated they would have liked more information about HIV and other STDs. The desire for information was especially strong among middle school students; according to data collected in our 1992 sample (Emihovich & Herrington, 1993), they were the least knowledgeable group about the transmission of STDs and the most likely group to report having been diagnosed with one.[6]

DISCOURSE OF HEALTH

A common refrain repeatedly voiced by all informants was that "children can't learn if they're not healthy." Sommerfeld (1992a) documented the fact that health problems among American children are rapidly rising. As one response, Roberta Doering, president of the National School Boards Association, recently issued a policy statement that corroborated the nurses' belief that healthy children are better learners, and she outlined the eight key components of comprehensive school health: health education; health services; healthy and safe school environment; school counseling, mentoring, and social services; healthy and nutritious food services; parent and community involvement; physical education; and health promotion for faculty and staff (Doering, 1996).

Cultural Biases in Student Outreach

All of these components were featured in one way or another in all of the projects, but they varied depending upon the community context and the nature of the student population. The fact that sexual discourses were highly contested was not surprising. What was unexpected is that even the provision of basic health information proved controversial in some areas. In general, when topics were focused on issues of basic student health (e.g., diet, nutrition, smoking prevention, physical checkups), project staff reported little opposition from parents and other community members to nurses taking an active role in this area. But as one of the case studies made clear, some parents viewed information about diet as a culturally biased attack on family eating habits. For both white and black families in rural areas, the nurses' stress on the idea that parents should prepare meals that were low in salt and fat was a direct affront to traditional southern diets. This finding paralleled other researchers' findings that health educators were ill trained to deal with controversy arising from even relatively benign health practices, such as stress management and deep breathing (Sommerfeld, 1992b).

Little agreement could be found even as to what these services would be called in schools. At first the term most often used was *school-based clinics* (SBCs); but once the Religious Right had appropriated this term to suggest that schools were providing services akin to abortion clinics (Glasow, 1988), the term was shifted to school health rooms. Dryfoos (1994) used the term *school-based clinic* to describe their distribution state by state but qualified it to include programs that were school-linked in providing primary health care, social support, and mental health services. Despite the best efforts of the Florida legislature and the state agency for health and human services to have project personnel use the term *health room*, people in the field on all our visits persisted in calling them a "clinic." Dryfoos accurately noted that "Whatever we call it, an enormous amount of activity and a modest amount of mostly state funding is being directed at new administrative arrangements to bring support services into schools" (1994, p. 207).

Students' access to health care was often framed by class- and race-based perspectives. Not surprisingly, the project personnel and school officials most sensitive to the lack of adequate health care coverage among their students were either minority members (such as the Haitian nurse and African-American principal in Gold County) or those who were located in desperately poor areas. Even though many of the projects were located in schools that had a high percentage of minority students, location alone is not a sufficient guarantee these students will come to the clinics. More intensive outreach efforts need to be conducted by school health personnel to ensure success. Earls (1993) noted that successful health promotion efforts among minority students needed to take into account the following variables: immigration status, family structure, degree of assimilation or accommodation to the majority culture, language use, child-rearing methods, religious beliefs and practices, health beliefs and practices, and educational aspirations. For example, our visits to Gold County demonstrated the importance of having school nurses who either shared the students' culture or who were knowledgeable about the validity of certain cultural practices. We recall the painful dilemma of one nurse in an elementary school who recognized Haitian parents' need to maintain control over their children through the traditional practice of caning yet who was legally obligated to report these punishments if the child complained about abuse. As young adolescents became more knowledgeable about the ways in which this practice was viewed by the school, they often used this information to gain an advantage over their parents, who were attempting to maintain discipline in the face of what they perceived were threats to their children's well-being in terms of living in a permissive American culture.

Cultural Issues in Adolescent Health

Specialists in the field of adolescent health have long recognized the major morbidities such as accidents, substance abuse, and disruptive behavior disorders (Holden & Nitz, 1995). What is of serious concern is the alarming increase in health problems related to sexual activity, such as sexually transmitted diseases and HIV infections. A further disturbing trend is that even within the more familiar categories of substance abuse and disruptive behaviors, the onset of these behaviors is occurring at increasingly younger ages, often even before early adolescence (Holden & Nitz, 1995). The findings from research were validated by our informants in both visits. In all of the projects, we heard over and over again stories of middle school children's involvement in behaviors that were simply unheard of even as recently as 10 years ago. Many of the project personnel attributed the problems to the lack of adult supervision after school, since most of the families with which they dealt consisted of family members who often worked two jobs to make ends meet and who were too tired or unavailable to keep track of young adolescents' activities.

Little consensus exists in the literature as to the most effective means of health promotion among this group. Theorists who have developed models to explain adolescent risk-taking behaviors disagree over whether the behaviors should be viewed from an individualistic perspective that emphasizes personality differences, an ecological perspective that emphasizes the role of peer pressure and community standards, a biological perspective that emphasizes hormonal or genetic influences, or a developmental perspective that emphasizes risk-taking as part of normal adolescent development (Millstein & Igra, 1995). Faced with this conflicting evidence, it is not surprising that project personnel found it difficult to implement effective strategies for reaching students to warn them about risky behaviors. Schoolwide health promotions tended to focus on topics that were unlikely to generate community opposition, such as a campaign in Silver County schools to increase seatbelt use among adolescents. Strategies for informing students about more controversial issues that seemed to be the most successful were the simplest: Nurses walked the halls and talked to students during recess or lunch; they set up a column in the student newspaper or established a telephone hot-line;

nurses or social workers set up small counseling groups in the privacy of their offices. The main advantage to all these strategies was that they afforded project personnel freedom to say in private what could not be said in public.[7]

Strikingly absent in medical discussions of adolescent risk-taking is the role of culture as it intersects with perceptions of risk, an omission that affected the thinking of many of the project personnel as well. Despite the fact that many projects were located in schools with large minority populations, we found only a few cases where these students' feelings and beliefs were incorporated directly into the curriculum. In both Silver County and Gold County, several schools had translated some health education materials into Spanish, but the project staff admitted that far more needed to be done. Discussions of teenage pregnancy were rarely cast in any perspective other than its being an impediment to success in later life, a very white, middle-class view; yet for low-income girls with few viable career prospects, pregnancy is often used as a negotiating tool to manage a relationship with a boyfriend, while for rural black girls it is an affirmation of adult status (Irvine, 1995). Discussions of condom use, when they happened at all, rarely took into account the fact that for African-American and Latina girls, persuading their boyfriends to use condoms is exceptionally difficult. As Irvine (1995) noted:

> Modes of intervention can be developed that address the deep meanings women hold about sexuality, gender, risk, and prevention. For example, Sobo suggests that rather than forcing a woman to give up the "wisdom narrative" or insisting that she persuade her partner to use condoms, the community needs to reframe the meaning of condom use so that it becomes symbolic of loving and intimate relationships. This would involve adjusting the cultural scripts of urban Latino and African-American heterosexuals in much the same way that gay men began to transform their cultural scenarios about sexuality. Ultimately, as with adolescent pregnancy, social and political changes will be necessary to effect the deepest change. In the meantime, programs that locate behavior change in the complicated social, cultural, and economic realities of people's lives will be the most effective ones. (pp. 140–141)

DISCOURSE OF POLITICS

The politicized struggles over school health services are indicative of contemporary American culture's inability to find common ground on an issue that should concern every citizen—the declining health and social conditions of children. Marian Wright Edelman (1996) has spoken forcefully about the abdication of the federal government's responsibility to provide services for poor children:

The Republican radicals are trying to eradicate the role of the federal government as a protector of last resort for children and the poor, and for ordinary people during a recession. This is a major attack on government, what I call an ideological coup d'etat—without any consideration for its consequences. (p. 24)

Who Advocates for Children?

Finkelstein (1995) succinctly articulated the dilemma of child advocates in the United States:

We live with a canon of political, moral and economic habits that is rich in the capacity to protect individual rights, religious and cultural diversity, family autonomy, economic abundance, and free-thinking. But we also live in a country that is poor in the capacity to protect the weak and dependent, support families, nurture community life, and otherwise secure the rights of children and families in need. (p. 5)

Both these comments parallel those of the social worker in Silver County who noted that being an advocate for children's needs led to her being called a *child-lover*, a term of contempt instead of praise. In many of our interviews there was widespread acknowledgment that politicians in both camps were divorced from understanding the reality of poor and working-class people's lives. At the same time, advocates for children's causes have too often assumed that just because they held the high moral ground by being focused on children's issues, they didn't have to get down into the political trenches and lobby for programs that served children's interests. Not surprisingly, politicians respond best to the incentives of money and votes; as a result, the needs of the elderly, through the intensive lobbying of the American Association of Retired Persons and senior citizens' stellar voting record, are met far beyond what is necessary. As one legislator candidly noted in a *Time* interview:

Is there a disproportionate amount of money being spent on people over the age of 65 versus under the age of three? Yes, unquestionably. Is it in part a function of their lobbying efforts? Yes, unquestionably. Is it largely a function of their need? No, it is not. (quoted in Gleick, 1996b, p. 34)

Community Politics and Children's Interests

Mobilizing a political agenda concentrated on children's issues is complicated by the lack of a community consensus as to what the most pressing issues and what the best means of addressing them are—a fact that was vividly illustrated in the three case studies. One of the recurring patterns we saw was that no county could be considered as a monolithic community in terms of the health services offered through the schools, despite the fact that the school board's role was to mandate policy for all the schools in that district. In determining who constitutes the community for mobilizing support of school health services, a reasonable place for project personnel to begin is the parents/guardians of the children being served in these schools.

When we visited the sites in both 1992 and 1995, we heard repeated references to one overriding fact: These services were desperately needed by families who had no other access to health care except through hospital emergency rooms. Every person interviewed stressed the need for schools to provide these services. Many parents stated that they wouldn't know what they would do if the services weren't there. Several parents noted that basic information about hygiene was not "getting done at home" and that "kids would be a mess without it." Other parents commented that with two people working, it was impossible to send children home with minor illnesses. In general, people in the community were "surprised and impressed" at the availability of services through this program. Several parents said that schools needed to focus more directly on AIDS prevention and human sexuality issues. Other parents stated that more attention also needed to be paid to alcohol abuse among teenagers, since that was a bigger problem in many communities than drug abuse. The shared feeling among those we interviewed was that many parents were abdicating their role in educating their children about sexual issues and that schools needed to become more involved in discussing them.

Many parents were aware of special programs that were presented by nurses and other project personnel, often on health-related issues, at PTA meetings. Almost all parents said they were informed about the program by a letter sent home describing the availability of services in the school. Several parents mentioned they would like to see the school open one or two nights a week to provide health services for children. They felt this would enable more working parents to meet the project personnel and ask questions about their children's health. Several parents said they had already asked about medical issues and received "very helpful information."

While there was fairly strong support for having basic health services available in schools, providing more specific birth-control information was a problem for many project personnel because of the fear of opposition from certain organized groups within the community and/or small groups of highly vocal parents. When we first visited the sites in 1992, we used the term *projected* because in many cases the opposition was more imagined than real. In cases where it did surface, project staff reported that this opposition was more likely to occur among people who did *not* have students enrolled in the project schools. Parents of students in these schools who were interviewed supported the idea of providing more access to contraceptive information, although clearly with some reluctance. As one parent put it, "I would be concerned about the nurse discussing it, but I would want her to do it. Kids need better information, and many parents are afraid to talk about it." In some schools where contraceptive information was discussed, parents were kept informed and were asked to sign permission slips for these discussions to take place. In other projects, this information could only be presented by a medical doctor to students for whom signed parental permission slips were on file.

In 1995 the opposition was highly visible and growing in intensity, as evident in the taping of school board meetings by members of certain religious groups, but there were clear-cut differences in schools' willingness to take risks to promote effective sex education through the clinics. Our visits sharply reminded us of Tip O'Neill's famous saying, "All politics are local." In some projects, the community's antennae went up when nurses tackled issues such AIDS and STD prevention and human sexuality. Several nurses said they were restricted to presenting only the medical aspects of these issues (e.g., identification of symptoms, description of body parts, etc.), although in other projects nurses or social workers could discuss more value-oriented issues.

In the case of the high school in Gold County that was successful in mobilizing community support for the clinic, parents and school health personnel used some of the tactics advocated by Rienzo and Button (1993) in their study of the political dynamics of school-based health clinics. As they noted:

> Key informants emphasized the importance of proactively assessing and demonstrating community support and, if legitimate, exposing the opposition as an outside group attempting to exert its will over the community. (Rienzo & Button, 1993, p. 270)

In Gold County, the parents were successful in portraying the school board members as hardhearted and unwilling to acknowledge the severity of poor children's health problems in the community, a community in which none of the board members resided. This use of both class and race issues worked to their advantage, and the services provided to children, including family-planning information, were maintained.

Silin (1995) has suggested that the question of whose values will prevail is indicative of a struggle within two kinds of communities over issues of sexuality and HIV/AIDS:

> Often these debates have been characterized by a tension between two
> co-existing communities in which we may hold joint membership: the
> community of compassion, celebrating connection and mutual engage-
> ment, and the community of fear, erecting barriers for protections
> against the unknown. (p. 31)

But his characterization may be too limited to sexual concerns, since
the interviews attested to the idea that people feared much more than the
loss of children's sexual innocence. What they were concerned about was a
whole constellation of behaviors, particularly evident among middle school
students, that indicated a disregard for personal safety and community
connection. Their concern is quite legitimate when the data on middle
school adolescent health care issues are examined: They reveal an alarming
rise in all categories of dysfunctional behaviors, such as smoking, drug use,
early sexual experience, teenage pregnancies, and sexually transmitted diseases (Centers for Disease Control, 1995). However, the risk is real that
the growing parents' rights movement will create considerable obstacles for
school personnel in providing badly needed health and counseling services
for students who need them, even in the face of parental opposition. In a
recent case in Georgia, the parents sued when they learned that the school
counselor had supposedly driven their daughters to a local clinic to procure
birth control pills ("Telling Tales," 1996). While the parents' lawyer was free
to malign the counselor's motives and to contest the idea that the school
should have jurisdiction over a student's access to family-planning services,
the school could not easily defend itself without violating the Buckley
Amendment, which guarantees a student's right to privacy. We heard stories in the sites we visited about desperate female students who sought
information on how to prevent a pregnancy in cases of familial incest or,
more chilling, counseling as to the best means of dealing with a pregnancy
that resulted from the same circumstance. In these cases the school officials
must make a judgment call as to whose rights prevail, the student's or the
parents'. The fact that the school in Georgia was so reluctant to provide
more details about the students' side of the story strongly suggests to us the
possibility that incest may have been a factor in the girls' desire to seek
birth control. Unfortunately, legislators who respond to pressures exerted
by outside groups by passing legislation that impacts on all students without hearing all the facts jeopardize the welfare of students who have no
other recourse but to go to school officials for help.

DISCOURSE OF CARE

In an ironic turn of events, the latter part of the twentieth century
has emulated the seventeenth century: We have too many "knowing chil-

dren" amidst adults who care very little about their welfare. Teenagers in particular are left to fend for themselves. In a provocative article, Whitehead (1994) stated that comprehensive sex education programs failed to account for the Hobbesian realities of teenage sex: "nasty, brutish, and short." The emphasis many programs placed on developing good communication skills and an openness about sexual matters does not reflect the fact that, for most girls under the age of 15, their first sexual experience is likely to be a coercive one and that decisions about pregnancy are interwoven with the girl's struggle to master the developmental tasks of adolescence. Furthermore, Whitehead charges that these programs absolve adults from their traditional responsibility of maintaining familial and institutional controls over teenage sexuality. By presuming that all adolescents need are the techniques of prevention and better knowledge of their sexuality, adults who advocate for these programs assume adolescents will be empowered to make the appropriate decisions about how to behave in a sexually responsible manner. As Whitehead (1994) sees it:

> Their job is to train teenagers in the management of their own sexuality and to provide access to contraceptives. In the new technology adults are called upon to staff teenagers in their sexual pursuits while teenagers themselves are left to decide whether or not to engage in sex. Refusing sex, no less than having sex, becomes a matter of following individual dictates rather than following socially instituted and culturally enforced norms. (p. 80)

Adult Responsibilities

Whitehead's critique is echoed by Males (1996) in his recent book, *The Scapegoat Generation;* he feels that adults have abdicated their role as protectors of the young while feeling justified in pursing their own pleasures at children's expense. Giroux (1996) has argued that nowhere is this attitude more highly visible than in the media, especially in the portrayal of young adolescents in the movie *Kids:*

> The relations between youth and adults have always been marked by strained generational and ideological struggles, but the new economic and social conditions that youth face today, along with a callous indifference to their spiritual and material needs, suggest a qualitatively different attitude on the part of many adults toward American youth— one that indicates the young have become our lowest national priority. Put bluntly, American society at present exudes both a deep rooted hostility and chilling indifference toward youth, reinforcing the dismal conditions under which young people are increasingly living. (p. 31)

Giroux agrees with both Males's and Whitehead's contention that adults have left teenagers to fend for themselves, ostensibly cloaking this abandonment in the guise of giving them the freedom to choose among many options, a choice that adults want to reserve for themselves. As Giroux (1996) pointedly noted, the filmmaker of *Kids* was in effect living out fantasies from his own troubled childhood and the desire for sexual freedom he never had, but "his narrative about youth plays on dominant fears about the loss of moral authority, while reinforcing images of demonization and sexual license through which adults can blame youth for existing social problems, and be titillated at the same time" (p. 33). Giroux further noted that the film fails to locate youth's problems (especially those of poor and minority youth) within a sociohistorical context of violence, oppression, and diminished lack of economic opportunities, and he states that the director "fails to understand—or at least represent— that it is precisely adult society with its celebration of market values and market moralities and its attack on a civil society that undermines the nurturing system and safety nets for children" (p. 33).

We find it both ironic and heartening that a neoconservative social commentator like Whitehead and a Marxist-oriented academic could be in so much agreement as to how the problems of today's youth are defined and managed. The critiques of all three writers were echoed in the voices we heard throughout our visits, in that children and youth were being abandoned by both their families and the larger social community. Over and over we heard the refrain expressed by one nurse, "For some kids, we're the only safe environment in their entire lives. It's the only place for six hours where they can feel they're not threatened by other people in their families." While she may have overstated the case to some extent (in some urban areas, schools have become equally threatening environments), her point remains valid that the project personnel and, by extension, those involved directly with children's health care were more cognizant of being on the front lines in a continuing battle to provide adequate health and social services for children in need.

Civic and Corporate Responsibility

The social problems that were highly visible in all three sites raise an interesting question about the role of business and community institutions. In every project we visited, we noted that the staff maintained an impressive list of agencies and community groups they used for referrals, especially for the coordination of care of students with chronic/serious illnesses or problems. These lists included the following groups: Children's Home Society, Junior League, the OB clinic at local hospitals, the county public health unit, Job Corps, juvenile justice system, county medical associations, the Lions Club, the American Red Cross, Teen Alliance programs, local church groups, private doctors and dentists willing to take charity cases, allergy clinics, vocational agencies, and so forth. One point stressed by project coordinators in rural areas was the lack of community agencies to provide mental health and drug or alcohol rehabilitation assistance. Assistance in these areas was unaffordable or simply unavailable for many rural parents. These communities even relied on the schools to provide second-hand clothing and shoes.

One statement frequently heard in Republican rhetoric is that private groups and social organizations will take up the slack once state and federal funding for social services is cut. At first glance the lists of agencies that all project personnel maintained lends credence to this notion. Yet when we listened closely to the comments made by people in the field, it was clear that they perceived this private beneficence to be sporadic, uncoordinated, and highly dependent upon a key person's commitment to the school and community. Because the needs were so great in many schools, nurses and social workers often found the task of coordinating services among the different agencies to be an overwhelming job.

At the same time, people were conscious of the fact that they lived in a cultural milieu that undercut many of their best efforts to focus attention on prevention and reduction of high-risk behaviors. The frustration of one principal was painfully evident as he talked about the lack of corporate responsibility in promoting socially responsible behavior, especially among adolescents. Echoing Hillary Clinton's belief, he told us:

> It takes a whole village to raise a child. Schools are on the firing line and we need to involve the whole community, churches, the Chamber of Commerce. And corporate America has to take responsibility, too. We can't let them evade their responsibility in pushing smoking and wine coolers on our young people. It's so obvious I can't see why they don't see it.

Finkelstein (1995) has a heated response to why corporations can't see their responsibility:

> We are heirs to traditions of public distrust, of near-Darwinian beliefs in the moral value of free markets, of commitments to individual liberties. We are also in possession of commitments to justice, egalitarian dreams, and visions of pluralistic possibilities. In my view, we have generated infant and child hating policies, not because we hate children, are ignorant of their needs, or unaware of our duties to them, but because we have elevated economic self-sufficiency over social compassion, material over moral matters, the needs of employers over the

needs of children. All of us—conservatives, liberals and moderates alike—shared a distrust of public involvement with families and in the process we are withering away the prospects for our children. (p. 12).

Other social science researchers and political commentators (Phillips, 1990; Wolff, 1996) have noted the failure of public discourse to recognize that the needs of free-market capitalism are often inimical to the needs of children and families and to the maintenance of community. The cultural contradictions of capitalism have been noted and feared for decades (Bell, 1968). But the more recent penetration of mass media and advertising into all aspects of daily life has elevated the dangers:

> We're a pluralistic culture struggling to find common beliefs, and unfortunately, our most central belief system is about the importance of money. Many of us reject a values system based on economics—a value system that says more is better, that money equals happiness, and that consumption is the goal of life. But in media and advertising, our children are being educated to believe that products are what matters. This will hurt them and ultimately, it hurts us all. (Pipher, 1996, pp. 16–17)

According to one of our informants, the true test of leadership is to find a way to unite "passionate conviction and community consensus around the need to care for children," a test that many in the political sphere are failing.

DISCOURSE OF MORALITY

The dilemma that faces everyone involved in providing health services to children, especially young adolescents, is to how to imbue adolescents and their families, and the public at large, with a greater sense of moral responsibility without returning to the days of the scarlet letter. In Silver County, one of the social workers mentioned the need for "consciousness raising" in the sense of returning a sense of conscience and purpose to talks about moral behaviors. As she put it:

> Parents and families aren't necessarily distraught when their teenager becomes pregnant. They had them when they were 14, 15, 16; there is acceptance that this is just the way it is. I would like to see those decisions come from people in the community and finding ways to reach their youth to make it not OK from a moral standpoint. And morality is very practical because it's living in this world.

Her comment seem to suggest that parents are co-conspirators in the breakdown of moral values among students today, but Rubin's work on working-class families, the kinds of families whose children attend the schools where these services were located, paints a more complicated picture. In her view, these parents seem to be bewildered by cultural changes that have negatively affected their children. As she described it:

> It's this sense that their children see the world so differently that's so hard for working class parents. For it seems to say that now, along with the economic dislocation they suffer, even their children are out of their reach, that they can no longer count on shared values to hold their family together. It doesn't help either that no matter where they look, they don't see a reflection of themselves. If they look up they see a lifestyle and values they abhor, the same ones that, they believe, are corrupting their children. If they shift their gaze downward, they see the poor, the homeless, the helpless—the denizens of the dangerous underclass whose moral degeneracy has, in the working class view, led to their fall. (Rubin, 1994, p. 47)

Centering Moral Behavior

But these parents are no longer able to articulate a sense of moral vision that can be transmitted to their children because they are unsure of the meaning traditional values now hold in a relativistic culture where any behavior seems possible and right, depending on one's point of view. Rubin (1994) perceptively noted their dilemma:

> As they struggle with the shifting cultural norms—with the gap between the ideal statement of the culture in which they came to adulthood and the one into which their children are growing—nothing seems to make sense anymore. . . . They yearn for a past when, it seems to them, moral absolutes reigned, yet they're confused and uncertain about which of yesterday's moral strictures they want to impose on themselves and their children today. (p. 63)

The dilemma faced by the parents in Rubin's study was evident throughout our visits to these three case study sites, indeed to all twelve sites we visited as part of the initial evaluation study. We were reminded of the principal in Silver County who spoke wistfully of a past when the problems he faced did not exist but who was realistic enough to recognize that those days were gone forever unless there was a public condemnation of the behavior at all levels, societal as well as individual.

A related problem is the normalization of deviant behavior that has occurred primarily through the media, especially daytime talk shows. According to Abt and Seesholtz (1994), social and moral order does not exist as a predetermined given but rather is constructed by human activity:

> Knowledge of how to behave in social situations is contained in cultural scripts or blueprints that are themselves the products of human interaction and symbolic communication about the nature of "reality." "Morality," norms, values, judgmental expressions of group conventions, create limits on social behavior. These limits are maintained either by "internalizing the scripts" or by reliance on external threats and punishments. Society is a result, then, of its boundaries, of what it will and won't allow. Shame, guilt, embarrassment, are controlling feelings that arise from "speaking the unspeakable" and violating cultural taboos. (p. 172)

Television, of course, is one of the main sources of cultural scripts for many people, including impressionable children and adolescents. And the scripts they are acquiring from the daytime talk shows in particular raise disturbing questions for parents and other adults charged with the task of inculcating a sense of moral restraint and balance among the young. As Abt and Seesholtz note, the most troubling aspect of presenting people who exhibit no shame in "sharing" their most intimate thoughts and desires—which often run counter to socially desired values of caring, concern, empathy for others, and a broader understanding of community—is that the hosts make no attempt to locate the narratives within a broader perspective or to suggest alternative viewpoints that challenge the speakers' comments. A case in point they cited was an episode on "The Phil Donahue Show" where the guest was a woman who had married her son's 14-year-old friend:

> The audience failed to comment on the boy/husband's dropping out of school, the couple's dependence on welfare, the boy/husband's threatening of his parents with violence if they didn't sign the permission form, as well as the boy/husband's wearing of a swastika on a torn t-shirt. At one point the boy/husband did say he "liked the way it looked," otherwise it had no meaning for him. (p. 181)

Hearing about accounts like these, we are reminded of the lines from Yeats's famous poem, "The Second Coming": "Things fall apart, the center cannot hold, mere anarchy is loosed upon the world. . . . The best lack all conviction, while the worst are full of passionate intensity" (Finneran, 1989, p. 187). How are parents and caretakers within the community to locate a moral center for children when there is no public condemnation of behavior like this?

Moral Convictions and Public Discourse

Clearly, television talk shows cannot be held solely accountable for the problem of moral relativism that prevails in today's culture. A few strong voices who speak with conviction can challenge the existing social order, as history has proven, but taking such an action entails a detailed understanding of where one is positioned. One difficulty liberals find in raising a dialogue about these issues is that too often they lack the courage of their convictions, and they are too aware of the shifting moral ground inherent in relativistic positions. In contrast, conservatives are unafraid to state strong opinions because they are convinced they are right, a justification that often stems from an adherence to a biblical code of morality. Liberals shrink from advocating a powerful role for government in creating policies that contribute to the public welfare, while conservatives, who once believed that government intrusion into an individual's private affairs was unwarranted, now want government to legislate aspects of private behavior in order to restore a sense of moral community. The irony is that these positions are almost a mirror reversal of previous public discourse, where, as Sandel (1996) noted, "From the Progressive era to the New Deal to the Great Society, American liberalism sought to cultivate a deeper sense of national community and civic engagement," and that now "it is conservatives, rather than liberals, who speak most explicitly of citizenship, community, and the moral prerequisites of a shared public life" (p. 38). Yet in many sites we discovered that the opposition to having health services available in schools was more imagined than real, while the children's needs were so much greater than one would suspect from the outside. Why, then, were people who were so committed to attending to these needs so unwilling to defend the clinics against the critics, apart from risking the chance that the clinics would be closed?

The reasons are complex, a meshing of philosophical values with self-interest. One reason we believe many school personnel were reluctant to take a more public stance was because they experienced a crisis of belief with respect to the realities of the daily lives of the children whom they served. They bought into the fashionable perspective of multiple values, which holds that no one set of beliefs about moral behaviors is privileged over another. The idea that certain practices detrimental to children's welfare cannot be openly addressed without infringing on parental rights or community values, or raising the specter of class- and race-based biases, has taken strong root in the mainstream culture, which in turn has contributed to what Himmelfarb (1994) has called the "demoralization of society":

Most of us are uncomfortable with the idea of making moral judgments, even in our private lives, let alone with the "intrusion" as we say,
of moral judgments into public affairs. We are uncomfortable not only
because we have come to feel that we have no right to make such judgments and impose them on others, but because we have no confidence
in the judgments themselves, no assurance that our principles are true
and right for us let alone for others. We are constantly beseeched to be
"nonjudgmental," to be wary of crediting our beliefs with any greater
validity than anyone else's, to be conscious of how "Eurocentric" and
"culture bound" we are. (p. 21)

But in all fairness to school health personnel, there were good reasons for them to believe that speaking out on these contested issues would
only bring public condemnation. All they had to do was look at how even
powerful public figures faced strident opposition when they spoke openly
about sexual matters that the general public was unwilling to acknowledge. The best example is the case of Joycelyn Elders, the former surgeon
general, who was not afraid to state her liberal views on adolescent sexuality, especially the idea that masturbation was the best means of dealing
with sexual impulses because it was safe, with no risk of STDs or pregnancy, and who paid a steep price in terms of her dismissal from office.
The project staff had to weigh the painful dilemma of hiding their true
views (many of the nurses admitted to us that they knew they weren't
giving the students sufficient information on which to make decisions
about sexual matters) against that of losing their jobs and, consequently,
any chance of reaching the students at all. Like Elders, many of the project personnel's position on the politics of health collided with the politics
of sex, but the spate of statistics on the decline in children's welfare suggests that we can no longer afford what Silin (1995) called the "passion
for ignorance." The reality of human nature, however, is that we cannot
expect people in public service to break their silence about what they
observe and what needs to be done to deal with the problems they encounter unless the general community is willing to support them.

Public Intellectuals and Practical Politics

In this chapter we examined the different discourses that were
voiced throughout the case studies based on Gee's (1991) notion that discourses are "ways of being in the world" (p. 142). We subscribe to Sapir's
(1970) idea that language use constitutes a kind of social reality, in that
the way in which people talk about their actions and roles reflects to some
extent how they behave in the world and view their position in it. Gee
(1991) noted that "social reality" refers to the "ever multiple and chang-

ing, and ever 'contestable' ways we humans have of 'acting out' our relationships to each other, whether in classrooms or communities or whole societies" (p. 9). In his view, one that we share, changing the world implies a need for a change in the way that people talk about current issues and problems, because it is through discourse that people become inspired or find the will to alter conditions that can no longer be tolerated.

We suggest that the time has now come to develop a different kind of public discourse about how best to meet the needs of children in our society. We argue that it is the role of public intellectuals to lead a conversation with all concerned parties about exploring ways to reconcile the issues we have raised in this chapter. The recent return of the public intellectual among the African-American intelligentsia has focused new attention on the question: What is a public intellectual? We believe such individuals to be people who recognize that the perceived contradictions between reason and passion are false dichotomies and that a search for rational solutions to pressing social problems can be pursued within a framework of commitment to the public good and caring for those in need. In the same vein, Vaclev Havel suggested that public intellectuals have a responsibility to speak out about issues of social justice and equity. He cautioned, however, against intellectuals who champion models that espouse holistic social engineering or who presuppose that a single model can explain all circumstances. Instead, he used the term *intellectuals* in the sense that these people would act as the "conscience of society" because they are able to see the interconnections among competing interests. He also argued that they should also become involved in public policy debates because "the more such people engage directly in practical politics, the better our world will be" (Havel, 1995, p. 37).

In the next chapter we take seriously Havel's admonition to become involved in these policy debates by sketching out a framework that balances children's needs with that of the public interest not to find solutions only in the infusion of more public funds into programs that have yet to document their worth. In a sense, this framework addresses a paradoxical challenge: how to ensure that children's needs will be cared for as part of a civic and government commitment, yet to instill a sense of individual and community responsibility for meeting these needs at the local level. We are concerned about breaking down the binary oppositions that have polarized the political discourse without losing the center. We argue that the center will hold if there is a genuine willingness on the part of all stakeholders to acknowledge that a society that does not care for its young is a society that truly has lost its moral compass.

Chapter 7

Imagining the Future

MAKING POLITICS WORK FOR CHILDREN

> Imagination is the power that enables us to perceive the normal
> in the abnormal, the opposite of chaos in chaos.
> —Wallace Stevens, *The Necessary Angel*

Threading our way through the multiple discourses that currently frame individual and institutional responses to the needs of children, we were struck repeatedly by the gap between the compassion most adults express for children and the miserable conditions in which so many children live; between the high levels of professional competence manifested by teachers, nurses, and administrators and the inability to translate the competence into dramatic improvements in children's lives; and between the resources deployed and the lack of demonstrable impact of the resources. We were impressed repeatedly by the determination in the voices of those involved in the projects under study to make these programs work for children. And yet, the many voices we heard seemed to be caught unwittingly in multiple discourses whose contradictions and limited vistas fell short of producing a unified vision or sustained course of action, one capable of breaking through the obstacles limiting these children's futures.

RECONCILING DISCOURSES

We argue that if the conditions of children are to be restored to a level that is consistent with the ideals of a just and democratic society, a critical set of preconditions must be met: a reconciliation of diverse discourses that honors compassion and consequences as well as rights and responsibilities; a public policy framework that respects diversity and strengthens community; a rethinking of the strengths and limitations of current institutions and the professionals who serve children; and the establishment of a system of accountability designed to improve children's and families' well-being.

What is needed is restoration of a public discourse in which people who believe that government and public institutions should ensure equality of services for the public good can articulate their viewpoint without denigrating the beliefs of those who believe strongly in individual responsibility and moral commitment. Such a discourse would merge the language of liberal perspectives on economics and government with that of conservatism's emphases on moral values, individual responsibility, and public accountability. Hunter (1991) suggested that the opposing strains of progressivism and conservatism could be reconciled on the basis of four premises: (1) a change in the environment of public discourse to allow for a more thoughtful and reasoned debate of issues; (2) a rejection by all factions of the impulses of public quiescence—for conservatives, a rejection of private resignation and for progressives, a rejection of radical subjectivism; (3) a recognition of the "sacred" within different moral communities, and a search for consensus on what constitute vital threats to a community's well being; and (4) a recognition of the inherent weaknesses, even dangers, in each side's moral commitments—for progressives, the inability to articulate issues of moral conviction in everyday discourse and for conservatives, an eagerness to set moral limits.

Finding Common Ground

One potent source for constructing a reasoned public discourse can be found in recent scholarship on Dewey's philosophy of American liberalism. As Michael Sandel (1996) noted in a recent book review of a new book, *John Dewey and the High Tide of American Liberalism:*

> The great service of Ryan's book is to remind us that liberalism was not always reluctant to speak the language of morality, community, and religion. "Deweyan liberalism," he writes, "is different. It is a genuine liberalism, unequivocally committed to progress and the expansion of human tastes, needs, and interests. . . . Nonetheless, it comes complete with a contentious view of what constitutes a good life; it takes sides on questions of religion, and it is not obsessed with the defense of rights. . . . The individual it celebrates is someone who is thoroughly engaged with his or her work, family, local community and its politics, who has not been coerced, bullied, or dragged into these interests but sees them as fields for a self-expression quite consistent with losing himself or herself in the task at hand." (p. 38)

Another source is the work by Haber (1994), who suggested that formulating a political position beyond postmodern politics entailed rethinking the relationship between the individual and the community. She proposed the concept of "subject-in-community" as a way of acknowledging the fact that people don't exist as autonomous individual selves, but always in relation to a defined community, and that multiple relations are possible. People's identities are formed within communities of similar interests and, for her, "a viable politics is one that can accommodate difference" (1994, p. 4). She further noted that:

> The more different community alignments are explored, the more problems concerning identities and goals are discovered. Sure. But the process of resistance is begun; those community/identity interests are no longer silent. They too are made part of the debates about rights, justice, and respect, and they therefore open new life possibilities. (p. 122)

Concern for Children: A Catalyst for Redefining Community

Increasingly, advocates at both ends of the spectrum are realizing that the rigid ideological and political stances of the contemporary cultures' wars are becoming impediments to pursuing the very courses of actions they are advocating. And more than anything else, concern for children's welfare is emerging as a unifying theme that holds the promise of moving public discourse beyond its current ideological impasse and opening the way for the crafting of a new kind of community of ideas and of people. In June 1996, for example, a rally for children held in Washington, D.C., attracted thousands of participants from a broad coalition of social and religious organizations. Friedan (1996) noted the emergence of a new paradigm, whose unifying construct is concern for children:

> The old paradigm of "identity politics"—a rights-based focus on narrowly defined grievances and goals—has increasingly shown its limitations. A future of separate and warring races, genders, and generations is in no one's interests. In seminars and schools, in community centers and union halls, in churches and the offices of public spirited businesses, a new paradigm has been quietly taking shape. Perhaps its strongest unifying theme is a concern for children, who represent not only the greatest vulnerabilities of our institutions but also the future of those institutions. (p. 6)

One critical element is that children have to be conceived of as an integral part of rebuilding democratic communities, ones where people share a common association and promote moral discourse and full participation of citizens in a variety of settings. Bellah, Madsen, Sullivan, Swidler, and Tipton (1985) referred to these kinds of communities as "communities of memory":

> The communities of memory that tie us to the past also turn us toward the future as communities of hope. They carry a context of meaning that can allow us to connect our aspirations for ourselves and those closest with us to the aspirations of a larger whole, and see our own efforts as being, in part, contributions to a common good. (p. 153)

The concept of "communities of memory" is of critical conceptual importance in suggesting a means to bridge the past with the future, affirming that the past, even if traditional and conventional by contemporary standards, must be reconciled with the future, no matter how progressive, in order to build connections among people and across time. A century earlier Alexis de Tocqueville (1899) wrestled with the same themes of changes and continuity, of private and civic virtue, as he tried to untangle the relationships between community and democratic governance. In his observation of nineteenth-century American life, he realized that the uniquely American predilection to band together in communities of like interest was a necessary correlate to democracy, a means to combat the otherwise unchecked individualism that democracy encourages. Tocqueville's observations of American life led him to the central import of "association" in developing caring human beings. In analyzing Tocqueville's observations, Berkowitz (1996) sums up his insight on human *association:*

> Associational life shifts the gaze of individuals away from themselves toward others; it generates in each an awareness of the needs and the limitations of others; it enlarges self-interest narrowly conceived by making vivid the private advantage that flows from cooperation for the public good; and it teaches the habits of cooperation and self-restraint by giving individuals regular opportunities to practice them. (p. 46)

For Tocqueville the American predilection for association or community was not just a good in and of itself but reflected, or derived from, fundamental traits of character, such as self-restraint and economy, which were aggressively fostered within the family and in certain Protestant religious beliefs and practices (Berkowitz, 1996). The triad of family, religion, and community formed a mutually reinforcing phalanx of values and personal traits that rooted individuals in their collective past and bound them together in their aspirations for the future.

However, contemporary public discourse consistently fails to recognize their importance. Given this, a recent study (Putnam, 1995) cites disturbing evidence that contemporary Americans are associating less— that they are living in self-imposed physical and psychological isolation from one another—and raises critical questions about how connections among individuals within families and across groups can be established and sustained in the absence of these connections. Modern-day public discourse, particularly in contemporary liberalism, is uncomfortable broaching traditional notions of religion as a medium for the teaching of virtues such as restraint and forbearance and for traditional notions of the family as the soil in which these and other civic virtues are fostered.

The appeal to "reason" as the only criterion for validity in public discourse has pushed questions of the metaphysical origins of morality outside of the parameters of acceptable public discourse. To invoke religious precepts in public discourse is considered an abridgment of the country's insistent separation of government and religion, even though, as Tocqueville realized, much of the individual behavior necessary to cultivate a healthy polity, such as perseverance and self-restraint, was fostered in individuals by religious teachings (Berkowitz, 1996). Liberals' insistence that the impact of large-scale social and economic dislocations on affected communities be recognized and their desire to avoid blaming the victims has led them to undervalue the importance of family and family cohesion in strengthening individuals and in promoting and developing "communities of memory" (Kamarck & Gaston, 1990). The family has suffered greatly in esteem from other societal trends in this century as well. In many respects, this primal locus of connection, identity, and "memory" has been replaced by the individual. The Freudian notion that individual pathology resides in the family and in interfamily relations has come to dominate commonplace understandings through its rapid popularization in the mass media (Pipher, 1996; Skolnick, 1991). The tendency to see the family as harmful as well as helpful was also exacerbated by feminists who branded the family as a locus of patriarchal oppression (Skolnick, 1991). The marking of the family as a source of individual pathology has discredited previous notions of the family as a place in which self-discipline and the virtues of selflessness and responsibility are fostered. Elkind (1995) noted that one defining characteristic of the postmodern family is that of autonomy, "whereby each family member pursues his or her own interests and puts these interests before those of the family" (p. 13). Instead of a setting where the boundaries between family and the outside world are clearly marked, we now have "permeable" homes where all information is disseminated to all members through electronic means, with few of the traditional filters imposed by parents in protecting their children from unseemly information.

Contemporary understanding of the relationship between the adolescent and the family have, in particular, underscored the importance for the adolescent of separating from the family as a necessary step in the passage to adulthood. The widely agreed-upon notion that adolescence is a time in which the emerging adult searches for and constructs an individual identity (Erikson, 1963) is often confused with the concept that adolescence is inescapably a time of stormy relations between teenager and parent, suggesting that identity can only be developed in conflictual reaction to the parent. This view gained widespread public acceptance in large part due to its forceful articulation by the psychologist Stanley Hall in a 1904 publication. Yet as many scholars have since shown, research does not bear this out (Esman, 1990). For example, Asian youth development is not marked by this period of hostility or anger. Pipher (1996), in a critique of the mental health community, notes:

> In the past when therapists saw troubled teenagers, they could generally assume that the parents had problems. That's because most teenagers were fine. Troubled teens were an exception and required some explaining. Today most teenagers are not fine. At one time we [therapists] helped kids differentiate from enmeshed families. Now we need to help families differentiate from the culture. President Clinton said that "governments don't raise children, parents raise children." But, especially with adolescents, communities raise children and electronic communities are doing a horrible job. Our culture of consumption has thoroughly confused most people about how to live in families. We live in the United States of Advertising and many therapists have inadvertently played a part in the spread of existential flu. Advertisers and pop psychology dovetail to produce a certain kind of adult—one who is shallow, self-absorbed, concerned about inadequacies. Popular psychology has implied that if one's intimate relationships are in order, life will be fine. But the situation is more complex than that. People cannot be whole and healthy unless they connect their lives to something larger than their own personal happiness. (pp. 31–32)

It is our contention that the revitalization of civic life and the development of mutual responsibility require the nourishing of the mediating institutions of religion, family, and community. The link between responsible individual and civic betterment resides to a large degree in these institutions.

As Himmelfarb points out, revitalization of democratic communities goes hand in hand with a restoration of the concept of the "responsible self." The social paradox is that you help yourself through service and contributions to the larger community. Our concept of the responsible self parallels the Victorian ethos of "self-help" that prevailed in the late nineteenth century, as described by Himmelfarb (1994):

> For the Victorians, the individual, or "self" was the ally rather than the adversary of society. Self-help was seen in the context of the community

as well as the family; among the working classes this was reflected in the virtue of "neighborliness," among the middle classes of philanthropy. Self-interest stood not in opposition to the general interest, but as Adam Smith had it, as the instrument of the general interest. Self-discipline and self-control were thought of as the source of self-respect and self-betterment, and self-respect as the precondition for the respect and approbation of others. The individual, in short, was assumed to have responsibilities as well as rights, duties as well as privileges. (p. 43)

Finally, the restoration of communities committed to caring for children requires a willingness among all groups to relinquish control over private agendas that conflict with the greater public good. Too often in the translation of public concern for children to public policy enactment, discussion of what is best for children degenerates into a debate over "who controls," not "what works." For example, even if sexuality education "worked" to reduce pregnancy, the conservative right might still reject it because the real issue is "control." Likewise, even if a religiously based abstinence program "worked," liberals might reject it because it violates the principle of separation of government and religion.

Public discourse has to expand beyond currently conflicting notion of individual rights versus community well-being. While, unquestionably, a cultural divide exists in this nation, there are common agendas across the liberal and conservative spectrum—things like safe streets, good schools, strong families, and caring communities, which are valued by all. Where we can bridge the divide, we should. Where we cannot, we must create places for honest, intense, and respectful debate. These public exercises in community understanding, in turn, will provide a foundation for community building that honors the sanctity of children and recognizes their centrality in democratic communities.

CREATING PUBLIC POLICY INITIATIVES

In investigating how one state and its citizens approached the problem of teenage pregnancy, we found enormous concern for children and widespread conflict about how to proceed. There was virtual unanimity in deploring the corrosive impact of too-early pregnancies on the lives of the parents and the babies and on the communities in general. At the same time, there were bitter differences over what programmatic strategies to pursue, one group's solution being the other group's problem. This forced the questions: Is there a community of interest around the issues of adolescent sexuality and the role of public schools? Are there shared foundational beliefs upon which to build community and to achieve reconciliation without denying differences? Can divided communities of interest be transformed into communities of caring?

In creating and funding the Florida Supplemental School Health Program, state policy makers tried to push beyond the disabling dichotomies of the ideological warfare through deploying a strategy of decentralization. The program was explicitly designed to maximize local discretion, based on the belief that issues of adolescent health and sexuality were so personal in nature, so intimately connected to religious and philosophical beliefs, and so contentious that they should not be subjected to a uniform policy design. In many respects, these assumptions were valid and the decentralized approach was one of the indisputable strengths of the program. By establishing the goals of the program as remarkably broad (reducing teenage pregnancy and promoting student health), by allowing local participants to select from established delivery models or design their own, by allowing funds to be used for objectives as loosely defined as "increase student self-esteem," and by permitting a wide variety of professional services, the state tried to create a program field in which a wide variety of services could be delivered, thus allowing for a matching of programs with the needs, preferences, and beliefs of diverse communities around the state.

But there were a number of assumptions behind the decentralized approach that were not sufficiently explored. The state clearly felt that consensus around the role of schools in addressing the "new morbidities" could be more easily achieved at lower governmental levels. School districts and schools, encompassing smaller jurisdictions and fewer people, would more easily find common ground by which to forge effective prevention and intervention strategies. In other words, the assumption among state policy makers was that both community and consensus would be found at the local level. However, in a stinging rejection of these assumptions, we did not find this to be the case at all. To the contrary, we found an overwhelming heterogeneity at all, even the lowest, levels. Religious, cultural, racial, and linguistic heterogeneity was the norm, not the exception. In other words, even at the school or neighborhood level, we found strikingly divergent communities of interests that cut wide swaths across neighborhoods and school communities and defied consensus.

How Divided Is the Public?

In 1994, Public Agenda, a nonpartisan, nonprofit research and education organization, developed and conducted an opinion research project to explore the public's perspective on these issues. The research focused specifically on controversies causing turmoil in school districts across the country, such as proposals to raise academic standards, establish learning goals, and reform curriculum and assessment; disputes over sex education; and, arching over all these subjects, questions of who should control the information presented to young people in public schools—teachers, administrators, state legislators, parents, or community representatives? The findings both confirmed a number of the findings of our own research as well as suggested a way to push past the divisions that, at times, seem beyond reconciliation.

On the one hand, the public opinion data found Americans sharply polarized in a number of areas regarding sex education and the role of schools in teaching about sexuality. At the same time, it affirmed a stronger unanimity on bedrock values critical to social justice and democratic governance. The study reported that, in general, Americans accept sex education and support a strong role for public schools in teaching students about human sexuality. Few Americans, only 14% according to the study, feel schools spend too much time on sex education, and a majority of Americans want sex education to begin by sixth grade. Ninety-five percent say the teaching of the biology of sex and pregnancy is an appropriate area for public schools, and 78% would start before high school. An even higher number (97%) say the schools should teach students about the dangers of sexually transmitted diseases, including AIDS, with 86% wanting this to begin before high school.

Consensus is strong in the general area of need for sexuality education. Division appears, however, on details and specifics. In fact, sex education was the area that resulted in the most dichotomized opinions in all the areas queried. And the divisions were sharp, suggesting that beliefs are strong and would not be easily swayed. The authors of the study report:

> Despite the consensus that schools should play an important role in sex education, it is the most divisive issue examined in this study. Americans have important disagreements about exactly what should be taught, when it should be taught, how it should be taught, and the degree to which moral judgments should play a part. Large numbers of Americans place themselves squarely in "for" or "against" categories, not in the middle, whenever they are asked about some especially candid sex and AIDS education practices—or those that suggest moral neutrality about premarital or homosexual sex. For example, 31% of Americans want the schools to teach that sex before marriage is *always wrong*, a message that receives their highest possible rating for appropriateness. But 22% say this is "not at all appropriate." In other words, more than half of Americans place themselves squarely at the extreme

ends of the scale. Similarly, 32% of Americans are comfortable with sex education textbooks that feature "nude photos of men and women showing their sexual organs," even before high school, but 34% think this is "never appropriate." Twenty-eight percent think it is appropriate for schools to discuss homosexuality as an acceptable lifestyle, even before high school, but 37% think this is "never appropriate." There is even strong disagreement about appropriate behavior at school: 36% "strongly favor" the idea of "banning hugging and kissing between students on school groups," but 19% "strongly oppose" such a ban. Fifty-six percent of Americans feel "using models of nude men and women to demonstrate the correct use of condoms and diaphragms" is appropriate, while 41% say this is "never appropriate." Fifty-five percent believe it is appropriate to allow schools to distribute condoms to students, while 43% oppose it; and 51% support allowing schools to supply students with telephone numbers of gay support groups, while 46% oppose it. A related area of disagreement concerns the age at which sex education is appropriate. Overall and not surprisingly, people feel more comfortable about sex education for older students. Only 21% support making condoms available to middle school students, as opposed to 55% who would allow high schools to distribute condoms. And while only 19% support the idea of allowing schools to give out the telephone numbers of homosexual support groups to elementary or middle school students, about half (51%) supports this idea for high schoolers. (Johnson & Immerwahr, 1994, pp. 27–28)

The researchers also noted that though geographic residence and religion are both clearly factors influencing opinions, neither are determining factors. Based on focus group discussions, they conclude that "for some Americans, discomfort with more explicit sex education does not stem primarily from moral or religious convictions, but rather from the sense that sexuality should be a private matter, not one for routine public discussion" (p. 30).

The authors stress the intensity of disputes on these issues and the potential for such disputes to intensify and amplify other, perhaps, latent areas of disagreement within a community and school setting. In particular, they note that people without children in the public schools were less supportive in general of frankness in sex education and that these issues attract press attention and the attention of people who do not normally pay that much attention to the public school issues. But the authors also suggest a way to bridge these divisions:

Perhaps the only solace this study offers educational leaders is the remarkable ability of individuals in focus groups—typical parents from all walks of life—to express conflicting viewpoints without rancor. People also seemed to desire, among themselves at least, to find some areas of agreement, or at least, to agree on reasonable mechanisms for making a decision. (Johnson & Immerwahr, 1994, p. 30)

These sentiments are reflected in other findings from public opinion research. An overwhelming majority of Americans—across geographic and demographic lines—believe it is "highly appropriate" for public schools to teach an inner circle of consensus values. And these are the very values critical to achieving harmony in the public arena: tolerance and equity. Johnson and Immerwahr (1994) report:

> People want schools to teach values, but they especially want schools to emphasize those values that allow a diverse society to live together peacefully. The public's lack of concern about "values issues" as defined by the press and leadership does not mean that Americans endorse a public school education that is value-neutral or makes no judgments about moral behavior. There is a circle of broadly agreed upon values people expect the schools both to teach directly and to reinforce by example. And there are some "lessons" that most Americans believe are not the business of the public schools—those that seem strident to people and aimed at dividing them, rather than helping them live together in harmony. The public's concerns about tolerance and equality extend beyond selection of textbooks and development of curricula and lesson plans. People expect the schools to enforce certain minimum standards of fair treatment for all children. Study participants were presented with this scenario: "If a teacher passes a group of students in a public school playground who are teasing another child about his race, should the teacher: A) let the students work it out themselves; B) break up the situation; or C) break up the situation and emphasize that teasing about race is wrong?" Ninety percent of Americans—across all geographic and demographic lines—want the teacher not only to break up the situation, but to explain that the behavior is wrong (Option C). Eighty-six percent would expect the same reaction if the child were being teased about religion. More than seven in ten (72%) would expect the same reaction if the child were being teased because a parent is homosexual; in this case, however, another 18% would have the teacher break up the situation, but not discuss the reason at length. (p. 24)

Their findings suggest that arching over the discord present in issues surrounding sex education—the age at which to introduce information on human sexuality and where to draw lines between public and domestic arenas of control—is a strong desire for harmony and peace in social relations. The report continues:

> The findings—strongly endorsing the teaching of "respect" for others and rejecting more contentious messages—suggest among the general public a longing for harmony and civility and some desire to put discord in the past. The public school system has played a historic role in enabling diverse Americans to learn about each other, and live together without bloodshed—a goal that many other nations have not been able to achieve. During the 1950s and 1960s, the public schools became the symbol of the nation's moral judgment that African-Americans and white Americans should live together in equality. Few would argue that the United States has lived up to all its goals, and it is indisputable that prejudice, anger, misunderstanding, and distrust continue to divide the country along racial and ethnic lines. Regardless of these failures, the vast majority of Americans accept the goal, and they want the public schools to play a central role in passing that goal along to their children. (Johnson & Immerwahr, 1994, p. 25)

Drawing on our own research, current thinking in both academic and public policy circles, and public opinion data, we suggest a policy framework to help create democratic communities with children at their center.

Creating Better Public Policies

The design of the Florida Supplemental School Health Program divided roles and responsibilities among the levels of governmental actors: the state, the school district and the schools, and the local county public health units. The divisions appeared to follow most of the best thinking on effective policy design. That is to say, the state's role was specific but limited: a stable and significant funding source; broad goal articulation; requirements for evidence of need, will, and capacity at the local level; evidence of willingness to cooperate across agencies and mandated statewide evaluation after two years. Locals were given considerable discretion in how they might choose to deploy their resources, in how to align this program with other existing programs, in staffing decisions and in prioritizing of state goals with particular, local objectives.

As seen in the middle chapters, we found that many of the design elements did seem to be effective, bearing out the validity of what many advocates of comprehensive children's service advocates have been saying for almost 30 years now: A deregulatory structure can prove to be sound and supportive. We found local discretion being used wisely and with ingenuity. We found no examples of abuse of state flexibility or of goal displacement. We found considerable programmatic distinctiveness, most of which seemed to be reasonable and productive adaptations to local contexts. We found that the state was able to maintain a supportive but not intrusive presence while assuring a steady source of funds.

At the same time, the flexibility designed into the program did not appear to be anywhere near fully exploited. Even though it was well understood that the students' risk-taking behaviors stemmed from a complex brew of psychosocial, cultural, and economic forces, educators and health professionals appeared reluctant to reach beyond their respective professional areas and institutional boundaries or to engage with other community and family members whose influence in the students' lives was great. In other words, the policy design, which was considered enlightened and "correct" in its recognition of the important limitations on having higher levels of government impose solutions on lower levels, failed to question whether the local governments receiving the flexibility had either the capacity or the desire to exploit it. The state acted somewhat naively in assuming that simply allowing discretion would be sufficient. There was a failure to recognize that regulation was only one and probably not the largest impediment to improved programming.

What we found to be the largest impediment was a crippling dependency on consensus prior to taking actions. This dependency was a potent, almost paralyzing, counterweight to developing programming powerful enough to achieve its objectives and to extra-institutional experimentation and exploration; it was also supported by powerful professional and institutional norms. As the public opinion data show, local strategies that depend on consensus to move forward will be severely compromised because the public is deeply divided on many of these issues. Repeatedly we found that the professionals in this program were effective and creative in finding programmatic strategies to achieve their objectives within the zone of consensus that they believed to exist in their communities, but they were extremely reluctant to probe beyond professionally sanctioned norms of conduct and to deal directly with the diversity of opinion that existed in their communities. As a result, the projects could be effective only in areas in which consensus existed.

The insistence on consensus, we believe, is part and parcel, both cause and effect, of the continued strength of the bureaucratic and professional models that dominate both education and health care in our country. The educational and health institutions, whether they were local schools or health clinics, were designed to buffer the professionals from lay influence. They were separate locales in which standards of conduct and programs were established and monitored by professional communities. Emerging from the progressive reforms of an earlier era, these models achieved remarkable success throughout most of this century in improving health care, delivering basic and advanced education, and improving the well-being of most Americans. We conclude, however, that these models have failed to adapt to a different set of challenges facing communities today. The bureaucratic and professional models assumed a lay consensus on basic strategies and goals and thus relied on uniform standards of professional conduct, bureaucratic institutional settings, and independence from lay involvement. These models proved remarkably effective over the last half-century for certain ends: providing basic education for virtually all students and eliminating the most menacing public health threats, such as contagious childhood diseases. They worked well because there was a tacit endorsement by the lay community that the values underlying the professional and institutional practices were consonant with the communities or when the problems required only technical solutions.

However, the very attributes that were determinants of success in the past become impediments when no community consensus exists or when the problems are socially constructed rather than technical. This is precisely the case in contemporary American communities and with the "new morbidities" of contemporary adolescents. Far from there being tacit community endorsement of professional approaches to preventing teenage pregnancies, opinions differ widely. James (1993), looking back into the formation of today's one-best-school system a century earlier, stresses that the reformers' ideas concerning effective organizational structures emphasized professional control and standardization, worked against nonprofessional or community-based leadership structures, and discredited attempts at local differentiation:

> The pattern of school governance that prevailed in American cities set maturing bureaucracies against innovative leadership developing from within the ranks and at the grass roots. It created organizational disincentives against encouraging the bubbling up of new ideas from the work force and local community. Perhaps most of all, this pattern removed effective bureaucratic control from schooling organizations at the community level and frustrated strategies of youth development attuned to local and culturally specific conditions. (p. 187)

The powerful institutional and professional norms that maintain the current organizational objectives and structures were based on "the dread unleashed by this nation's swift passage from traditional and agrarian communities to an industrial society" (James, 1993, p. 191). The *dread* was focused on:

> the behaviors that seem to tear at the most fundamental of societal values, as the young enter boldly and publicly into "adult" arenas of be-

havior: producing offspring; establishing commercial enterprises (often underground and crime linked); and defying schools by defacing and ignoring them. (James, 1993, p. 190)

It was fear that united mainstream political, professional, and philanthropic communities to develop a bureaucratic model that set high standards of professional conduct at the expense of lay influence and local control. Where we did find reaching out beyond institutional boundaries, it was primarily to other youth-serving organizations in the communities. Many have suggested that through forging alliances with the nonprofit volunteer sector in local communities, schools can magnify their effectiveness in serving young people. Heath and McLaughlin's (1993) work, particularly with community-based youth organizations, offers considerable promise. Unfortunately, James suggests that these agencies—even though much smaller and presumably more autonomous in organization and control—are subject to the same powerful institutional and professional norms that constrict the responsiveness of schools. He points in particular to the roles of charities and philanthropies in reinforcing social values identical to those that determine public schooling institutional character:

> A look back at youth organizations in this century reminds us that formal schooling and informal organizations for youth are interconnected agents of socialization. Out-of-school organizations cannot be treated merely as alternatives to dysfunctional schooling practices. They are part of a combined reality with mainstream institutions. To be understood in all their complexity, both must be viewed in their relation to institutional norms that neither school reformers nor those who offer alternatives through youth-serving organizations have managed to overcome. To help young people find some place for themselves in family, community, workplace, and public bureaucracies, youth organizations must reexamine the highly problematic but powerful nexus of institutional rules that supports or impedes the growth of particular types of organizations. (James, 1993, p. 191)

James's analysis of the similarity between formal schooling and community-based youth services organizations leads to his conclusion that a policy agenda for young people must reach beyond presumed synergies that can be sought in closer working relations between community-based organizations and schools and enter the realm of philosophy and ideology.

So once again we return to the question of values. The structures of both schooling and community youth organizations inherited from nineteenth-century reformers were based on the desire to curb adolescent risk-taking behaviors and placed strong emphasis on the values of social efficiency and administrative control, all of which demanded professional—not lay—control, standardized—not tailored—responses, and separate institutional settings. Change will require not just new organizational structures and professional norms but a honest confrontation with all members of a community and a reconstruction of authentic community. As James (1993) writes:

> Deep change requires a recasting of underlying categories, not just temporary new players among youth-serving organizations. That means more than restructured, high-performance grass-roots or local organizations to serve the young based on client or consumer preferences. The supreme task is to construct new values in the nation's public life, a phalanx of understanding robust enough to open the way for democratic, collective action unmediated by present institutional norms that govern social service for the young. (p. 191)

Professional and Institutional Reengagement with Community

We agree with James that the "supreme task" is the construction of new values—values that derive from the students', the parents', and other citizens' understanding of the world and their place in it. The task of construction requires open acknowledgment of differences in fundamental values and recognition that certain religious beliefs, family practices, and social arrangements are not amenable to professional solutions. What is needed from professionals is a willingness to concede moral, religious, and ideological legitimacy to parents and other community members and to construct programs, approaches, and strategies that build upon an assumption of ideological diversity. There must be a willingness to concede moral authority to private, community-based groups and to support them in or elicit from them programmatic content and strategies. This is not an abdication of professional standards, competence, or responsibility but a redefinition of them and a rethinking of their fundamental sources of authority—legal and moral. Sarason (1995), in his essay on parental involvement in schools, insists upon the radicality of the notion that parents' values must be a factor in determining institutional practice. He formulates a seemingly simple political principle but one whose implications are radical. "When you are going to be affected, directly or indirectly, by a decision, you should stand in some relationship to the decision making process" (p. 5). This is not, he repeats, a technical shift in responsibility but an absolute redistribution of power based on a change in the source of legitimacy.

In our study, we found creative responses within the profession's traditional view of its role, but we did not find activities in the community arena that were as creative or as clever, actions which at their heart are more political than professional; their lack, we feel, retarded the impact of the programs. For example, reaching out to different constituencies in the community—not so much drawing them into a preset agenda but trying to understand what their agenda was and trying to respond in differentiated and tailored ways. Because the state did not work through or find a successful accommodation to the deep ideological cleavages that exist around teenage sexual activity and the role of the schools, these issues remained to be dealt with at the local level. We found the health educators, administrators, and teachers struggling to balance their control function with the service mandate. These are political issues, which most professionals are loathe to get involved in. The walls that professionals have successfully erected around themselves and the distance they have kept from those they are committed to serve—their disdain of things political—make them ill equipped to deal with the value-laden realities these program confront daily.

Some scholars question whether modern bureaucracies, no matter how reformed or reinvented, are capable of fulfilling a mandate to serve. McKnight (1995), in *The Careless Society: Community and Its Counterfeits*, pulls no punches: "Service systems can never be reformed so they will 'produce' care. Care is the consenting commitment of citizens to one another. Care cannot be produced, provided, managed, organized, administered or commodified. Care is the only thing a system cannot produce" (p. x).

In sharp contrast to this view, several educational scholars have challenged the view that bureaucratic structures, especially schools, cannot care for students by providing services on-site that meet their educational and social needs. Nel Noddings (1984, 1995a, 1995b) suggested that schools should not be considered only as places where children achieve high educational standards, but as places where they acquire an understanding of their role in society. As she put it:

> Our society does not need to make its children first in the world in mathematics and science. It needs to care for its children—to reduce violence, to respect honest work of every kind, to reward excellence at every level, to ensure a place for every child and emerging adult in the economic and social world, to produce people who can care competently for their own families and contribute effectively to their communities. (1995a, p. 366)

In a similar vein, Jane Roland Martin (1995) noted that schools should become the "moral equivalent of home," in the sense that schools share responsibilities with parents for imparting basic values and creating a curriculum that integrates academic tasks with life functions. Finally, Epstein (1995) argued forcefully that the creation of school/family/community partnerships is necessary in a society undergoing rapid change where children's needs are given short shrift. Mindful of the need to recognize and respond to local and regional differences, she established a framework of six kinds of caring and involvement from which programs can be developed to meet community needs.

Like these scholars, we do not share McKnight's profound pessimism toward institutional capacity. We remain much too respectful of the remarkable advances in education and health produced this century by these very bureaucracies. And we remain in awe of the energy and commitment we found repeatedly as we visited the projects in our field visits. At the same time, we found the programming to be too limited by institutional and professional blindness.

The conditions we found facing health educators, teachers, and students served in the projects required multiple and multifocused responses. They required lateral and horizontal connections between school and community, while the bureaucracies in which they operate continued with hierarchical and across-the-board responses. We found the bureaucracies continuing to operate as if they had a monolithic purchase over the communities they served, ignoring the vast multiplication of activities and organizations in the nongovernmental arena.

No doubt, much of this hesitancy comes from the continued dominance of the direct-service orientation of both health and school educators. Human behavior is stressed to the relative neglect of theories of social behavior. We found the tools of community needs assessment, coalition building, and advocacy for children relatively untried in these programs. In a recent study of collaborative human service programs at the local level, Agranoff (1986) points out that because of increasing devolution of fiscal and regulatory responsibility to the lowest governmental levels and the requirements of multiple-agency involvement, front-line workers often end up with considerable managerial flexibility in how they go about designing, delivering, and collaborating in their programs.

We certainly found this to be the case with the Florida Supplemental School Health Program. Agranoff (1982) points out that in the interstices of the collaborative programs there are vast gray areas requiring interpretation, priority, and direction, and it is in these areas that the potential for creative, nonbureaucratic, and mutually beneficial solutions may be found. However, precisely because of this flexibility, much of what the program managers need to do to be successful is political, not professional or technical, in nature.

Social agencies and private organizations were not seeking out schools either. We found a void in connections with or the development of local quasi-political leadership structures around the broader needs of children, even though the necessity, the efficacy, and the feasibility of doing so have been repeatedly seen in research on the War on Poverty programs and restressed in 1990s versions of community development strategies. Growing demands exist for a more radical decentralization—a replacement of administrative elites not by a cadre of front-line workers but by the clients themselves. The only possible option in a highly diverse world is a system that is distributive, not centralized. However, the remarkable strength of the institutionalized resources of schools is needed, too—the staff, the facilities, the expertise. We agree with Heath and McLaughlin (1993) that some of the bureaucratic features of schools are critical attributes necessary for sustaining programs. These include facilities, staff development, and management information systems for tracking student progress and outcomes.

We conclude our analysis by arguing for a rethinking of the bureaucratic paradigm, acknowledging its strengths and its formidable record of accomplishment. But we join a host of other voices, who, as the twenty-first century approaches, are questioning how the public sector can best be organized and managed to provide better services and to improve democratic accountability. While we fall far short of recommending the abolition of public organizations, we recognize the limitations of current school organizational structures and the system of incentives to combat the threats facing many of our children and our communities. We look hopefully to some of the new public management concepts, such as quality management, customer focus, distributive information technologies, decentralized organizational structures, and privatization of some services. However, more importantly, we stress the need to reexamine the interaction among public-sector management, democracy, and politics. Regarding the stresses and controversies that arise from adolescent risk-taking behaviors and adults' reactions to them, public-sector responses will need to be developed within a democratic community setting.

RETHINKING ACCOUNTABILITY

Large-scale government programs, whether funded at the state or federal level, have had a checkered evaluation history. On the one hand, there is a legitimate concern for acquiring data that document to the taxpayers' satisfaction whether or not programs have made a difference. On the other hand, politicians have long been reluctant to use data as a primary determinant of whether to fund programs or not; instead, they have based their decisions primarily on the political muscle exhibited by the group (or groups) who would be the most affected by the loss of a particular program. In our case, our evaluation report was presented to the Florida legislature in 1993, yet almost none of our recommendations were heeded. While this is an old story in evaluation circles—the failure of policy makers to use empirical data for informed decisions—as we noted in Chapter 2, it cannot be attributed to the lack of stakeholder involvement. The real issue is the power of politicians who support or oppose funding programs that match their constituents' interests.

The Language of Power

Establishing accountability through a process that is meaningful and useful for all concerned stakeholders requires a rethinking of the issues raised in evaluating models where collaboration across groups is the norm. Knapp (1995, p. 7) listed some of the issues confronting researchers who evaluate comprehensive collaborative services for children and families: (1) engaging divergent participants' perspectives; (2) characterizing and measuring the elusive independent variable; (3) locating and measuring the bottom line; (4) attributing results to influences; and (5) studying sensitive processes and influences.

Nowhere were some of the issues Knapp raised more visible than in the preparation of the final evaluation report. In keeping with our belief that the stakeholders who had a major investment in the program's successful implementation should be consulted throughout the evaluation process, agency program personnel played a key role in shaping the structure of the final report. This belief is consistent with the utilization-focused approach we took in the design. While acknowledging the need to acquire data that are quantifiable, reliable, and valid, evaluators using this approach also recognize that a corresponding need exists to acquire information from stakeholders' and clients' viewpoints that is more qualitative in nature. The extensive evaluation and policy analysis literature also supports the proposition that a utilization-focused evaluation is enhanced by stakeholder involvement in, and commitment to, the evaluation process (Dawson & D'Amico, 1985; Drake, 1989; Mark & Shotland, 1985; Schensul, 1987; Siegel & Tuckel, 1985; van Willigen, Rylko-Bauer, & McElroy, 1989; Weiss, 1981).

Throughout the process of developing the final report, we learned to speak what has been called the "language of power" (Fetterman, 1993) to the various policy-making constituencies involved in the Supplemental School Health Program in Florida. As Fetterman (1993) noted:

> Policy making is fundamentally a political process in which research—ethnographic or otherwise—plays one part. The exchange of information, however, does not presuppose a substantial voice in policy decisions; it only ensures participation in the game. The insights and findings of the most capably conducted research are useless if researchers abdicate their responsibility and chose not to play in this game. (p. 164)

We chose to play on the terms established by agency program personnel, but we also maintained our ground on issues of data collection and analysis where we felt our expertise qualified us to determine the rules. The final document was a compromise between our needs to produce a study that met social science standards while still being sensitive to the stakeholders' concerns that the findings of the program evaluation could be used to marshal or deflect political support for continued funding.

Evaluators as Moral Agents

Evaluation has traditionally been conceived of as an activity that involves the dispassionate judgment of an external reviewer who provides an objective and rational assessment of a given program's merit and worth. The underlying assumption of this position has been that human affairs can be subjected to the same standards of scientific rationality that characterize practices in the natural sciences. Evaluators who violate this assumption by acknowledging their own values in relation to the program being evaluated run the risk of being perceived as too subjectively involved to render an impartial judgment. Values are seen as messy and confusing to the overall purpose of the evaluation, which is to determine (objectively, of course) the self-evident "facts" of how the program operated, independent of the context in which it was applied. And as for any moral judgments about whether the program served the interests of social justice, or whether benefits were equally distributed, or whether program funds could be better applied elsewhere, these are issues no evaluator wishes to acknowledge, except on those rare occasions when conversations are "off the record" and people are willing to admit their deep-seated concerns.

One intent of this book was to examine the risks and responsibilities inherent when evaluators relinquish an objective, noninvolved role for a more subjective, partisan role in an evaluation where issues of design, outcome indicators, and program recommendations are continually renegotiated throughout the process. Specifically, we raised questions as to how our personal and political commitments to specific social programs affected our judgments of them, and whether the interests of social justice can be served in promoting the interests of the clients for whom these programs were intended. Schwandt (1989) noted that evaluators should "recapture a moral discourse," a point of view shared by Ericson (1990), who suggested that evaluators have a moral obligation to consider the normative content of evaluation practice. These ideas are in line with the recent work of other theorists who have suggested that evaluation practices should reflect changes in philosophical orientations from a rationalist, utilitarian approach to a more humanistic, value-laden approach (Guba & Lincoln, 1989; Lincoln & Guba, 1985; Sirotnik, 1990; Stake, 1986). A similar point of view has been espoused by Noddings (1984) and Soltis (1989), who argue that ethical considerations should frame the choice of educational and social research problems. The position can be taken that social researchers have a responsibility to the larger public that cannot be evaded by simply appealing to abstract goals such as the pursuit of knowledge for its own sake (Emihovich, 1990). Those who conduct research within an evaluative context are obligated to consider the moral implications that their findings may carry for those who are affected by the program in question. Several minority researchers have gone even further by suggesting that social science researchers should assume part of the responsibility for enhancing the quality of people's lives through their work, a position that completely belies the concept of the disinterested scientist or evaluator (hooks & West, 1991; King & Mitchell, 1990).

We close this section with our belief that university-based researchers can play a valuable role in the process of establishing accountability by functioning as relatively unbiased outsiders. Although complete objectivity is not possible, since we bring our own agendas into the field, we can play the role of critical skeptics, people who have been educated to ask the hard questions. We chose to write this book because, in the words of David Fetterman (1993), a well-known ethnographic evaluator, "Researchers have a moral responsibility to serve as advocates—after the research has been conducted—if the findings merit it" (p. 162). One conclusion we reached from conducting the evaluation study in 1992 was that we could not maintain the ethical neutrality so highly prized in the social sciences in light of the overwhelming needs children had for services beyond what the program was able to deliver. As the paradigms for doing behavioral and social science research rapidly shift, it is axiomatic that the researcher's or evaluator's role will change as well. The idea that evaluators should become moral agents is admittedly a radical one, but the increasingly bleak conditions of marginalized people's lives, especially those who are poor and nonwhite, necessitate more radical actions than academic evaluators are often willing to admit. As the feminist Naomi Wolf (1993) described it:

> Radicalism is understanding the nature of discrimination, arming yourself with as much power as possible, and forcing unjust institutions to learn and legislate and change. A real radical does not stand in the margins admiring her own purity. Rather, she is a warrior to bring outsiders' views into the center, asking, How can my actions spark change for the good in the real lives of as many people as possible. (p. 115)

What we learned from the accountability process is that both educators and health care providers need to realize that there is no incompatibility between demonstrating caring, competency, and humanitarianism that is centered on children's welfare, and focusing on efficiency and demonstrable effectiveness. Ironically, the power of placing a greater emphasis on outcomes is that it returns professionals' attention to the important issue of community. Outcomes that measure client impact are fundamentally about a community's values and goals. Outcome measures without community consensus on goals are just numbers. Collaboration across agencies and across the whole community is essential for outcomes to have meaning. Outcomes are meaningless without being closely related to the goals that they measure. The goals, in turn, are meaningless unless they reflect a community's consensus developed by collaboration across agencies and neighborhoods (Gardner, 1994, p. 194).

IMAGINATION AND CHILDREN'S WELFARE

Imagining the future is a favorite theme for those interested in science fiction, and if popular culture is any guide, the overriding anxiety of the late twentieth century is that aliens will invade Earth and threaten the American way of life. We suspect that this anxiety about aliens attacking masks a more fundamental anxiety about the kind of society we envision for ourselves in the twenty-first century. Too little imagination is evidenced by too few policy makers in conceptualizing a future for children where poverty is eradicated, where schools are places that provide both a life-enhancing education as well as services that allow children and their parents to live lives of dignity and worth, where caring and concern for children's welfare are the values that define communities. In a provocative essay, the educational philosopher Maxine Greene argued persuasively that imagination plays a key role in promoting a dialogue about the possibilities inherent in the future. As Greene (1988) noted:

> Indeed, it takes imagination to bring people together in these times in speech and action, to provoke them to try to understand each other's perspectives, to tap into others' desires, even others' dreams. To me,

one of the possibilities (one of the imaginative possibilities before us) is that of drawing diverse people together to project, to reach out towards a more humane and fulfilling order of things. . . . Perhaps, if imaginative possibilities are made dramatically visible, more people may act together to repair certain of the reparable deficiencies, to do something about the flaws. In doing so they may create values in their own lives, make commitments that are new, invent ways of acting that may radiate through the community and beyond. (p. 55)

In the previous chapters of this book we presented evidence to suggest that in one sense we don't have to wait for aliens to arrive to destroy the world, because they have already arrived. Clearly, it is an alien impulse for people not to care for its young, since no society can survive far into the future when it sacrifices its young. If the struggle over scarce resources is cast only in political terms, children will be the losers since they don't vote, and the groups organized to serve their interests often do not know how to develop or maintain an effective lobbying force. Our purpose in writing this book was to draw public attention to these issues with the intent of contributing to the burgeoning national dialogue as to how they can best be resolved. Given the enormous wealth and resources available in this country, why can we not envision a better future for all children, and then take the necessary actions to ensure it? The question is one that all American citizens should ponder deeply.

Notes

CHAPTER 2

1. In the evaluation report we did standardize the data on project cost per student so that comparisons could be made across projects. Even just the descriptive data were very revealing, since the full-service school projects (which had the full array of professionals, including, in some places, a physician) had the highest cost per student when compared to projects that had a nurse and health aide. However, we also noted that one of the full-service school projects where the physician was able to write prescriptions for contraceptives at the school site had the most dramatic decrease in the number of pregnancies.

2. Our site visits validated the truth of this assumption. Schools that were not funded received constant pressure from parents to provide services, since they had heard about them from other parents, and it was one of the many public relations problems superintendents had to address in terms of how the project schools were selected. The concept of control, one derived from laboratory studies, falls apart in the field when indignant parents want to know why their children aren't receiving the same benefits.

3. Little did we know at the time how prophetic this statement was to become. Just before we sent out our surveys in March 1992, a major controversy erupted in one of the project areas we had selected in our random sample. One of the school districts had been using a sex education program known as Teen Aid, and the school staff had surveyed middle school students about their sexual behaviors (without securing parental permission) to determine if the program had had any impact in changing students' attitudes. Irate parents flooded the district office with calls, and the incident received so much negative publicity that we lost not only this county for our sample but five surrounding counties as well.

4. To their credit in terms of getting meaningful data, HRS and DOE personnel added questions on both issues to the survey that was sent to secondary students. They did so even though they knew they would take political heat from conservative school districts who would raise protests about these questions with their legislators.

5. Although HRS and DOE decided that creating their own survey questions would be more helpful, since they would specifically target relevant program aspects, the two surveys were modeled after the Florida Youth Risk Behavior Survey developed by the Centers for Disease Control (1992).

6. The statistical analysis of the survey data indicated that the students who engaged in high-risk behaviors (e.g., drug abuse, sexually active, considered suicide in the last 12 months) were also the most likely to visit the health rooms to

seek services. We concluded that "the linkage between at-risk students and health room utilization strongly suggests that the program services are reaching those students most in need of them" (Emihovich & Herrington, 1993, p. 75). It is not an entirely unwarranted assumption to believe that as a result of these visits, some students did change their behavior.

7. See Zabin and Hirsch (1988) for a detailed discussion of the problems of collecting pregnancy data in a school setting.

8. Before readers conclude this statement to be self-serving in that we were seeking another contract, we had already decided that we would not conduct a second evaluation if one had been proposed. This study consumed two years out of our professional lives from beginning to end, and given the demands of satisfying the key stakeholders' concerns at every step of the process, we felt everyone's interests would be better served if a new evaluation team was selected. When we returned to the field three years later as independent researchers, we learned that a new evaluation was underway that was being conducted by the University of South Florida, with a final report issued in the summer of 1995 (University of South Florida, 1995).

CHAPTER 3

1. The category "other" now included a growing population of Asian people, primarily Vietnamese, who came to work on the shrimp boats.

2. Two of the best beaches in the United States are located in a nearby county. The area also enjoys a mild climate year-round that is cooled by Gulf breezes; it has acquired a reputation as the "Redneck Riviera," since the tourists come primarily from southern Georgia and lower Alabama.

3. Within just our evaluation study, our statewide survey of schools involved in this program revealed that 33% of the middle school students were already sexually active (Emihovich & Herrington, 1993).

4. This controversy flared into the open after Memorial Day in 1993, when a local gay activist declared on a TV interview that the area had become the "Gay Riviera." Coming on the heels of the murder of a local doctor by an antiabortion activist, it raised fears of rising hatred and potential violence among right-wing groups (Griffin, 1993). The controversy soon died down and the feeling toward the gay community became more muted.

5. In the 1992 evaluation study, two versions of the student health survey were developed. The first one was for elementary students in grades 3 to 5, and none of the questions pertained to sexual issues. The secondary school survey was designed for students in grades 6 to 12, and many questions focused on sexual behaviors, with the exception of questions pertaining to either homosexuality or rape. A complete copy of all questions for both surveys is available in the evaluation report (Emihovich & Herrington, 1993).

6. Because she was interested in the possibility of running for superintendent, she refused to name the group, saying only that it was part of a nationally funded, religious network.

7. Additional support for her contention comes from the first author's experience of working with a teenage pregnancy-prevention program in another county in northwest Florida. The program was also housed in several local churches, and information about birth-control methods was disseminated with full knowledge of church officials (Emihovich, 1993).

8. The coordinators were conscious of the fact that this method excluded very poor families, since they were unlikely to have telephone service. However, they noted that within the boundaries of each school district, they conducted additional sampling to ensure that some of these families' concerns were represented.

9. In several parts of Florida SACs experienced direct conflict with their school board over their right to establish a plan that was appropriate for a particular school. The best-known case occurred in Lake County, where the State Education Department threatened to bring legal action against the board for their failure to allow a SAC to establish their school improvement plan.

10. One of the coordinators clarified this issue by explaining that there was money available, but only for 26 counties that had no school health services at all. One county refused to accept the money because it did not want any state control over how it dealt with sex education in the curriculum.

CHAPTER 4

1. She was referring to a health survey given by the Centers for Disease Control in 1990 just before the Supplemental School Health Program was funded. This county was one of the few where the schools selected in the sample fully cooperated and where there was no discernible public reaction against it.

2. During the time we were conducting the evaluation study, there were some counties that we were prevented from visiting or from collecting data because the local politics concerning students' access to school-based health services was so contentious.

3. She mentioned the issue of trust because she was previously known for having fairly liberal views on health services in schools, particularly the idea that condoms should be distributed by school nurses. However, once she was elected to the school board she quickly realized that this idea was, as she put it, "light years" away from being implemented, and she has since gone on record as opposing condom distribution until there is more community support for it.

4. All the principals at the time of our first interview were white males.

5. Although there are acknowledged problems with self-report questionnaires for assessing sexual behavior, especially among adolescents, it's difficult to imagine how one would learn about frequency of condom use other than from self-report measures.

6. In several cases we found that the state auditing team had just visited the site the week before we came. The timing was fortuitous for us, because people were primed to talk about their experiences in the program to someone who was not there to judge or evaluate it for program continuation.

7. Two bills were proposed in the 1995 session to restrict students' access to school-based health services. One bill would have required parents to sign a form opting in for health services, instead of opting out. Such a bill would have the effect of disenfranchising most poor children from receiving services, since their parents would be unlikely to know about the need to request the services. The second bill proposed that the names of students who received health services in schools be linked to the database maintained by the Department of Transportation. Once these students turned 16 and applied for a driver's license, they would pay an extra fee if the computer indicated that they had received services from a school nurse or other health care professional. In effect, it would be a tax on those students who received the services. Both bills failed to pass, but they were expected to be revived in the 1996 session.

CHAPTER 5

1. We learned on our return visit that this rate had to be qualified somewhat due to errors in how the pregnancies had originally been counted. The nurse told us that a more realistic figure was about a 40% drop in the pregnancy rate.

2. Admittedly, we are presenting only one side of the story. We did not interview the school superintendent to learn why he had pulled his school out of the SSHP program, and it may well be that he felt better services could be provided by the hospital. However, parents would still face transportation problems in getting their children to the hospital to obtain health services, especially those who lived in more rural areas.

3. Interestingly, the first author learned about an almost identical situation in a urban high school in the Northeast. The school had a male student who could only be described as an outrageous transvestite (including the wearing of full makeup and dresses to school), yet the students were relatively tolerant of his behavior. It was the adults who couldn't wait for him to graduate, since they felt he was a public embarrassment.

4. His words proved to be prophetic. One year later, the media began featuring articles on the problem of teenage pregnancies being linked to older men. In January 1996, an article appeared in *Time* magazine indicating that California had recently allocated $2.4 million for a pilot program to prosecute men who engaged in sex with underage girls (Gleick, 1996a). In May 1996, the *New York Times* reported that Florida was considering legislation to prosecute statutory rapists under child abuse laws (Navarro, 1996).

5. A positive result simply means that a person has been exposed to someone who is a carrier, but it does not necessarily mean that he or she will develop tuberculosis. It does mean, however, that the person needs to seek medical treatment over a prolonged period of time.

6. We should add the qualifier that none of the people we interviewed taught health education. These teachers were presumably the most threatened by the idea of having school nurses assume a more educational role by giving

classroom presentations, and they might have been less than enthusiastic about the expansion of the school nurse's functions beyond the health room.

CHAPTER 6

1. It may well be that the advent of new technologies, such as the abortion pill, will alter the nature of the opposition from conservative groups. Access to safe, reliable birth control has always been an issue in the United States (Snitnow, Stansell, & Thompson, 1983).

2. She cites the example of Furstenberg, Brooks-Gunn, and Morgan (1987), where a 17-year follow-up study was performed on their 1972 Baltimore study of pregnant African-American teens. Only a minority (13%) were on welfare, and one-quarter of them had incomes that placed them in the middle class.

3. For this reason, programs designed to prevent teenage pregnancy are more likely to succeed in community-based settings, where such conversations can take place without fear of censorship. Emihovich (in press) analyzed the discourses of adolescent African-American females in a community-based pregnancy-prevention program and concluded that:

> Young women (of all social class backgrounds) have few opportunities to engage in multiple discourses that allow them to voice their feelings and concerns about their reproductive options, their relationships with men, their conflicting desires, and their self-esteem and worth. Creating contexts for such discourses to emerge is, as feminists argue, critical if young women are to take control of their sexuality and their health by making informed choices.

4. The one exception was the nursing coordinator in Gold County, who mentioned in her interview how her staff had to develop a public relations plan to deal with a case of an HIV child who was going public in one of the service schools.

5. In several focus group interviews that we conducted with adolescents in our 1992 visit, boys often mentioned that their primary reason for using condoms was because of their fear of getting AIDS or other STDs. As one Hispanic male described it, "I don't mind having no babies, but I don't want no diseases."

6. Among the seventh-grade students in our sample, 12% of the girls and 14% of the boys reported having had a sexually transmitted disease. Among the sixth-grade boys, the rate was an astonishing 19%.

7. We suspect that the project staff's availability for private discourse was one of the main reasons why conservative groups were opposed to the idea of providing these services in schools. Even if the use of various contraceptive methods, for example, could not be openly discussed in classrooms, nurses and social workers could, and did, counsel students in private as to the best means of prevention or where to seek help in dealing with an unwanted pregnancy.

References

Abt, V., & Seesholtz, M. (1994). The shameless world of Phil, Sally, and Oprah: Television talk shows and the deconstructing of society. *Journal of Popular Culture, 28* (1), 171–191.

Agranoff, R. J. (1982). Meeting the challenges and changes in human service administration: Devolution, deregulation education, and privatization. *Journal of Health and Human Resources Administration, 4*(2), 384–385.

Agranoff, R. J. (1986). *Intergovernmental management.* Albany: State University of New York Press.

Annual Conference of School Nurses. (1996, June). *The leaders in you: Advocating for a healthy school community.* Washington, DC: National Association of School Nurses.

Appadurai, A. (1991). Global ethnoscapes: Notes and queries for a transnational anthropology. In R. G. Fox (Ed.), *Recapturing anthropology: Working in the present* (pp. 190–210). Santa Fe, NM: School of American Research Press.

Bell, D. (1968). *Cultural contradictions of capitalism.* New York: Basic Books.

Bellah, R. N., Madsen, R., Sullivan, W. M., Swidler, A., & Tipton, S. D. (1985). *Habits of the heart.* Berkeley: University of California Press.

Berkowitz, P. (1996, June 24). The art of association. *The New Republic,* 44–49.

Brindis, C. (1991). *Adolescent pregnancy prevention: A guidebook for communities.* Palo Alto, CA: Stanford University Health Promotion Resource Center.

Brooks-Gunn, J., & Paikoff, R. L. (1993). "Sex is a gamble, kissing is a game": Adolescent sexuality and health promotion. In S. G. Millstein, A. C. Petersen, & E. O. Nightingale (Eds.), *Promoting the health of adolescents* (pp. 180–208). Oxford: Oxford University Press.

Brown, N. O. (1966). *Love's body.* New York: Random House.

Brown, S. S., & Eisenberg, L. (Eds.). (1995). *The best intentions: Unintended pregnancy and the well-being of children and families* (Report of the Committee on Unintended Pregnancy, Institute of Medicine). Washington, DC: National Academy Press.

Burdell, P. (1995). Teen mothers in high school: Tracking their curriculum. *Review of Research in Education, 21,* 163–207.

Carlson, D. L. (1992). Ideological conflict and change in the sexuality curriculum. In J. T. Sears (Ed.), *Sexuality in the curriculum* (pp. 34–58). New York: Teachers College Press.

Carter, D. M., Felice, M. E., Rosoff, J., Schwab-Zabin, L., Beilenson, P. L., & Danneberg, A. L. (1994). When children have children: The teen pregnancy predicament. *American Journal of Preventive Medicine, 10*(2), 108–113.

211

Center for the Future of Children. (1992). *School linked services*. Los Altos, CA: Author.

Centers for Disease Control. (1992). *Florida Youth Risk Behavior Survey*. Atlanta, Ga: Author.

Centers for Disease Control. (1995). *Youth risk behavior surveillance*. Atlanta, GA: Author.

Cremin, L. A. (1988). *American education: The metropolitan experience, 1876–1980*. New York: Harper & Row.

Cummings, K. (1993). Of purebreds and hybrids: The politics of teaching AIDS in the United States. In J. C. Fout & M. S. Tantillo (Eds.), *American sexual politics* (pp. 353–380). Chicago: University of Chicago Press.

Dawson, J. A., & D'Amico, J. J. (1985). Involving program staff in evaluation studies: A strategy for increasing information use and enriching the data base. *Evaluation Review, 9*(2), 173–188.

Doering, R. (1996, January 23). Schools boards must address the needs of the whole child. *School Board News*.

Drake, H. M. (1989). Using stakeholders in the research process: A case study in human services. In J. van Willigen, B. Rylko-Bauer, & A. McElroy (Eds.), *Making our research useful: Case studies in the utilization of anthropological knowledge* (pp. 237–255). Boulder, CO: Westview.

Dryfoos, J. G. (1994). *Full service schools*. San Francisco: Jossey-Bass.

Earls, F. (1993). Health promotion for minority adolescents: Cultural considerations. In S. G. Millstein, A. C. Petersen, & E. O. Nightingale (Eds.), *Promoting the health of adolescents* (pp. 58–72). Oxford: Oxford University Press.

Edelman, M. W. (1996, January 15). Children of a lesser country. *The New Yorker*, pp. 23–24.

Elam, S. M., Rose, L. C., & Gallup, A. M. (1993). The 25th annual Phi Delta Kappa/Gallup poll of the public's attitudes toward the public schools. *Phi Delta Kppan, 75*(2), 137–157.

Elkind, D. (1995). School and family in the postmodern world. *Phi Delta Kappan, 77*(1), 2–14.

Ellwood, D. (1988). *Poor support: Poverty in the American family*. New York: Basic Books.

Emihovich, C. (1990). Reopening the conversation: The ethic of caring in educational research. In M. J. M. Brown (Ed.), *Proceedings of the fifth annual Qualitative Research in Education conference*. Athens: University of Georgia.

Emihovich, C. (1993). *A longitudinal evaluation of the Brighter Futures Program*. Tallahassee: Florida State University.

Emihovich, C. (1994, November). *Crossing cultural borders: The politics of morality in social services evaluations*. Paper presented at the annual meeting of the American Anthropological Association, Atlanta, GA.

Emihovich, C. (in press). Bodytalk: Discourses of sexuality among adolescent, African-American girls. In S. M. Hoyle & C. T. Adger (Eds.), *Kids talk: Strategic language use in later childhood*. Oxford: Oxford University Press.

Emihovich, C., & Davis, T. (1994). *Brighter Futures revisited: A longitudinal evaluation of the Brighter Futures program*. Final report submitted to Gadsden Citizens for Healthy Babies, Quincy, FL.

Emihovich, C., & Herrington, C. (1993). *An evaluation of the effectiveness of Florida's Department of Health and Rehabilitative Services Supplemental School Health Services Projects.* Tallahassee, FL: Learning Systems Institute, Florida State University.

Epstein, J. L. (1995). School/family/community partnerships: Caring for the children we share. *Phi Delta Kappan, 76*(9), 701–712.

Ericson, D. (1990). Social justice, evaluation, and the educational system. In K. A. Sirotnik (Ed.), *Evaluation and social justice: Issues in public education* (pp. 5–22). San Francisco: Jossey-Bass.

Erikson, E. H. (1963). *Childhood and society* (2nd ed.). New York: Norton.

Esman, A. H. (1990). *Adolescence and culture.* New York: Columbia University Press.

Fetterman, D. M. (1993). Ethnography and policy: Translating knowledge into action. In D. M. Fetterman (Ed.), *Speaking the language of power: Communication, collaboration and advocacy* (pp. 156–175). Washington, DC: Falmer.

Fiedler, T., & Kempel, M. (1993). *Almanac of Florida politics, 1994.* Miami, FL: Miami Herald Publishing Co.

Fine, M. (1992). Sexuality, schooling, and the adolescent female: The missing discourse of desire. *Harvard Educational Review, 58,* 29–53.

Finkelstein, B. (1995, April). *Child hating as public policy: An American dilemma.* Paper presented at the annual meeting of the American Educational Research Association, San Francisco.

Finneran, R. (1989). *The collected works of W. B. Yeats.* New York: Macmillan.

Florida Center for Children and Youth. (1992). *Conditions of children in Florida.* Tallahassee, FL: Author.

Florida Center for Children and Youth. (1994). *Conditions of children in Florida.* Tallahassee, FL: Author.

Foucault, M. (1978). *The history of sexuality* (Vol. 1) (R. Hurley, Trans.). New York: Random House.

Friedan, B. (1996, June 3). Children's crusade. *The New Yorker,* pp. 5–6.

Furstenberg, F. F., Brooks-Gunn, J., & Morgan, B. P. (1987). *Adolescent mothers in later life.* Cambridge, UK: Cambridge University Press.

Gamson, J. (1993). Rubber wars: Struggles over the condom in the United States. In J. C. Fout & M. S. Tantillo (Eds.), *American sexual politics* (pp. 311–331). Chicago: University of Chicago Press.

Gardner, S. (1994). Conclusion. In L. Adler & S. Gardner (Eds.), *The politics of linking schools and social services* (pp. 189–199). Washington, DC: Falmer.

Gee, J. (1991). *Social linguistics and literacies.* New York: Falmer.

George, J. (1992). *Expanding role of school nurses.* Tallahassee: Center for Policy Studies, Florida State University.

Giroux, H. A. (1996). Hollywood, race, and the demonization of youth: The "kids" are not all right. *Educational Researcher, 25*(2), 31–35.

Glasow, R. D. (1988). *School based clinics: The abortion connection.* Washington, DC: National Right to Life Fund.

Gleick, E. (1996a, January 29). Putting the jail in jailbait. *Time,* pp. 29, 33–34.

Gleick, E. (1996b, June 3). The children's crusade. *Time,* pp. 31–39.

Gold, S. D. (1989). *Reforming state and local relations: A practical guide.* Washington, DC: Author.

Greenberg, D. (1992, February 27). State probes teen-aid's use of sex ed funds. *The Gainesville Sun*, p. 1.

Greene, M. (1988). What happened to imagination? In K. Egan & D. Nadaner (Eds.), *Imagination and education* (pp. 45–56). New York: Teachers College Press.

Gregor, T. (1990). Male dominance and sexual coercion. In J. W. Stigler, R. A. Shweder, & G. Herdt (Eds.), *Cultural psychology: Essays in comparative human development* (pp. 477–495). Cambridge, UK: Cambridge University Press.

Griffin, L. (1993, October 11). A city fights over inviting gay strangers on its shore. *New York Times*, pp. 1B, 10B–11B.

Guba, E. G., & Lincoln, Y. S. (1989). *Fourth generation evaluation*. Newbury Park, CA: Sage.

Haber, H. F. (1994). *Beyond postmodern politics*. New York: Routledge.

Haffner, D. (1994). Schools should provide candid education on sexuality topics. In K. L. Swisher (Ed.), *Teenage sexuality* (pp. 141–145). San Diego, CA: Greenhaven.

Harbeck, K. (1992). Introduction. In K. Harbeck (Ed.), *Coming out of the classroom closet: Gay and lesbian students, teachers, and curricula* (pp. 1–7). New York: Harrington Park Press.

Havel, V. (1995, June 22). The responsibility of intellectuals. *New York Review of Books*, pp. 36–37.

Heath, S. B., & McLaughlin, M. W. (Eds.). (1993). *Identity and inner-city youth: Beyond ethnicity and gender*. New York: Teachers College Press.

Hennessy, J. (1992, April 29). Teen-aid suit cites inaccuracies, bias in sex-ed curriculum. *The Florida Times Union* (Jacksonville) p. 8A.

Herrington, C. (1991a). (Ed.). *The conditions of children in Florida*. Tallahassee: Florida State University, Learning Systems Institute.

Herrington, C. (1991b). *Public policy and children: An intergovernmental analysis*. Tallahassee: Florida State University, Center for Policy Studies in Education.

Herrington, C. (1994). Schools as intergovernmental partners: Administrator perceptions of expanded programming for children. *Education Administration Quarterly, 30*(3), 301–323.

Himmelfarb, G. (1994). A de-moralized society: The British/American experience. *American Educator, 18*(4), 14–21, 40–43.

Holden, E. W., & Nitz, K. (1995). Epidemiology of adolescent health disorders. In J. L. Wallender & L. J. Siegel (Eds.), *Adolescent health problems: Behavioral perspectives* (pp. 52–71). New York: Guilford.

Holtzman, P., Green, B. Z., Ingraham, G. C., Daily, L. A., Demchuk, D. G., & Kolbe, L. (1992). HIV education and health education in the United States: A national survey of local school district policies and practices. *Journal of School Health, 62*(9), 421–427.

hooks, b., & West, C. (1991). *Breaking bread: Insurgent black intellectual life*. Boston: South End Press.

Hunter, J. D. (1991). *Culture wars: The struggle to define America*. New York: Basic Books.

Irvine, J. M. (1995). *Sexuality education across cultures*. San Francisco: Jossey-Bass.

James, T. (1993). The winnowing of organizations. In S. B. Heath & M. W. McLaughlin (Eds.), *Identity and inner-city youth: Beyond ethnicity and gender* (pp. 176–195). New York: Teachers College Press.

Johnson, J., & Immerwahr, J. (1994). *First things first: What Americans expect from the public schools.* New York: Public Agenda.

Kamarck, E. C., & Gaston, W. A. (1990). *Putting children first: A progressive family policy for the 1990's.* Washington, DC: Progressive Policy Institute.

Katz, J. (1995, September). Guilty. *Wired,* 128–133, 188.

Kimball, B. A. (1992). *The "true professional ideal" in America.* Cambridge, MA: Blackwell.

King, J. E., & Mitchell, C. A. (1990). *Black mothers to sons: Juxtaposing African American literature with social practice.* New York: Lang.

Kirby, D. (1991). School based clinics: Research results and their implications for future research methods. *Evaluation and Program Planning, 14*(1–2), 35–47.

Kirby, D. (1992). School-based programs to reduce sexual risk-taking behaviors. *Journal of School Health, 62*(7), 280–287.

Kirby, D., Waszak, C., & Ziegler, J. (1989). *An assessment of six school-based health clinics: Services, impact, and potential.* Washington, DC: Center for Population Options.

Kirst, M. W. (1991). *Integrating children's services.* Menlo Park, CA: EdSource.

Kirst, M. W. (1994). Equity for children: Linking education and children's services. *Educational Policy, 8*(4), 583–590.

Knapp, M. S. (1995). How shall we study comprehensive, collaborative services for children and families? *Educational Researcher, 24*(4), 5–16.

Kochan, F., & Herrington, C. (1992, Fall). Restructuring for today's children: Strengthening schools through strengthening families. *Educational Forum, 57,* 42–49.

Kolbe, L. J. (1986). Increasing the impact of school health promotion programs: Emerging research perspectives. *Health Education, 17*(5), 47–52.

Larson, C. S. (Ed.). (1992). *School linked services, 2*(1) [special issue].

Lawson, A., & Rhode, D. L. (Eds.). (1993). *The politics of pregnancy: Adolescent sexuality and public policy.* New Haven, CT: Yale University Press.

Lazar, I., Darlington, R., Murray, H., Royce, J., & Snipper, A. (1982). Lasting effects of early intervention: A report from the Consortium for Longitudinal Studies. *Monographs of the Society for Research in Child Development, 47*(2–3, Serial No. 195).

Lincoln, Y., & Guba, E. (1985). *Naturalistic inquiry.* Beverly Hills, CA: Sage.

Lindsay, D. (1995, May 3). Abstinence bills gaining popularity and momentum. *Education Week,* pp. 17, 20.

Magnet, M. (1993). *The dream and the nightmare.* New York: Morrow.

Males, M. A. (1993). School-age pregnancy: Why hasn't prevention worked? *Journal of School Health, 63*(10), 429–432.

Males, M. A. (1996). *The scapegoat generation: America's war on adolescents.* Monroe, ME: Common Courage Press.

Mark, M. M., & Shotland, R. L. (1985). Stakeholder based evaluation and value judgments. *Evaluation Review, 9*(5), 605–625.

Martin, J. R. (1995). A philosophy of education for the year 2000. *Phi Delta Kappan, 76*(5), 355–359.

McKnight, J. (1995). *The careless society: Community and its counterfeits.* New York: Basic Books.

Millstein, S. G., & Igra, V. (1995). *Theoretical models of adolescent risk-taking.* New Haven, CT: Yale University Press.

Morgan, L., & Nickens, T. (1989, October 13). Abortion foes say deal was broken. *St. Petersburg Times,* p. 1.

Murray, C. A. (1984). *Losing ground: American social policy 1950–1980.* New York: Basic Books.

Musick, J. S. (1993). *Young, poor, and pregnant: The psychology of teenage motherhood.* New Haven, CT: Yale University Press.

Nathanson, C. A. (1991). *Dangerous passage: The social control of sexuality in women's adolescence.* Philadelphia: Temple University Press.

National Commission on Children. (1991). *Beyond rhetoric: A new American agenda for children and families.* Washington, DC: Author.

Navarro, M. (1996, May 19). Teenage mothers viewed as abused prey of older men. *New York Times,* p. 1.

Newton, J. (1989). *The new school health handbook: A ready reference for school nurses and educators.* Englewood Cliffs, NJ: Prentice Hall.

Nickel, J. (1992, September 21). Growing up gay in America. *Christopher Street* (New York), pp. 3–7.

Noddings, N. (1984). *Caring: A feminine approach to ethics and moral education.* Berkeley: University of California Press.

Noddings, N. (1995a). A morally defensible mission for the schools in the 21st century. *Phi Delta Kappan, 76*(5), 365–368.

Noddings, N. (1995b). *The challenge to care in schools.* New York: Teachers College Press.

Owens, R. G. (1991). *Organizational behavior in education.* Needham Heights, MA: Allyn & Bacon.

Patton, M. Q. (1986). *Utilization-focused evaluation.* Beverly Hills, CA: Sage.

Peterson, P. E., Rabe, B. G., & Wong, K. K. (1986). *When federalism works.* Washington, DC: Brookings Institute.

Phillips, K. P. (1990). *The politics of rich and poor: Wealth and the American electorate in the Reagan aftermath.* New York: Harper Perennial.

Phoenix, A. (1991). Mothers under twenty: Insider and outsider views. In A. Phoenix, A. Wooleth, & E. Lloyd (Eds.), *Motherhood: Meanings, practices and ideologies* (pp. 86–102). London: Sage.

Pipher, M. (1996). *The shelter of each other: Rebuilding our families.* New York: Putnam.

Pizzo, P. (1983). Slouching toward Bethlehem: American federal policy perspectives on children and their families. In E. Zigler, S. Kagan, & E. Klugman (Eds.), *Children, families, and government: Perspectives in American social policy* (pp. 10–32). Cambridge, NY: Cambridge University Press.

Putnam, R. D. (1995, January). Bowling alone: America's declining social capital. *Journal of Democracy, 6*(1), 65–78.

Rienzo, B. A., & Button, J. W. (1993). The politics of school-based clinics: A community level analysis. *Journal of School Health, 63*(6), 266–272.

Rubin, L. B. (1994). *Families on the fault line.* New York: Harper.

Sandel, M. J. (1996, May 9). Dewey rides again. *New York Review of Books,* pp. 35–38.

Sapir, E. (1970). Linguistics as a science. In G. Mandelbaum (Ed.), *Culture, language and personality* (pp. 65–77). Berkeley: University of California Press.

Sarason, S. (1995). *Parental involvement and the political principle: Why the existing governance structure of schools should be abolished.* San Francisco: Jossey-Bass.

Schensul, J. J. (1987). Knowledge utilization: An anthropological perspective. *Practicing Anthropology, 9*(1), 6–8.

Schmalz, J. (1989, October 12). Abortion access stands in Florida. *New York Times,* p. 5.

School poll in favor of condoms. (1992, August 28). *Tampa Tribune,* p. 15.

Schorr, L. B., & Schorr, D. (1989). *Within our reach: Breaking the cycle of disadvantage.* New York: Anchor Press/Doubleday.

Schwandt, T. A. (1989). Recapturing moral discourse in evaluation. *Educational Researcher, 18*(8), 11–16.

Sears, J. T. (1992a). Dilemmas and possibilities of sexuality education. In J. T. Sears (Ed.), *Sexuality and the curriculum* (pp. 7–33). New York: Teachers College Press.

Sears, J. T. (1992b). Educators, homosexuality, and homosexual students: Are personal feelings related to professional beliefs? In K. Harbeck (Ed.), *Coming out of the classroom closet: Gay and lesbian students, teachers, and curricula* (pp. 29–80). New York: Harrington Park Press.

Sedway, M. (1992). *Far right takes aim at sexuality education.* SIECUS Report, *20*(3), 13–19.

Scidman, S. (1992). *Embattled eros: Sexual politics and ethics in contemporary America.* New York: Routledge.

Siegel, K., & Tuckel, P. (1985). The utilization of evaluation research: A case analysis. *Evaluation Review, 9*(3), 307–328.

Silin, J. G. (1995). *Sex, death, and the education of children.* New York: Teachers College Press.

Sirotnik, K. (Ed.). (1990). *Evaluation and social justice: Issues in public education.* San Francisco: Jossey-Bass.

Skolnick, A. (1991). *Embattled paradise: The American family in an age of uncertainty.* New York: Basic Books.

Snitnow, A., Stansell, C., & Thompson, S. (Eds.). (1983). *Power of desire: The politics of sexuality.* New York: Monthly Review Press.

Soltis, J. S. (1989). The ethics of qualitative research. *Qualitative Studies in Education, 2*(2), 123–130.

Sommerfeld, M. (1992a, September 23). Survey charts rise in health problems among pupils. *Education Week,* p. 8.

Sommerfeld, M. (1992b, September 8). Health educators seek help in handling controversy. *Education Week,* p. 8.

Stake, R. E. (1986). An evolutionary view of program improvement. In E. R.

House (Ed.), *New directions in educational evaluation* (pp. 89–102). Philadelphia: Falmer.

Strehlow, M. S. (1987). *Nursing in educational settings.* San Francisco: Harper & Row.

Stevens, W. (1965). *The necessary angel.* New York: Vintage Books.

Stover, D. (1994). School curricula should support gay teens. In K. L. Swisher (Ed.), *Teenage sexuality: Opposing viewpoints* (pp. 178–184). San Diego, CA: Greenhaven Press.

Telling tales out of school. (1996, February 14) *Education Week,* 27–31.

Tocqueville, A. de (1899). *Democracy in America.* New York: Appleton.

Trudell, Bonnie N. (1993). *Doing sex education: Gender politics and schooling.* New York: Routledge.

Tyack, D. B. (1974). *The one best system: A history of American urban education.* Cambridge, MA: Harvard University Press.

Tyack, D. B. (1992, Spring). Health and social services in public schools: Historical perspectives. *The Future of Children, 2*(1), 19–31.

University of South Florida. (1995, August). *Florida comprehensive school health projects 1995 program evaluation.* Tampa: Author.

U.S. Department of Education. (1988). *Digest of education statistics.* Washington, DC: Author.

U.S. Department of Justice. (1995). *Violence against women—Estimates from the redesigned survey.* Washington, DC: Author.

van Willigen, J., Rylko-Bauer, B., & McElroy, A. (1989). (Eds.). *Making our research useful: Case studies in the utilization of anthropological knowledge.* Boulder, CO: Westview.

Weeks, J. (1985). *Sexuality and its discontents.* London: Routledge & Kegan Paul.

Weiss, C. H. (1981). Measuring the use of evaluations. In J. A. Ciarlo (Ed.), *Utilizing evaluation* (pp. 17–33). Beverly Hills, CA: Sage.

Whatley, M. H. (1992). Whose sexuality is it anyway? In J. T. Sears (Ed.), *Sexuality in the curriculum* (pp. 78–87). New York: Teachers College Press.

Whitehead, B. (1994, October). The failure of sex education. *Atlantic Monthly,* pp. 55–80.

Wolf, N. (1993). *Fire with fire.* New York: Random House.

Wolff, E. N. (1996). *Top heavy: The increasing inequality of wealth in America and what can be done about it.* New York: New Press.

Youth and HIV/AIDS: An American agenda (Report to the President). (1996). Washington, DC: U.S. Government Printing Office.

Zabin, L. S., & Hirsch, M. B. (1988). *Evaluation of pregnancy prevention programs in the school context.* Lexington, MA: Lexington Books.

Zigler, E., Kagan, S., & Klugman, E. (Eds.). (1987). *Children, families, and government: Perspectives in American social policy.* Cambridge, UK: Cambridge University Press.

Zigler, E., & Muenchow, S. (1992). *Head Start: The inside story of America's most successful educational experiment.* New York: Basic Books.

Index

About the Authors

Catherine Emihovich is Associate Professor of Educational Psychology and Director of the Buffalo Research Institute on Education for Teaching (BRIET) at the State University of New York at Buffalo. Her research interests focus on action research in teacher education, sociolinguistic studies of classroom discourse, metacognitive processes in computer instruction, race, class, and gender equity issues in education, teen pregnancy and health services in schools, and applied evaluations of educational and social services programs. She has published widely in journals such as *Language in Society, Theory into Practice, The Elementary School Journal, Linguistics in Education, Education and Urban Society,* and *Qualitative Studies in Education.* She has edited one book, *Locating Learning: Ethnographic Perspectives on Classroom Research,* and is one of several authors of a forthcoming book, *Preparing Tomorrow's Educators in Tomorrow's Schools of Education.* She is the former editor of the *Anthropology and Education Quarterly* and has guest edited special issues of five other journals. She has worked as an evaluation consultant for local, state, and national organizations, including the Educational Testing Service and the Getty Foundation.

Carolyn Herrington is Associate Professor of Educational Policy and Director of Florida Education Policy Studies at the Learning Systems Institute at Florida State University. Her research interests focus on educational politics and policy, public school governance, and the changing conditions of children. Her research has been published in journals such as the *Journal of Education Policy, Educational Administration Quarterly,* and the *International Journal of Education Reform.* She has written or edited numerous other articles, book chapters, monographs, and book reviews on education and children's policy. She is past editor of the *Politics of Education Bulletin* and she currently serves on the Board of Directors of the American Educational Finance Association. Her professional affiliations include core researcher for the Consortium for Policy Research in Education, state network coordinator for the Education Commission of the States, and board of directors for the Hardee Center for Women in

227

Higher Education Administration. She currently serves as Co-Principal Investigator for a Carnegie Commission-funded ethnographic study of immigrant and native-born minority students in four high schools in Miami.